CROSSING DIVIDES

CROSSING DIVIDES

Exploring Translingual Writing Pedagogies and Programs

EDITED BY
BRUCE HORNER
ELLIOT TETREAULT

UTAH STATE UNIVERSITY PRESS
Logan

© 2017 by University Press of Colorado

Published by Utah State University Press
An imprint of University Press of Colorado
5589 Arapahoe Avenue, Suite 206C
Boulder, Colorado 80303

 The University Press of Colorado is a proud member of
The Association of University Presses.

The University Press of Colorado is a cooperative publishing enterprise supported, in part, by Adams State University, Colorado State University, Fort Lewis College, Metropolitan State University of Denver, Regis University, University of Colorado, University of Northern Colorado, Utah State University, and Western State Colorado University.

∞ The paper used in this publication meets the minimum requirements of the American National Standard for Information Sciences—Permanence of Paper for Printed Library Materials. ANSI Z39.48-1992

ISBN: 978-1-60732-619-9 (paperback)
ISBN: 978-1-60732-620-5 (ebook)

Library of Congress Cataloging-in-Publication Data

Names: Horner, Bruce, 1957– editor. | Tetreault, Elliot, editor.
Title: Crossing divides : exploring translingual writing pedagogies and programs / edited by Bruce Horner, Elliot Tetreault.
Description: Logan : Utah State University Press, [2017] | Includes bibliographical references and index.
Identifiers: LCCN 2016034817| ISBN 9781607326199 (pbk.) | ISBN 9781607326205 (ebook)
Subjects: LCSH: English language—Rhetoric—Study and teaching (Higher)—United States. | Multilingualism—United States. | Critical pedagogy—United States. | Intercultural communication—United States. | Sociolinguistics—United States.
Classification: LCC PE1404 .C756 2017 | DDC 808/.042071173—dc23
LC record available at https://lccn.loc.gov/2016034817

Cover illustration © PsychoShadow / Shutterstock

CONTENTS

Acknowledgments   *vii*

Introduction   Crossing Divides: Exploring Translingual Writing
    Pedagogies and Programs
    Bruce Horner and Elliot Tetreault   *3*

PART 1   THEORIZING TRANSLINGUALITY IN WRITING
AND ITS TEACHING
1   Toward a New Vocabulary of Motive: Re(con)figuring
    Entanglement in a Translingual World
    Juan C. Guerra and Ann Shivers-McNair   *19*

2   Translingual Practice, Ethnic Identities, and Voice in Writing
    *Sara P. Alvarez, Suresh Canagarajah, Eunjeong Lee, Jerry Won Lee,
    and Shakil Rabbi*   *31*

PART 2   PEDAGOGICAL INTERVENTIONS
3   Enacting Translingual Writing Pedagogy: Structures and
    Challenges for Two Courses in Two Countries
    William B. Lalicker   *51*

4   Who Owns English in South Korea?
    Patricia Bizzell   *70*

5   Teaching Translingual Agency in Iteration: Rewriting Difference
    Bruce Horner   *87*

PART 3   INSTITUTIONAL/PROGRAMMATIC
INTERVENTIONS
6   Disrupting Monolingual Ideologies in a Community College:
    A Translingual Studio Approach
    Katie Malcolm   *101*

7   Writing Assessment as the Conditions for Translingual
    Approaches: An Argument for Fairer Assessments
    Asao B. Inoue   *119*

8   Seizing an Opportunity for Translingual FYC at the University of Maine: Provocative Complexities, Unexpected Consequences

Dylan B. Dryer and Paige Mitchell   *135*

9   Becoming Global: Learning to "Do" Translingualism

Chris Gallagher and Matt Noonan   *161*

PART 4   RESPONSES

10   Crossing, or Creating, Divides? A Plea for Transdisciplinary Scholarship

Christine M. Tardy   *181*

11   The Ins and Outs of Translingual Work

Thomas Lavelle   *190*

12   Language Difference and Translingual Enactments

Kate Mangelsdorf   *199*

About the Authors   *207*
Index   *211*

ACKNOWLEDGMENTS

We thank Michael Spooner for his support of this project, and the editorial team at the University Press of Colorado/Utah State University Press—especially Laura Furney, Darrin Pratt, and Beth Svinarich—for helping see the collection through to completion, and Linda Gregonis for providing our index. We also thank the two anonymous reviewers for their valuable comments on earlier versions of the collection.

We are deeply grateful to our contributors for their insights and patient hard work in developing translingual approaches to writing pedagogy and for making this collection possible. We would also like to thank the participants in the 2013 and 2014 Conference on College Composition and Communication preconvention workshops on Crossing BW/ESL/FYW Divides, I and II: Pedagogical and Institutional Strategies for Translingual Writing, from which this collection emerged. Special thanks to the workshop and discussion leaders Patricia Bizzell, Suresh Canagarajah, Debarata Dutta, Dylan Dryer, Chris Gallagher, Juan Guerra, Asao Inoue, Jay Jordan, William Lalicker, Steve Lamos, Min-Zhan Lu, Kate Mangelsdorf, Tamera Marko, Paul Kei Matsuda, Matt Noonan, Wendy Olson, Tony Scott, Gail Shuck, Christine Tardy, and John Trimbur. We also offer our gratitude to all who attended these workshops and participated in the lively discussions about translingual writing and pedagogy and crossing disciplinary divides.

CROSSING DIVIDES

INTRODUCTION
Crossing Divides: Exploring Translingual
Writing Pedagogies and Programs

Bruce Horner and Elliot Tetreault

This collection participates in an ongoing movement in the teaching and study of US college writing to respond productively to language difference in writing. Previous efforts to do so have focused on two kinds of such difference: differences in the varieties of English thought to manifest themselves in writing and differences in the specific languages of students. The first of these, represented most prominently by the 1974 Conference on College Composition and Communication statement Students' Right to Their Own Language (SRTOL), defended the legitimacy of varieties of English that appeared to deviate from what was purported to be standard English, most prominently the legitimacy of the language practices of African Americans, as in African American Vernacular English (AAVE) (Conference on College Composition and Communication 1974). Against charges that these varieties represented deficient forms of English or deficiencies in the cognitive abilities of the users, linguists demonstrated the linguistic legitimacy of those practices—their grammar—and thereby, in turn, the racism underlying denials of that legitimacy (see Bruch and Marback 2004; Smitherman 1999; Rouse 1979; Wible 2013). The second of these, building on theories and programs of second language learning, often took the form of the institutional development of distinct programs and curricula for students for whom English was an additional language—often incorrectly identified as only, and all, international students (see Matsuda 1999, 2006)—as well as distinct professional organizations and journals, such as TESOL and its journal *TESOL Quarterly* and the Symposium on Second Language Writing and its accompanying *Journal of Second Language Writing.*[1]

Both such efforts have been salutary in countering deficit notions of the language practices of minoritized groups and in countering the treatment of members of those groups as somehow cognitively deficient

DOI: 10.7330/9781607326205.c000

in light of differences in their language practices. But those efforts have been founded on assumptions about languages, relations between languages, and relations between languages and their users that scholarship in these fields and in the contributing and intersecting fields of bilingualism, English as a lingua franca, World Englishes, intercultural rhetoric, sociolinguistics, and second language acquisition is increasingly calling into question (Baker 2013; Belcher 2014; Blommaert 2010; Calvet 1999, 2006; Canagarajah 2011, 2016; Firth and Wagner 1997; Heller 2007; Khubchandani 1998; Leung 2005, 2013; Leung , Harris, and Rampton 1997; Matsuda 1997; Parakrama 1995; Pennycook 2010). In a critique of these assumptions, Bruce Horner and John Trimbur have observed that composition courses themselves emerged out of a chain of reifications of language, social identities, and the links between them whereby individuals are assumed to have only a single social identity tied to a single language (e.g., "Chinese"), competence with which develops in a linear fashion toward mastery (Horner and Trimbur 2002, 596). But increasingly, the identities and language practices of students, teachers, and the larger social realm are defying such reifications. While monolingualism—the language ideology that dictates a single, reified language and social identity for all—remains dominant, its own legitimacy is increasingly in question, as, in the United States and globally, populations, and languages, move, intermix, and fluctuate in identity. And, in response, a flurry of neologisms have emerged from a variety of disciplines and locations globally to name this alternative state of affairs—including "postmonolingualism" (Yildiz 2012), "plurilingualism" (Zarate, Lévy, and Kramsch 2008), "diversalité" (Bernabé, Chamoiseau, and Confiant 1989, 1999), "translanguaging" (García and Li 2014), "code-meshing" (Young and Martinez 2011), "transculturation" (Zamel 1997), and "translingualism" (Canagarajah 2013; Horner et al. 2011). While these terms are not to be equated with one another and are each in dispute as to their meaning, and while this volume deploys the still unsettled term *translingualism* to name this state of affairs and the appropriate orientation to adopt toward it (see Lu and Horner 2016), we can identify some shared alignments among these terms in the orientation they adopt and advocate toward language and the relations among languages and user identities.

First, they signal the acceptance of the copresence of more than one language as the norm of communicative situations rather than a deviation from that norm. Second, they signal the fluidity of the defining boundaries between these languages. Third, and relatedly, they position language use as entailing the mixing and changing of different languages, and fourth, and also relatedly, they grant agency to language users to do so rather than seeing such mixing and changing as evidence of linguistic failure, cognitive incompetence, or cultural threat. Fifth, they posit the identities of not only languages but also language users as fluid. And finally, they locate languages not outside material social history, as timeless, discrete universals against which language practices are to be measured, but in the material social realm as the always-emerging outcome of those practices.

Such principles redress the gap between actual language practices and identities and relations between these, on the one hand, and, on the other hand, what the ideology of monolingualism claims about these. While often couched in terms of language theory, it is theory developing out of and intervening in the practical effects of monolingualism, part of a larger movement in the politics of language and its teaching. Two phenomena related to forces of globalization have made that gap increasingly difficult for scholars and teachers of composition to ignore. First, there has been a growth in the number of students (and faculty) at US colleges and universities (as well as at colleges and universities outside the United States) whose language identities defy monolinguallanguage ideology's norm of one language/one identity/one nation (Hall 2014). Second, institutions of higher education have increasingly sought not only to recruit such students (as chapters in this collection by Dryer and Mitchell and by Gallagher and Noonan discuss) but also to extend their reach through internationalization of their campuses and programs (see Hesford, Singleton, and García 2009; Martins 2015). Institutions, as well as their students and faculty, are increasingly and constantly on the move, creating satellite and exchange programs that put their identification with a specific location in question and produce new challenges to writing faculty and writing program administrators, as well as to their students, now dispersed globally (see Cross-Border Education Research Team 2016; Doiz, Lasagabaster, and Sierra 2013; Horner and Kopelson 2014; Jenkins 2014; Seawright 2014; Wingate 2015; Ziguras 2005).

The chapters in this collection describe and reflect on current efforts by composition teachers, scholars, and writing program administrators to address the gap between what the ideology of monolingualism claims is the norm for student and faculty language practices and institutional home identities and the increasingly undeniable fact of students' and faculty's linguistic heterogeneity, the inherent instability of languages as the always-shifting outcome of practices, and the dispersed and shifting location of faculty, students, and programs. While responsive to previous attempts to address language difference in composition teaching, these current efforts aim to move beyond the limitations monolingualism has placed on conceptions of language difference and how it might best be addressed in our thinking, teaching, and research (see, for example, Canagarajah 2006, 2009; Horner 2001; Horner and Kopelson 2014; Horner, NeCamp, and Donahue 2011; Lu 2004, 2009; Matsuda 2006; Young 2009). In place of maintaining sharp institutional, programmatic, disciplinary, curricular, and pedagogical divides on the basis of the putatively stable language identities and backgrounds ascribed to students, compositionists are attempting to develop alternative ways of imagining and putting to useful work alternative conceptions of language, language relations, and users' language practices and identities.

Those making such attempts draw on disparate traditions in and beyond composition's traditional—that is, monolingualist—disciplinary purview, including (though not limited to) not only scholarly and teaching traditions in what has passed as the norm for first-year writing but also traditions in the study and teaching of second language writing and basic writing, and scholarship on English as a lingua franca, world Englishes, second language acquisition, intercultural and comparative rhetorics, bilingualism, and translation studies. In so doing, of course, compositionists are building on the insights of these traditions. However, given the dominance of monolingualist ideology, those drawing on these traditions must also confront the inevitable, if residual, strands of monolingualism they carry within them, as Thomas Lavelle notes in his response chapter in this book. Further, as Christine Tardy notes in her response chapter, in drawing on diverse traditions of scholarship and teaching, compositionists will inevitably find themselves rediscovering what those well versed in those traditions may see as old news (e.g., the mythic character of the native speaker), though put to possibly different uses. Finally, in efforts to apply insights taken from these diverse traditions to what appear to be novel situations, compositionists will inevitably give new, unauthorized meanings to terms and concepts with established meanings within those traditions—most notoriously, for example, code switching (see Guerra and Shivers-McNair, this volume ; Lu 2009; Matsuda 2013; Young 2009). As Min-Zhan Lu (2004) has noted, composition teachers and scholars have a long history of "poaching" from a variety of "other" fields to address new, or newly discovered, and above all urgent, challenges they face: taking what is claimed to belong to others as, instead, part of the commons and putting what is taken to uses different than what others see as either appropriate or legitimate.

But the chapters in this collection attest that there is a further facet to the challenge compositionists face as they rework old tools to put them to different ends. Not only are the readily available terms and concepts inadequate to describe the reality we face and the ends we aim for—as suggested by the roughly simultaneous emergence of such neologisms as *translingualism, plurilingualism, translanguaging, transcultural literacy, code meshing,* and *diversalité* to replace such terms as *multilingual* and *bilingual.* There is the challenge that the ideology of monolingualism inheres not merely in our discourse but in the academic institutional structures of programs and curricula as well as pedagogies and placement and existing assessment technologies and daily practices. For, to recall Pierre Bourdieu's warning, language ideology "is inscribed, in a practical state, in dispositions which are impalpably inculcated, through a long and slow process of acquisition, by the sanctions of the linguistic market" (Bourdieu 1991, 51). To combat monolingualist ideology, then, requires working not merely on professions of belief but on the inculcation of language dispositions and on sanctions of the linguistic market. In short, those attempting to explore translingual writing pedagogies and programs by crossing institutional disciplinary divides have their work cut out for them.

At the same time, as all the chapters in this collection make clear, there is both excitement and urgency driving such efforts. Resisting the temptation to stabilize (for purposes of analysis) and to parse out differences in the theoretical positions various of these efforts might align or conflict with, the contributors' chapters, and this collection as a whole, are driven by a shared sense of the need to work against monolingualism in writing and its teaching, issuing a resounding "No!" to monolingualism's insistence that students marked by (marked) language difference be quarantined as ESL or BW or (merely) FYW students and kept from admission to the academic community as full members, and to the normalizing of those writers that monolingualist ideology treats as unmarked by language difference. Following the lesson of the Buddhist parable of the poisoned arrow (see Hanh 1991, 299–300), we recognize that what matters most—to our students, ourselves, and our shared work and lives together—is finding the antidote to monolingualism's poison.

This is not, of course, to discount the value of theoretical parsing to verify the effectivity of the antidotes to monolingualism being pursued. As Juan Guerra and Ann Shivers-McNair argue in their chapter, discussions of translingualism have "evolved," shifting from a focus on disenfranchised students to all writers, and in the process have come to be marked by debates on how best to understand the problem, producing a

Bourdieuian "battlefield" of competing terms and concepts both drawn and reworked from a range of disciplinary traditions. Participating in this transdisciplinary effort, Guerra and Shivers-McNair themselves draw on feminist quantum physicist Karen Barad's notions of entanglement and diffraction. These concepts enable them to read (diffractively) the figurations of translingualism with quantum notions of entanglement and diffraction to further understand the significance of the temporal dimension of utterances (and the attendant difference this brings) and its intertwining with the spatial, and to better grasp the sedimentation of language practices and conceptualize the key concept of agency on which much of the debate on translingual writing has focused (see, for example, Lu and Horner 2013).

From a quite different perspective, in their chapter, Sara P. Alvarez, Suresh Canagarajah, Eunjeong Lee, Jerry Won Lee, and Shakil Rabbi take up the charged issue of the relationship between ethnic identities and heritage languages, a relationship a translingual perspective challenges. Noting that "ethnic identities and heritage languages are always already translingual," the authors also recognize the ideological reality of the "unique identity" of the mix of practices identified with any one of these (e.g., Korean, Spanish, Tamil [as ethnolinguistic categories]) (33). Using instances from their own teaching and learning experiences, the authors show the dialectical dance between ascribed ethnolinguistic identities and translingual practice. Acknowledging that there is no escape from ascriptions of "voice, identity, or ethnicity" but also that these are never stable or pure, the authors' accounts show the need to be strategically "proactive" in response to these ascriptions, using whatever linguistic and other resources are available, and those ascriptions themselves, to engage in performances of identity (45).

The chapters in part 2, "Pedagogical Interventions," describe specific efforts to work against the inscription of monolingualist ideology in pedagogy. In "Enacting Translingual Writing Pedagogy: Structures and Challenges for Two Courses in Two Countries," William Lalicker describes two composition courses he identifies as translingual. Not only are the courses intended to enroll students with a diverse range of language backgrounds and practices, but the design of the courses takes that diversity as the norm and context to be engaged in and through assigned course work. Rather than restricting the course focus to students identified as international and/or ESL, and rather than assuming the myth of linguistic homogeneity (all students as "native" English-speaking monolinguals [Matsuda 2006]) as the norm for students to represent and follow, Lalicker's courses take the presence of, and need to work across, English(es) and other languages as the (translingual) statistical and cultural norm, making "translingual rhetorical interaction central" to the pedagogy and to students' writing (52). However, in the efforts Lalicker describes at achieving equitable exchange in his courses between and among students from China and the United States, he also cautions that "extend[ing] translingualism to its fully international enactment" requires attention to the material conditions necessary to such enactment, conditions currently available only to students with significant financial means (65). Otherwise there is a risk that any international enactment of translingual approaches will come to be both a means and sign of privilege.

In "Who Owns English in South Korea," Patricia Bizzell explores the implications of notions of language ownership by attending to the various senses in which contemporary South Koreans might be said to "own" English despite the status of English in South Korea as a second rather than first language without official status. Drawing on the South Korean history of language politics, Bizzell's own experience teaching English in South Korea, and her study of the teaching of English in South Korea and the employment experiences of expat English teachers in South Korea, Bizzell identifies a range of conflicting treatments of English." These including significant flexibility in the conceptualization and use of English (including an acceptance of Konglish), a racialized concept of English and a racialized, gendered, ageist, and regionalist ideal for teachers of English (with young white female North Americans preferred), a complacent view of the intermixing of languages—such as Chinese, Japanese, and English with Korean—and a progressive view of language learning. Bizzell's account of English "ownership" in South Korea thus throws into sharp relief those approaches to and conceptions of language and language relations dominating practices of US educational institutions and culture while also offering a cautionary tale on celebrations of extending language ownership, highlighting the need to attend to the location and specific ways such ownership is instantiated.

Both Lalicker and Bizzell focus on international exchanges and differences in languages (e.g., Korean, English, Chinese, Japanese) as sites for and means of advancing translingual approaches to writing. In "Teaching Translingual Agency in Iteration: Rewriting Difference," Bruce Horner takes a different route, focusing not on how to accommodate those differences in language monolingualism has already disposed us to recognize as differences but, rather, on differences inherent to any and all utterances, including those monolingualism disposes us to view not as different at all but, instead, as instances of "the same."

Cautioning that pedagogies that might seem to work against monolingualism may inadvertently perpetuate it by accepting its definitions of what counts as language difference, and that pedagogies that might superficially appear to perpetuate monolingualism might call it into question, Horner asks that we design assignments that help us and our students "rethink what differences might be made through and in all writing practices, whether marked by the dominant as conventional writing or as unconventional" (92). And he offers double translation as a means of calling into question monolingualist notions of languages as stable and uniform "codes."

The chapters in part 3 address interventions in the monolinguistic frameworks dominating the teaching of postsecondary writing at the programmatic level: matters of curriculum, assessment, and the larger shifts in student demographics and institutional missions to which writing programs must respond. In "Disrupting Monolingualist Ideologies in a Community College: A Translingual Studio Approach," Katie Malcolm focuses on using acceleration programs in community colleges to advance translingual approaches to writing and its teaching. By calling for "institutional and classroom practices that examine, critique, and resist the monolingualist ideologies that deem certain students in need of remediation from the outset" (103), Malcolm draws attention to the necessity of questioning monolingualist assumptions at the level of programmatic reform. While the elimination or reduction of remedial course requirements that acceleration programs accomplish is a step in the right direction, Malcolm reminds us that the new requirements taking their place must work to instill "pedagogical practices that help students recognize their language differences as iterative assets for disseminating and creating knowledge"(103) to avoid playing into the same monolingualist ideology that has long marginalized multilingual students placed into remedial courses. And to benefit all students, Malcolm calls for an explicit pedagogical focus on seeing differences as important resources, instilling dispositions of openness to negotiate these differences and providing strategies for uncovering and critiquing the systems of valuation that construct some language practices as different and others as the norm.

To investigate how language ideologies inform the ways in which instructors evaluate students, Asao B. Inoue, in "Writing Assessment as the Conditions for Translingual Approaches: An Argument for Fairer Assessments," considers assessment as one site where writing programs can "find ways to cultivate a degree of fair conditions that agree with the basic assumptions translingual approaches hold" (119). Proceeding from the premise that we need new ways to assess writing if writing teachers and programs are to adopt translingual approaches to language, Inoue posits that "writing assessments must honor and value in tangible ways students' language practices and histories and not punish students for producing language difference (to a hegemonic norm)" (120). To help develop these kinds of assessments that see language difference as a much richer matter than correct or incorrect usage, Inoue argues specifically for assessment approaches that give more power to students through careful respect, listening, and negotiation. Inoue's examination of assessment demonstrates how translingual approaches call for a reconsideration of previously entrenched practices at the pedagogical and programmatic levels and how translingual conditions for learning can be constructed through revised assessment practices.

In "Seizing an Opportunity for Translingual FYC at the University of Maine: Provocative Complexities, Unexpected Consequences," Dylan Dryer and Paige Mitchell argue for a "documentary" approach to writing program administration. Attending to the ways institutional "documents 'enact' intentions tangential to or counter to our efforts" (148), they explore "networks of documents and administrative structures" with which translingual dispositions can be scaffolded (135). Their efforts at Maine show the productive complexities that arise from attempting to teach students within the framework of a translingual curriculum, how translingual approaches may be impacted by a university's recruitment efforts for international students, and how documents such as rater responses to student portfolios can influence dispositions toward language use.

Chris Gallagher and Matt Noonan address similar tensions in "Becoming Global: Learning to 'Do' Translingualism." Gallagher and Noonan examine the dynamic between Northeastern University's "branding" as a global university and the writing program's efforts to develop translingual approaches to instruction and assessment. Their analysis of that dynamic leads them to the realization that translingualism is "not a state of being, but rather a process we must learn and learn again" (165), and that this process will likely look different in various institutional contexts. Treating translingual dispositions as learning practices, Gallagher and Noonan also draw attention to the necessity of preparing teachers and administrators for encountering what is recognized as language difference in student work, which involves "learning about and from students how to teach them" (166). Fostering these learning processes also involves confronting the labor conditions within a writing program that may enable or constrain the ability to prepare instructors for encounters with language difference. Gallagher and Noonan explore how to foster translingual approaches at two levels—programmatic policy and pedagogy in specific courses—leading them to argue that for such an approach to be "meaningful and productive for students, it must be integrated into, must emerge from, their reading and writing practices" (175), which are also continually evolving.

The chapters by Christine Tardy, Thomas Lavelle, and Kate Mangelsdorf comprising part 4 offer considered responses to and perspectives on the efforts at crossing divides represented by the other chapters. Writing from the perspective of applied linguistics, Tardy cautions that the use of new terminology—such as *translingualism*—for naming language ideologies, practices, and pedagogies may have the unintended effect of cutting off attention to extant relevant and aligned knowledge represented under the guise of more established terms in fields traditionally kept at arm's length from composition—for Tardy, especially the fields of second language writing, World Englishes, and second language acquisition. And, echoing Dryer and Mitchell and others (see, for example, Kilfoil 2014), Tardy calls for reforming graduate education in composition to give renewed emphasis to language study as central, rather than ancillary, to the study of writing and its teaching and thereby to support crossing of the disciplinary divides currently segregating work in all these fields.

In "Ins and Outs of Translingual Labor," Thomas Lavelle uses Imre Lakatos's distinction between centrifugal and centripetal forces in disciplinary work to draw out a tension in contributors' chapters between attempts to articulate translingual beliefs about language and ideology and attempts to enact these in curricula, programs, and pedagogy. In line with the caution from Bourdieu we note above about the inscription of dominant language ideologies in dispositions and institutional structures, Lavelle notes what he terms the "seepage" of monolingualist ideology even into those practices intended to combat it as teacher-scholars and program administrators confront that inscription. This leads Lavelle to offer, as a kind of heuristic for such work, attention to an "arc linking language ideology > individual and institutional complicity > insufficient training in thinking about language > unfair portfolio assessments" (196). While he sees the need for more attention to the third link in this arc as an antidote to monolingualist seepage, he also acknowledges that every link in such cycles has the potential to be simultaneously a point of reinforcement of and break in that cycle.

Kate Mangelsdorf offers a similar assessment. Noting the diversity of pedagogical, curricular, and programmatic practices being pursued under the translingual rubric, she argues for the need to see efforts at translingual enactments described in the collection's chapters as "developmental," and, in light of the intransigence of institutional structures, she cautions that these will "take a long time to implement, involve a great deal of compromise, and can initially lead to resistance and confusion" (199). Furthering Tardy's call for changes to graduate-program curricula to address language issues, Mangelsdorf also highlights the challenges attempts at such changes face in overcoming entrenched claims to curricular space in graduate programs and the threat renewed attention to language might appear to pose to the privileged space occupied in graduate-program curricula by courses in, say, rhetorical theory and history. But she also calls for pursuing additional avenues by which a translingual orientation might advance, such as its relation to teaching and scholarship addressing the multimodal character of communicative practices.

In the article "Language Difference in Writing: Toward a Translingual Approach," the authors acknowledge that in fact "we are still at the beginning stages of our learning efforts in this project" (Horner et al. 2011, 310). *Crossing Divides* helps those efforts by providing specific, concrete explorations, from a wide variety of institutional conditions and perspectives, of what might be involved in taking up a translingual approach in our work as composition teachers, scholars, and program administrators. To attempt to cross divides means, first and foremost, recognizing the presence of the institutional, disciplinary, programmatic, curricular, and pedagogical divides we face, just as cross-language work must take as its point of departure the presence of languages to be "crossed." Simultaneously, however, crossing these divides requires that we refuse to accept the inherent stability of the borders separating us, recognizing that, though real, those borders are also the outcome of, and are therefore dependent on and vulnerable to, our practices—in our work as teachers, scholars, and program administrators. As Louis-Jean Calvet has warned of linguists' representations of language practices, these representations "act on practices and are one of the factors of change" (Calvet 1999; 2006, 241), noting that, for example, "*the invention of a language* and consequently the *way it is named* constitute an intervention in and modify the ecolinguistic niche" (Calvet 1999; 2006, 248).

Those attempting to cross divides produced by and maintaining the ideology of monolingualism must contend with this dialectic: confronting, by reworking, those representational practices in their work as teachers, scholars, and program administrators that heretofore have helped maintain the hegemonic position of monolingualism, whether by giving new inflections to these representational practices, twisting

their shape and significance, or finding in putatively monolinguistic traditions the bases for monolingualism's demise. Like national borders,
divides meant to keep separate can unwittingly bring the underlying
continuities they deny into visibility. The divides we cross—of differences in language, identity, discipline, program, curriculum, and pedagogy—while bringing into often sharp relief the work cut out for us, also
offer the means by which we can, and must, take up that work. The chapters in this collection show us the shape this work can take.

Note

1. The focus of the Symposium on Second Language Writing and the *Journal of Second Language Writing* is not restricted to writing only in English as a second language.

References

Baker, Will. 2013. ""Interpreting the Culture in Intercultural Rhetoric: A Critical Perspective from English as a Lingua Franca Studies." 2013." In *Critical and Corpus-Based Approaches to Intercultural Rhetoric*, edited by Diane Belcher and Gayle Nelson, 22–45. Ann Arbor: University of Michigan Press.
Belcher, Diane. 2014. "What We Need and Don't Need Intercultural Rhetoric for: A Retrospective and Prospective Look at an Evolving Research Area." *Journal of Second Language Writing* 25 (1): 59–67.
Bernabé, Jean, Patrick Chamoiseau, and Raphaël Confiant. 1989. *Éloge de la créolité*. Paris: Gallimard.
Bernabé, Jean, Patrick Chamoiseau, and Raphaël Confiant. 1999. *In Praise of Creoleness*. Translated by Mohamed B. Taleb Khyar. Baltimore, MD: Johns Hopkins University Press.
Blommaert, Jan. 2010. *The Sociolinguistics of Globalization*. Cambridge: Cambridge University Press.
Bourdieu, Pierre. 1991. *Language and Symbolic Power*. Edited by John B. Thompson. Translated by Gino Raymond and Matthew Adamson. Cambridge, MA: Harvard University Press.
Bruch, Patrick, and Richard Marback, eds. 2004. *The Hope and the Legacy: The Past, Present, and Future of "Students' Right to Their Own Language."* Cresskill, NJ: Hampton.
Calvet, Louis-Jean. 1999. *Pour une écologie des langues du monde*. Paris: Plon.
Calvet, Louis-Jean. 2006. *Towards an Ecology of World Languages*. Translated by Andrew Brown. London: Polity.
Canagarajah, A. Suresh. 2006. "The Place of World Englishes in Composition: Pluralization Continued." *College Composition and Communication* 57 (4): 586–619.
Canagarajah, A. Suresh. 2009. "Multilingual Strategies of Negotiating English: From Conversation to Writing." *JAC* 29 (1–2): 17–48.
Canagarajah, A. Suresh. 2011. "Afterword: World Englishes as Code-Meshing." In *Code-Meshing as World English: Pedagogy, Policy, Performance*, edited by Vershawn Ashanti Young and Aja Y. Martinez, 273–81. Urbana, IL: NCTE.
Canagarajah, A. Suresh. 2013. *Translingual Practice: Global Englishes and Cosmopolitan Relations*. London: Routledge.
Canagarajah, A. Suresh. 2016. "Crossing Borders, Addressing Diversity." *Language Teaching* 49 (3): 438–54.

Conference on College Composition and Communication. 1974. "Students' Right to Their Own Language." Special issue, *College Composition and Communication* 25. http://www.ncte.org/library/NCTEFiles/Groups/CCCC/NewSRTOL.pdf.

Cross-Border Education Research Team. (2016). "Branch Campus Listing." Last updated June 17, 2016. http://www.globalhighered.org/?page_id=34.

Doiz, Aintzane, David Lasagabaster, and Juan Manuel Sierra, eds. 2013. *English-Medium Instruction at Universities: Global Challenges.* Bristol, UK: Multilingual Matters.

Firth, Alan, and Johannes Wagner. 1997. "On Discourse, Communication, and (Some) Fundamental Concepts in SLA Research." *Modern Language Journal* 81 (3): 285–300.

García, Ofelia, and Wei Li. 2014. *Translanguaging: Language, Bilingualism and Education.* New York: Palgrave Macmillan.

Hall, Jonathan. 2014. "Multilinguality Is the Mainstream." In *Reworking English in Rhetoric and Composition: Global Interrogations, Local Interventions*, edited by Bruce Horner and Karen Kopelson, 31–48. Carbondale: Southern Illinois University Press.

Hanh, Thích Nhất. 1991. *Old Path White Clouds: Walking in the Footsteps of the Buddha.* Berkeley, CA: Parallax.

Heller, Monica, ed. 2007. *Bilingualism: A Social Approach.* Basingstoke, UK: Palgrave Macmillan.

Hesford, Wendy, Eddie Singleton, and Ivonne M. García. 2009. "Laboring to Globalize a First-Year Writing Program." In *The Writing Program Interrupted: Making Space for Critical Discourse*, edited by Donna Strickland and Jeanne Gunner, 113–25. Portsmouth, NH: Boynton/Cook.

Horner, Bruce. 2001. "'Students' Right,' English Only, and Re-Imagining the Politics of Language." *College English* 63 (6): 741–58.

Horner, Bruce, and Karen Kopelson, eds. 2014. *Reworking English in Rhetoric and Composition: Global Interrogations, Local Interventions.* Carbondale: Southern Illinois University Press.

Horner, Bruce, Min-Zhan Lu, Jacqueline Jones Royster, and John Trimbur. 2011. "Language Difference in Writing: Toward a Translingual Approach." *College English* 73 (3): 303–21.

Horner, Bruce, Samantha NeCamp, and Christiane Donahue. 2011. "Toward a Multilingual Composition Scholarship: From English Only to a Translingual Norm." *College Composition and Communication* 63 (2): 269–300.

Horner, Bruce, and John Trimbur. 2002. "English Only and U.S. College Composition." *College Composition and Communication* 53 (4): 594–630.

Jenkins, Jennifer. 2014. *English as a Lingua Franca in the International University: The Politics of Academic English Language Policy.* London: Routledge.

Khubchandani, Lachman M. 1998. "A Plurilingual Ethos: A Peep into the Sociology of Language." *Indian Journal of Applied Linguistics* 24 (1): 5–37.

Kilfoil, Carrie Byars. 2014. "The Language Politics of Doctoral Studies in Rhetoric and Composition: Toward a Translingual Revision of Graduate Education in the Field." PhD diss., University of Louisville.

Leung, Constant. 2005. "Convivial Communication: Recontextualizing Communicative Competence." *International Journal of Applied Linguistics* 15 (2): 119–44.

Leung, Constant. 2013. "The 'Social' in English Language Teaching: Abstracted Norms versus Situated Enactments." *Journal of English as a Lingua Franca* 2 (2): 283–313.

Leung, Constant, Roxy Harris, and Ben Rampton. 1997. "The Idealised Native Speaker, Reified Ethnicities, and Classroom Realities." *TESOL Quarterly* 31 (3): 543–75.

Lu, Min-Zhan. 2004. "Composing Post-Colonial Studies." In *Crossing Borderlands: Composition and Postcolonial Studies*, edited by Andrea Lunsford and Lahoucine Ouzgane, 9–32. Pittsburgh, PA: University of Pittsburgh Press.

Lu, Min-Zhan. 2009. "Metaphors Matter: Transcultural Literacy." *JAC* 29 (1–2): 285–93.

Lu, Min-Zhan, and Bruce Horner. 2013. "Translingual Literacy, Language Difference, and Matters of Agency." *College English* 75 (6): 586–611.

Lu, Min-Zhan, and Bruce Horner. 2016. "Translingual Work." *College English* 78 (3): 207–18.

Martins, David S., ed. 2015. *Transnational Writing Program Administration.* Logan: Utah State University Press.

Matsuda, Paul Kei. 1997. "Contrastive Rhetoric in Context: A Dynamic Model of L2 Writing." *Journal of Second Language Writing* 6 (1): 45–60.

Matsuda, Paul Kei. 1999. "Composition Studies and ESL Writing: A Disciplinary Division of Labor." *College Composition and Communication* 50 (4): 699–721.

Matsuda, Paul Kei. 2006. "The Myth of Linguistic Homogeneity in U.S. College Composition." *College English* 68 (6): 637–51.

Matsuda, Paul Kei. 2013. "It's the Wild West Out There: A New Linguistic Frontier in U.S. College Composition." In *Literacy as Translingual Practice: Between Communities and Classrooms,* edited by A. Suresh Canagarajah, 128–38. London: Routledge.

Parakrama, Arjuna. 1995. *De-Hegemonizing Language Standards: Learning from (Post)Colonial Englishes about "English."* London: Palgrave.

Pennycook, Alastair. 2010. *Language as a Local Practice.* London: Routledge.

Rouse, John. 1979. "The Politics of Composition." *College English* 41 (1): 1–12.

Seawright, Leslie E., ed. 2014. *Going Global: Transnational Perspectives on Globalization, Language, and Education.* Newcastle-upon-Tyne: Cambridge Scholars.

Smitherman, Geneva. 1999. "CCCC's Role in the Struggle for Language Rights." *College Composition and Communication* 50 (3): 349–76.

Wible, Scott. 2013. *Shaping Language Policy in the U.S.: The Role of Composition Studies.* Carbondale: Southern Illinois University Press.

Wingate, Ursula. 2015. *Academic Literacy and Student Diversity: The Case for Inclusive Practice.* Bristol, UK: Multilingual Matters.

Yildiz, Yasemin. 2012. *Beyond the Mother Tongue: The Postmonolingual Condition.* New York: Fordham University Press.

Young, Vershawn Ashanti. 2009. "'Nah, We Straight': An Argument Against Code Switching." *JAC* 29 (1–2): 29–46.

Young, Vershawn Ashanti, and Aja Martinez, eds. 2011. *Code-Meshing as World English: Policy, Pedagogy, Performance.* Urbana, IL: NCTE.

Zamel, Vivian. 1997. "Toward a Model of Transculturation." *TESOL Quarterly* 31 (2): 341–51.

Zarate, Geneviève, Danielle Lévy, and Claire Kramsch, eds. 2008. *Précis du plurilinguisme et du pluriculturalisme.* Paris: Éditions des Archives Contemporaines.

Ziguras, Christopher. 2005. "International Trade in Education Services: Governing the Liberalization and Regulation of Private Enterprise." In *Globalizing Education: Policies, Pedagogies, and Politics,* edited by Michael W. Apple, Jane Kenway, and Michael Singh, 93–112. New York: Peter Lang.

PART 1

Theorizing Translinguality in Writing and Its Teaching

1

TOWARD A NEW VOCABULARY OF MOTIVE
Re(con)figuring Entanglement in a Translingual World

Juan C. Guerra and Ann Shivers-McNair

In the few years since Bruce Horner, Min-Zhan Lu, Jacqueline Jones Royster, and John Trimbur introduced the term *translingualism* to composition and literacy studies (Horner et al. 2011)—four years after Mary Louise Pratt and the MLA foreign-language committee she chaired published their position on the critical role *translingualism* and *transculturation* play in the foreign-language classroom (Ad Hoc Committee on Foreign Languages 2007; Pratt et al. 2008)—scholars in the field have immersed themselves in conversations about what translingual writing is, as well as where it ends and where everything else—ESL, basic, multilingual *and* mainstream writing—begins (Matsuda 2014). As more voices have joined the conversation, translingualism has evolved from an approach to language difference designed for specific intervention in the lives of disenfranchised students to one intended to address the needs of all student writers (Lu and Horner 2013, 585). Not surprisingly, recent efforts to explicate the concept's core characteristics have led to implicit debates about the kind of vocabulary that best explains the motives of scholars who have embraced the term and all it signifies.

In what follows, we argue that the emergence of translingualism as a new approach to language difference is symptomatic of efforts by transdisciplinary scholars interested in challenging the ideological constraints of monolingualism, an approach that for far too long has colonized the writing classroom, as well as in demonstrating dissatisfaction with efforts by proponents of multilingualism—referred to as the "traditional multilingual model" by Bruce Horner, Samantha NeCamp and Christiane Donahue—to rectify monolingualism's shortcomings (Horner, NeCamp, and Donahue 2011, 287) (for a discussion

DOI: 10.7330/9781607326205.c001

of the difference between interdisciplinarity and transdisciplinarity, see Hawhee 2009). Because critiques designed to respond to the vicissitudes ignored by monolingualism and multilingualism require the introduction of a new vocabulary of motive, efforts to establish the legitimacy of a translingual approach have reflected a collective, albeit unorchestrated, search for a figurative language that provides fresh insights and a vocabulary of motive that takes us beyond worn and tired conceptualizations with little generative power.

We begin our effort to describe a vocabulary of motive (we acknowledge ours is provisional, one others will want to refine and modify in situ) by locating translingualism in the context of approaches to language difference. We then review various efforts among scholars in composition and literacy studies to informally identify what C. Wright Mills (1940) refers to as a "vocabulary of motive"[1] and Rosi Braidotti (1994) calls "figurations."[2] We conclude by introducing a generative vocabulary developed by Karen Barad (2007) in her work on material-discursive phenomena to illustrate a critical shift taking place in the field toward the use of a more precise vocabulary that addresses the rhetorical and discursive needs of our students as they tackle the array of conflicts and contradictions language difference produces in their lives.

APPROACHES TO LANGUAGE DIFFERENCE

In light of current conversations in composition and literacy studies about how best to approach language difference, and in keeping with our effort to unpack the vocabularies of motive that have informed them, we begin by first reviewing the three approaches to language difference that have emerged as most salient in the course of various critiques by proponents of translingualism (see table 2.1). Historically, the monolingual approach has maintained hegemonic control in the teaching of first-year writing since its inception at Harvard University in 1885 (Horner and Trimbur 2002, 597). The entailments listed under the first column below emphatically demonstrate its ideological attributes: it is assimilative and grounded in a superficial understanding of language and culture that suggests English monolingualism reflects a national commitment in the United States to a traditional and singular linguistic identity unwilling to acknowledge a role for any other language in public discourse. The ideological trajectory also identifies its commitment to monolingual English as a consequence of the nation's colonial past. Because the United States was founded by an English-speaking people, proponents of monolingualism contend it must maintain that linguistic

Table 2.1. Social and ideological approaches to language and cultural difference

Monolingual/Monocultural	Multilingual/Multicultural	Translingual/Transcultural
Code Segregation	Code Switching	Code Meshing
Assimilation	Acculturation	Transculturation
Eradication	Accommodation	Hybridization
Language Understanding	Language Awareness	Critical Language Awareness
Cultural Understanding	Cultural Awareness	Critical Cultural Awareness
Life in the Either/Or	Life in the Both/And	Life in the Neither/Nor
Conservative	Liberal	Progressive
Traditional	Modern	Postmodern
National	International	Transnational
Colonial	Neocolonial	Decolonial

identity under any circumstances. As a consequence, Bruce Horner and John Trimbur argue, "a tacit language policy of unidirectional English monolingualism has shaped the historical formation of U.S. writing instruction and continues to influence its theory and practice in shadowy, largely unexamined ways" (Horner and Trimbur 2002, 594–95).

Because a monolingual paradigm has been in place for so long, efforts to challenge, much less dismantle, it have faced great odds. In the 1980s and 1990s, for example, the battle cry against monolingualism was taken up by multidisciplinary scholars in the field who formulated a strategy grounded in multilingualism and multiculturalism, a counternarrative that argued that because the United States is a nation of immigrants, the teaching of writing should reflect a respect for the linguistic and cultural practices of multilingual students who at the time were enrolling in increasing numbers in colleges and universities across the country. As the second column in table 2.1 suggests, a multilingual approach to language difference was grounded in the idea that students in writing classes should be encouraged to engage in code switching as they move from one cultural context (the home or community) to another (the academy). Because it is aligned with a liberal commitment to accommodation and encourages both students and teachers to become increasingly aware of how language and culture influence their writing, a multilingual approach substitutes the salad-bowl metaphor for the melting-pot metaphor favored by proponents of monolingualism (Severino, Guerra, and Butler 1998, 1). While the multilingual effort has produced a lot of scholarship we simply do not have space and time to present here, the key arguments put forth by its proponents are well represented in Carol Severino, Juan C. Guerra and Johnnella E. Butler's edited collection *Writing in Multicultural Settings* (Severino, Guerra, and Butler 1998). Several essays in the collection, for example (as is also true of most scholarship with a traditional multilingual perspective), demonstrate a tendency to fix language, culture, and identity, framing each of them as discrete and nonporous entities proponents of translingualism have found problematic. At the same time, however, a number of essays in the collection resist the tendency to fix language, culture, and identity, among them Esha Niyogi De and Donna Uthus Gregory's "Decolonizing the Classroom: Freshman Composition in a Multicultural Setting," which Stephanie Kerschbaum (2014) praises for its effort to think of student identities as "the embodiment of a complex set of identifications that must be considered together" rather than in terms of "single identifiers" (De and Gregory 1998, 10).

A quick glimpse at the third column in table 2.1 readily demonstrates the affiliation proponents of translingualism have with what in cultural studies and critical theory are considered progressive positions designed to challenge the constraining elements that inform both a monolingual and a multilingual approach to language difference. According to Horner, Lu, Royster and Trimbur (2011) (see also Horner, NeCamp, and Donahue 2011; Lu and Horner 2013), who as we noted earlier introduced the concept of translingualism to the field of composition and literacy studies, a monolingual approach is problematic because it takes as the norm "a linguistically homogeneous situation: one where writers, speakers and readers are expected to use Standard English or Edited American English—imagined ideally as uniform—to the exclusion of other languages and language variations" (Horner, Lu, Royster and Trimbur 2011, 303). Unfortunately, the multilingual approach that emerged to challenge that norm did not go far enough because the multilingual approach assumed "that each codified set of language practices is appropriate only to a specific, discrete, assigned social sphere: 'home' language, 'street' language, 'academic' language, 'business' language, 'written' language, and so on" (306). In Horner, Lu, Royster and Trimbur's view, a translingual approach offers a meaningful alternative because it "(1) [honors] the power of all language users to shape language to specific ends; (2) [recognizes] the linguistic heterogeneity of all users of language both within the United States and globally; and (3) directly [confronts] English monolingualist expectations by researching and teaching how writers can work with and against, not simply within, those expectations" (305). While the recent appearance of the term *translingualism* gives this approach an air of newness, of something scholars in the field have not considered before, the string of entailments listed under the third column of table 2.1 suggests that the ideology informing a translingual approach is by no means a new phenomenon but instead reflects a system of dispositions that provides an alternative to the colonial and neocolonial ideologies reflected, respectively, in a monolingual and a multilingual approach.

Although the introduction of a translingual approach has destabilized the binary and the dichotomous relationship implied by the relationship between a monolingual and a multilingual approach, the translingual approach has also raised questions about the extent to which it in turn is establishing a hegemonic presence in composition and literacy studies, especially as it relates to long-standing positions reflected in the work of scholars who have challenged "the myth of linguistic homogeneity" (Matsuda 2006) in basic (through work on the dialect practices of underrepresented minority students) and ESL (through work on the multilingual practices of immigrant students) writing. Part of the problem, as we see it, is the tendency among proponents of translingualism to borrow figurations from allied disciplines that serve its purposes in making a case against both monolingualism and multilingualism. In some respects, the tension between these related but varied perspectives signals a new and unanticipated contestation as proponents of the various approaches work together or against one another to demarcate the role of their respective takes on language difference. In an effort to address some of these tensions, we will examine in the next section a range of neologisms as well as standard terms given new meanings that proponents, allies, and, at times, detractors of translingualism have introduced to identify what we consider an emerging vocabulary of motive that provides a critically grounded and progressive response to language difference.

COMPETING VOCABULARIES OF MOTIVE

The vocabulary of motive that has taken root in the work of transdisciplinary scholars involved in forging a new language that critiques the constraints inherent in the vocabularies of motive informing monolingual and multilingual approaches to language difference is certainly not unique to them. Because they are interested in disrupting and destabilizing ideological efforts to fix reality inside discrete borders, transdisciplinary scholars in the broader field of language, culture, and rhetoric have also identified neologisms and given standard terms new meanings. In their effort to develop "a framework for the analysis of identity as constituted in linguistic interaction," for example, Mary Bucholtz and Kira Hall approach identity "as a relational and socio-cultural phenomenon that emerges and circulates in local discourse contexts of interaction rather than as a stable structure located primarily in the individual psyche or in fixed social categories" (Bucholtz and Hall 2005, 585–86). In so describing identity, they posit five principles—emergence, positionality, indexicality, relationality and partialness—that describe identity as "a discursive construct that emerges in interaction" (587). In her effort to develop a new rhetoric of difference, Stephanie Kerschbaum (2014) uses similar language in challenging efforts in composition and literacy studies to fix difference by taxonomizing and redefining it. Although such efforts have enhanced the way we teach with and across difference, these kinds of approaches "to studying and writing about difference still freeze particular subjects, details and interpretations within the research literature" (12). In arguing for what she calls "marking difference," Kerschbaum uses language similar to Bucholtz and Hall's to accent the importance of making visible "the dynamism, the relationality, and the emergence of difference" (7). Although they do not directly identify themselves as proponents of translingualism, the vocabulary of motive accented by these transdisciplinary scholars nevertheless hints at an attitude, orientation, or perspective that defines in similar terms a position that has emerged in the literature on translingualism.

In the course of introducing translingualism to the field of composition and literacy studies, Horner, Lu, Royster and Trimbur (2011) accent many of these same characteristics in languages and language users in an effort "to develop alternatives to conventional treatments of language difference" (304). In the process, they invoke several of the figurations we have shared in our review of scholarly work on the periphery of translingualism. For example, they acknowledge that "the formation and definition of languages and language varieties are fluid" (304) and contend that a translingual approach "takes the variety, fluidity, intermingling, and changeability of languages as statistically demonstrable norms around the globe" (305). They also make every effort to demonstrate how a translingual approach "counters demands that writers must conform to fixed, uniform standards" by addressing "how language norms are actually heterogeneous, fluid and negotiable" (305). Horner, NeCamp and Donahue (2011) add a degree of nuance in their critique of what they call the "traditional multilingual model" by pointing out how the translingual model they support demonstrates how "languages and language boundaries are fluctuating and in constant revision" and the reasons "code-switching, borrowing, and blending of languages are [now] understood as the norm" (287). Together, Horner, Lu, Royster and Trimbur (2011) and Horner, NeCamp and Donahue (2011) engage in the critical process of highlighting figurations that signal the emergence of a vocabulary of motive that must come into play in our emergent understanding of language difference.

In "Translingual Literacy, Language Difference, and Matters of Agency," Min-Zhan Lu and Bruce Horner invoke a number of figurations that reflect an unwillingness on their part to treat languages, language users or doers, practices, conventions, and contexts "as discrete, preexisting, stable, and enumerable entities" (Lu and Horner 2013, 587)—among them, *translation, renegotiation of meaning, always emergent, in process* (a state of becoming), *relational, mutually constitutive* and *dynamic*. In so doing, they accent the ways in which a translingual approach is different from either a monolingual or multilingual approach. Lu and Horner also borrow and distill the ideas from a number of transdisciplinary scholars, among them Judith Butler, Anthony Giddens, and Alastair Pennycook, who provide a vocabulary for developing "an alternative conception of language difference in writing: one that, by insisting on the temporal character of utterances, recognizes difference not as deviation from a norm of 'sameness' but as itself the norm of language use" (584). In the course of borrowing different figurations from them, especially from Butler (e.g., the politics of the performative, the social iterability of linguistic practice, iteration as agentive), Lu and Horner signal an implicit desire to bring together a vocabulary of motive that will provide proponents of translingualism with the tools they need to challenge approaches to language difference that presume a discrete and stable universe of matter and meaning. In the course of reflecting on the array of figurations transdisciplinary scholars have invoked in their varied efforts to establish a theoretical and ideological perspective that can both inform and complicate our understanding of how language functions in a world where continuous change is the one constant, we are persuaded that the basic elements for constructing a shared vocabulary of motive exist. Before we close, however, we would like to review what we consider one of the more coherent and comprehensive vocabularies of motive we have come across, one with the potential to frame and enrich our understanding of translingualism as a viable alternative for engaging language difference.

AT THE PRECIPICE OF AN ALTERNATIVE
TRANSLINGUAL VOCABULARY OF MOTIVE

In *Meeting the Universe Halfway: Quantum Physics and the Entanglement of Matter and Meaning*, Karen Barad (2007) provides a comprehensive vocabulary of motive we believe resonates with the elements of translingualism. Because the number of figurations she coins to frame her complex argument is larger than we can accommodate in the space and time this chapter offers, we will focus our discussion on two figurations— *entanglement* and *diffraction*—that best capture the shift in orientation she argues for. Barad, a quantum physicist and feminist scholar working at the entanglement of the "natural" (material) and "social" (discursive), plainly states that "language has been granted too much power" by social constructivist theories that posit it as the "stuff of reality" (Barad 2007, 132–33), and we recognize the potential irony of applying her figurations to the study of language difference. But we argue that it is precisely her skepticism of the determining and representational powers of language that resonates with what we see as the motive of translingualism. To understand language difference as entanglement, we must first understand Barad's use of entanglement, which draws upon a quantum notion of existence. "To be entangled," Barad explains, "is not simply to be intertwined with another, as in the joining of separate entities, but to lack an independent, self-contained existence. Existence is not an individual affair. Individuals do not preexist their interactions; rather, individuals emerge through and as part of their entangled intrarelating" (ix). We add to Barad's posthumanist notion of "individuals" both language users and languages-in-use; after all, translingualism challenges notions of languages as discrete systems within which people operate and instead emphasizes the dynamic, situated nature of language practices.

How, then, do we understand language difference as entanglement? This concept, too, requires a rethinking: understanding difference not as an inherent property but as contingent. As Barad has more recently explained, "The key is understanding that identity is not essence, fixity or givenness, but a contingent iterative performativity, thereby reworking this alleged conflict into an understanding of difference not as an absolute boundary between object and subject, here and there, now and then, this and that, but rather as the effects of enacted cuts *in a radical reworking of cause/effect*" (Barad 2014, 173–74). Thus, the marking of difference, to return to Kerschbaum's phrase, is a matter of entanglement.

Understanding difference in this way can strengthen the work of translingualism scholars to disrupt the ways language, language users, and difference are figured in monolingual and multilingual paradigms. We observe that one of the major contributions of Lu and Horner (2013) is the addition of temporality to prior paradigms' spatial conceptions of context, structures, agency, power, language, and practice. While spatial conceptions rely on static borders, temporal conceptions emphasize change and dynamism, and we see Lu and Horner as trying to balance both. Barad's quantum notion of entanglement emphasizes, similarly, that boundaries (of selves, of languages) are not preexisting; they are in negotiation, in formation, deformation, and reformation. And that negotiation does not happen *in* time; it *is* time. Difference, space, and time are made and marked, remade and remarked.

This figuring of space and time has implications for a translingual understanding of the sedimenting of language practices. Both Barad (2007) and Pennycook (2010) use the term "sedimenting," but while Pennycook is referring to the sedimenting of language practices and the observability of repetition in those practices within (presumably) linear time, Barad describes sedimenting as "an ongoing process of differential mattering" in which "the past matters and so does the future, but the past is never left behind, never finished once and for all, and the future is not what will come to be in an unfolding of the present moment; rather the past and the future are enfolded participants in matter's iterative becoming" (Barad 2007, 181). Considering sedimentation both through Pennycook's understanding and Barad's quantum understanding allows us to account for the experience and observation of repetition of language practices and strengthen our resistance to an overly deterministic understanding of that repetition. Negotiation *is* time, and time *is* negotiation. The unfolding actions of language users and languages-in-use allow certain people and practices to matter and exclude other people and practices from mattering, and they also *create* (rather than *result from*) a past and *create* (rather than *cause*) a possible future, an argument similar to the one Karin Tusting (2000) offers about memory in "New Literacy Studies and Time: An Exploration." The simultaneity of possibility and exclusion, of repetition and difference, invites us to broaden not only our understanding of time and space but also of performativity, another important figuration in translingualism.

As we noted at the beginning of this section, Barad believes language has been granted too much power to determine reality, and Barad's reading of performativity is at the heart of her argument against what she sees as Butler's (and Foucault's) erroneous assertion that matter is a product of a linguistic or discursive act. Butler's "performative account of mattering thinks the matter of materiality and signification together in their indissolubility," Barad acknowledges, but, she adds, "for both Butler and Foucault, agency belongs only to the human domain" (Barad 2007, 145). So while Butler's notion of performativity, as it has been taken up in translingualism (particularly by Lu and Horner 2013), does indeed enliven a view of agency-in-action, Barad's rearticulation of performativity sees agency not only in humans and language but also in mattering itself: thus, "matter is not a linguistic construction but a discursive production in the posthumanist sense that discursive practices are themselves material (re)configurings of the world through which the determination of boundaries, properties and meanings is differentially enacted" (Barad 2007, 151). We see this quantum account of entangled performativity and meaning making as resonating with and enriching the work of translingualism to recognize agency in relations.

As Barad argues, an understanding of agency as entanglement allows us to see that agency is not an attribute, but "*is 'doing' or 'being' in its intra-activity*" (178). This means "possibilities for (intra-)acting exist at every moment, and these changing possibilities entail an ethical obligation to intra-act responsibly in the world's becoming, to contest and rework what matters and what is excluded from mattering" (178). We can see a similar move in Jay Jordan's (2015) call for a materialist, ecological approach to translingualism that does not limit its focus to humans and language alone: "An expanded material-rhetorical ecology does not eliminate possibilities for human agency so much as embed such possibilities in and among others, substituting attention, comportment and humility for a strong sense of humans' masterful extraction of resources" (372). Emphasizing a materialist view of agency as intra-activity unsettles the human-focused binary of social structure and individual humans. After all, as Barad notes, "'others' are never very far from 'us'; 'they' and 'we' are co-constituted and entangled through the very cuts 'we' help to enact. Intra-actions cut 'things' together and apart. Cuts are not enacted from the outside, nor are they ever enacted once and for all" (179). The figuration of an agentive entanglement folds back over into the rethinkings of difference, time, space, and sedimenting (as well as agency) not as a priori properties themselves but as entanglements: cutting together-apart. Thus, reading translingualism's emerging figurations with Barad's understanding of entanglement allows us to both extend the purview of entanglement to language practices and further nuance translingualism's vocabulary of motive.

CODA

As generative and important as the work of translingualism is in resisting the deleterious effects of the assumptions of the monolingual and multilingual paradigms, we believe a word of caution is in order. In framing the translingual paradigm as a corrective to monolingual and multilingual paradigms, the fact that translingualism is still itself a paradigm can be elided. Here again Barad is helpful: she reminds us that "both the phenomenon and the embodied concepts that are used to describe them are conditioned by one and the same apparatus" (174). In other words, the apparatus (in this case, the translingual paradigm and its figurations) is not external to the phenomenon itself (in this case, language practices). Or, as Juan Guerra (2013) reminds us, "We find what we look for, and we look for what the conceptual lenses we use allow us to see" (83). We are reminded, furthermore, of Raúl Sánchez's (2012) call to recognize "every framework or interpretation as itself part of the system being described rather than a privileged perspective on that system" (238). Just as a translingual vocabulary of motive encourages and enables us to account and intervene ethically in the entanglements of difference and agency, as well as in time and space, it also reminds us to account for our apparatus (the translingual paradigm) as part of those entanglements.

Notes

1. According to Mills (1940), motive consists of "the terms with which interpretations of conduct *by social actors* proceeds [*sic*]" (904). Motives and actions, he points out, often originate "not from within but from the situation in which individuals find themselves" (904). This particular conception of motive, he argues, "translates the question of 'why' into a 'how' that is answerable in terms of a situation and its typal vocabulary of motive, i.e., those which conventionally accompany that type situation and function as cues and justifications for normative actions in it" (906).

2. Braidotti (1994) defines a figuration as a politically informed account of an alternative subjectivity designed to help us "learn to think differently about the subject, invent new frameworks, new images, new modes of thought" (1). Because this figurative mode functions according to what she calls "the philosophy of 'as if,'" that is, "as if some experiences were reminiscent or evocative of others" (5), a figuration has the potential to open up, "through successive repetitions and mimetic strategies, spaces where alternative forms of agency can be engendered" (7).

References

Ad Hoc Committee on Foreign Languages. 2007. "Foreign Languages and Higher Education: New Structures for a Changed World." Modern Language Association. https://www.mla.org/Resources/Research/Surveys-Reports-and-Other-Documents /Teaching-Enrollments-and-Programs/Foreign-Languages-and-Higher-Education -New-Structures-for-a-Changed-World.

Barad, Karen. 2007. *Meeting the Universe Halfway: Quantum Physics and the Entanglement of Matter and Meaning*. Durham, NC: Duke University Press.

Barad, Karen. 2014. "Diffracting Diffraction: Cutting Together-Apart." *Parallax* 20 (3): 168–87.

Braidotti, Rosi. 1994. *Nomadic Subjects*. New York: Cambridge University Press.

Bucholtz, Mary, and Kira Hall. 2005. "Identity and Interaction: A Sociocultural Linguistic Approach." *Discourse Studies* 7 (4–5): 585–614.

De, Esha Niyogi, and Donna Uthus Gregory. 1998. "Decolonizing the Classroom: Freshman Composition in a Multicultural Setting." In *Writing in Multicultural Settings*, edited by Carol Severino, Juan C. Guerra, and Johnnella E. Butler, 118–32. New York: MLA.

Guerra, Juan C. 2013. "Cultivating Transcultural Citizenship in a Discursive Democracy." In *Texts of Consequence: Composing Rhetorics of Social Activism for the Writing Classroom*, edited by Christopher Wilkey and Nicholas Mauriello, 83–115. Cresskill, NJ: Hampton.

Hawhee, Debra. 2009. *Moving Bodies: Kenneth Burke at the Edges of Language*. Columbia: University of South Carolina Press.

Horner, Bruce, Min-Zhan Lu, Jacqueline Jones Royster, and John Trimbur. 2011. "Language Difference in Writing: Toward a Translingual Approach." *College English* 73 (3): 303–21.

Horner, Bruce, Samantha NeCamp, and Christiane Donahue. 2011. "Toward a Multilingual Composition Scholarship: From English Only to a Translingual Norm." *College Composition and Communication* 63 (2): 269–300.

Horner, Bruce, and John Trimbur. 2002. "English Only and U.S. College Composition." *College Composition and Communication* 53 (4): 594–630.

Jordan, Jay. 2015. "Material Translingual Ecologies." *College English* 77 (4): 364–82.

Kerschbaum, Stephanie. 2014. *Toward a New Rhetoric of Difference*. College Composition Studies in Writing and Rhetoric. Urbana, IL: NCTE.

Lu, Min-Zhan, and Bruce Horner. 2013. "Translingual Literacy, Language Difference, and Matters of Agency." *College English* 75 (6): 582–607.

Matsuda, Paul Kei. 2006. "The Myth of Linguistic Homogeneity in U.S. College Composition." *College English* 68 (6): 637–51.

Matsuda, Paul Kei. 2014. "The Lure of Translingual Writing." *PMLA* 129 (3): 478–83.

Mills, C. Wright. 1940. "Situated Actions and Vocabularies of Motive." *American Sociological Review* 5 (6): 904–13.

Pennycook, Alastair. 2010. *Language as a Local Practice*. Milton Park, UK: Routledge.

Pratt, Mary Louise, Michael Geisler, Claire Kramsch, Scott McGinnis, Peter Patrikis, Karin Ryding, and Haun Saussy. 2008. "Transforming College and University Foreign Language Departments." *Modern Language Journal* 92 (2): 287–92.

Sánchez, Raúl. 2012. "Outside the Text: Retheorizing Empiricism and Identity." *College English* 74 (3): 234–46.

Severino, Carol, Juan C. Guerra, and Johnnella E. Butler. 1998. *Writing in Multicultural Settings*. New York: MLA.

Tusting, Karin. 2000. "New Literacy Studies and Time: An Exploration." In *Situated Literacies: Reading and Writing in Context*, edited by David Barton, Mary Hamilton, and Roz Ivanič, 35–51. New York: Routledge.

2

TRANSLINGUAL PRACTICE, ETHNIC IDENTITIES, AND VOICE IN WRITING

Sara P. Alvarez, Suresh Canagarajah,
Eunjeong Lee, Jerry Won Lee, and Shakil Rabbi

Scholars in language-related fields have recently deconstructed the one language—one ethnicity notion that has dominated popular discourses and academic studies. Linguistic anthropologists, for example, assumed that when speakers switch from one language to another, they also index different ethnic identities (Gal and Irvine 1995). Similarly, Jacqueline Jones Royster (1996) has critiqued the expectation of her composition colleagues that to voice her African American identity she must use what may be understood as Black English. While dominant ideologies represent ethnicities and heritage languages as primordial, pure, and monolithic, the reality is that diverse language resources index plural and hybrid ethnicities each of us may (or may not) practice, and these identities are not a priori but constructed and evolving. In fact, some scholars consider ethnicity itself as a construct formulated in modernist and colonial contexts for political purposes (see Dirks 2001). They argue that ethnicity should no longer be treated as an exclusive category and that we ought to consider the intersectionality of identities as they are relevant to people in different situations, where ethnicity may or may not be salient and certainly may not be realized according to the ethnic categories at our disposal.

It is less clear where we go from here after the one language—one ethnicity ideology has been deconstructed. John Maher has recently introduced the notion of "metroethnicities," treating ethnic identities as playful, ironic, and parodic forms of community and identity. Maher (2010) argues that "ethnicity can be a toy. Something you play with" (584). For Maher, a fluid ethnic identity can allow individuals from conservative or fundamentalist communities to playfully adopt alternative identities and to resist the seriousness of imposed ethnicities (584). Similarly, Alastair Pennycook and Emi Otsuji have borrowed the term

DOI: 10.7330/9781607326205.c002

metroethnicity to explore "metrolingualism" as a form of language in practice in urban spaces (Pennycook and Otsuji 2015). They demonstrate how people may adopt a range of identities and languages they do not traditionally own to construct new communities and interactions in urban contexts.

However, there is a danger in exaggerating this "ludic" (Maher 2010, 584; Pennycook 2010, 133; Rampton 1999, 499) component of ethnicity and language ideology in practice, as it might give the impression of a levity that lacks serious purposes or objectives. Ethnicity has served as a form of "strategic essentialism" (Spivak 1993) for people from minority communities around the world. Their ethnicity and heritage language have become strategic in resisting the homogenizing tendencies of dominant communities. These considerations have motivated some scholars to criticize and contest what we identify as *translingual practice*, which refers to both the practice and orientation of language as translingual (Canagarajah 2013; Horner, Lu, Royster, and Trimbur 2011). That is, language is dynamically used and negotiated between language users and the socially reinforced parameters of normative language discourses. For the scholars concerned, translingual practice threatens the cultural identities of their communities. For instance, Scott Lyons (2009) has stated that code meshing[1] is a "hybrid" form of language that "violates the elders' rule of mutually assured separatism" (102). Lyons raises concerns with code meshing—and consents to code switching—because in his view the shuttling between languages encouraged by the translingual orientation and practice could hinder the ability of tribal students to maintain their heritage languages and national sovereignty. Lyons does acknowledge that his language, Ojibwe, has incorporated many words from French during colonial contact, and it is enriched by these borrowings. Yet, a concern remains that translingual writing pedagogies might lead to students' losing proficiency in their heritage languages.

Here, we would like to clarify that we see both code meshing and code switching as important visions and ways of capturing various aspects of what translingual practice can and does entitle, and for this reason we see this concern as related to the development and understanding of translingualism. However, we must move beyond Saussurean language ideologies, which describe and, to some extent, prescribe languages as monolithic systems and sets of situated codes (Burke, Crowley, and Girvin 2003; Cooper 2014). The limitation to expressions such as *code switching* or *code mixing* is their tendency to reinforce the view of languages as discrete and bounded objects. In contrast, translingualism is an ongoing effort to disabuse any analysis of such distinctions and sheds light on processes and practices people engage in during their signifying moments beyond the product or form of their language use.

In response to concerns regarding translingualism as a threat to ethnicity and heritage, such as those raised by Lyons, we point out that ethnic identities and heritage languages are always already translingual. They have emerged out of centuries of language and cultural contact. However, what gives a unique identity to the mix of cultural resources and communicative practices labeled as *Bangla, Korean, Spanish,* or *Tamil* is language ideology. It is the community's definition of what constitutes its separate identity that makes it appropriate linguistic and cultural resources for its self-fashioning.[2] In this sense, the notions of heritage languages and ethnic identities are constructed and appropriated in contested ways through individual as well as collective ideologies of heritage and ethnicity (Blackledge and Creese 2008). To consider this possibility, we must treat ideology in the post-Marxian sense, not as false consciousness but as enabling social interpretations and practices. These language ideologies shape how certain translingual practices index specific ethnic identities and constitute heritage languages through sedimented language use through time and space. Individuals can work within communally defined notions of heritage to *sustain* traditional notions of heritage but also choose to redefine and reconfigure what constitutes ethnicity through their own language practices. In this way, our focus is on the sustainability of ethnic and group affiliations as situated within particular contexts in relation to dominant ideologies and is specifically based on how students can and do situate their multilingual and multicultural writing experiences.

In the narratives below, four of us describe and analyze how we experience ethnicity in and through our translingual practice, especially as it relates to our writing and teaching. As our narratives demonstrate, we are unable to locate our identities in predefined constructs. In presenting these narratives, we aim to emphasize the complex and often unexpected ways in which ethnicity and translingual practice, as performative practices, influence each other dialectically and how these exchanges play out in our everyday professional lives. This inherent interrelationship, as we will elaborate in the discussion that follows the narratives, has significant implications for the teaching of writing.

THE LIMITS OF ESSENTIALIZATION: EUNJEONG

It was during my master's program that I first became keenly aware of my ethnic identity. In an English department where the majority of students were white, I was one of the three Asian, "nonnative" speakers of English (as monolithically imagined) out of a fifty-or-so graduate-student body. One night while discussing Edward Said's (1978) *Orientalism*, the professor specifically pointed at me and asked, "What do you think, Jeong? I was curious about what you thought of the reading since you were the only non-American here. You're from Korea, right?" The question struck me quite strongly as it meant a number of things. First, I was not quite sure whether the professor wanted my personal opinion as "non-American" or as a representative of a country, Korea, or something else. This was particularly eye opening to me, as my ethnic difference was understood as something meaningful in the classroom, or something that could be universalized for the Korean experience on reading a text, which analyzes the construction of the "Orient" from the Western perspective.

This classroom confrontation left me somewhat conflicted toward my own identity; the fact that the professor expected me to have a "unique" and "special" answer from a Korean perspective did not settle in me well, as I saw myself not just as *the* Korean but as a multilingual, multicultural person. Reflecting further back on my personal history, I did not think I was an adequate person to represent traditional assumptions of Koreans. In addition, I knew that the way in which I communicate with an audience in English, heavily influenced by my "unique" conversational fashion of writing, is not typical or welcome in academia, so bringing up my Korean voice almost seemed like another disciplinary test. I responded to the "test" with a final paper that analyzed a Korean movie in which the main character is silent throughout the entire film instead of a work written in English. My paper was returned with a number of red question marks, presumably asking for clarification on some of the word choices and appropriation of my indirect and somewhat repetitive rhetorical features in the paper compared to what is more common in English academic writing.

When I became a teacher of English for multilingual writers, I became keener about the different identities I was bringing in to my students in the classroom. Whenever I introduced myself at the beginning of the semester, I knew I needed to be ready for moments like the one with the professor. This time, however, I was not just a student but needed to bear another name, *teacher*, and more specifically, *a teacher of English writing*. How I speak and write English mattered much more in this space, not less or in a different way, which my students often extrapolated in order to place me on the continuum of various Korean students in the United States. My silent *t*, big gestures, occasionally dropped *y'all*, double modals, and reduced *ing* led my students to ask questions.

"How long have you been in the US?"

"Are you like 교포?"[3]

"Are you like us F1?"

"But you don't sound so much like Korean, like us Korean!"

"How come you have your parents living here but you're still F1?"

"Why didn't you come to US with them?"

"You could have learned English better then!"

One day, a student gave me the answer: "So, you're like half American already!"

I did not really know what to say to that comment other than, "You think so?" I did not actively or explicitly resist the identity my students ascribed to me either because I was not quite sure what my students meant by "half American." Instead, I shared my experience, such as strategies for adapting to a new environment, difficulties of living abroad, how to vote for elections in Korea while being abroad, and anecdotes about what it meant to live here as an international student and ethnic minority in the United States and on campus. This was my way of connecting to my students, about half of whom were Korean and the other half Chinese. Perhaps I was resisting the "half American" label this way. Still, what my students seemed quite curious about was whether or not I actually knew how to speak Korean or how to write my name in Chinese characters. On the last day of the class, a group of students came up to me and asked, "Can you just speak Korean to us once? We really want to hear!" Once I nonchalantly said, "그래!"[4] The students shrieked with amusement with the confirmation they probably had been wanting to obtain throughout the entire semester. My students then asked one question after another, checking to see whether I was really qualified to be Korean—that is, speaking Korean not as a Korean American or 1.5 generation Korean but as a Korean *like them*. This was the moment my innocent act of filling in Koreanness was finalized. All the stories I had been telling in "America's language" needed to be confirmed in the language they knew best to be fully legitimized and recognized as such.

When my ethnic identities were ascribed and challenged, it was my translingual practice that helped perform (Butler 1999) an ethnic category: *a* Korean and not *the* Korean ethnicity—and sometimes the other way around. Sometimes more successfully heard than other times, translingual practice—as rhetorically situated—functioned as my way of practicing or accentuating *a* Korean ethnicity in multiple contact zones (Pratt 1991). Speaking a "pure" language did not give me a feeling of belonging to a particular ethnic identity, a myth, as stated earlier in our chapter, that language studies have deconstructed (Makoni and Pennycook 2005). Rather, it was my translingual practice that enabled me to draw on my ethnic identity and go beyond—be it Korean (or non-Korean), non-American, half American, or *like American*, the latest label I have received from my students after marrying a self-identified Hispanic person—more specifically, a Texacan. One's ethnic identity in this sense is never static and given; it is always evolving, emerging, and enacted through our moments of translingual practice.

EMERGING BILINGUAL AND BICULTURAL PRACTICES: SARA

Unlike many undergraduate students, I did not leave home to attend college. I lived with my family, and I enrolled at a commuter college in Queens, New York. The rapid beat of Cali *salsa*, my neighbors' K-pop music blasting from their car, and the neurotic fast pace of one of the most populous cities on this planet were too much to stay away from. Translingual Queens is the overt representation of Jonathan Hall's (2014) argument that "multilinguality is the mainstream" (31), where speaking multiple Englishes and approximately two hundred other languages is the norm (New York City Department of City Planning 2015). My choice to stay at home may be one of the things that could have begun my academic marking as ethnically Latina, as my family has always been the center of my life. As García and Wei (2014) note in *Translanguaging*,[5] being and living bilingual means that I "could not avoid having had language inscribed on [my] body" (18). I was my family's unofficial translator for various events, such as my younger brother's parent-teacher conferences, my mother's life-threatening and life-saving surgeries, and my father's travails with the gas company. Told from this monolingualist perspective, my parents' efforts in my higher education could be overlooked.

But monolingualist views of bilingualism cannot account for the ways in which translingual practice has allowed individuals like me, a Colombian New Yorker, to sustain our critical bilingualism so it enhances our academic and teaching practices. That is, views of bilingualism as a practice that consists of two standardized systems of language that individually correspond to particular identities cannot realistically capture my emerging identity or language practices. In fact, as I elaborate below, it could have silenced that value of my Colombian New Yorker Spanish-speaking identity in English. Thus, scholars who carefully note the rhetorical and dynamic strategies multilingual students use not only confront linguistic hegemony but also open paths for students to sustain their bilingual and bicultural practices.

As emergent bilinguals (García and Kleifgen 2010), my parents were very involved in my academic discourse in English. During college, I could not start writing the body of my final paper if I did not feel like I had the "perfect" introduction. I was taking one of the required special-topics courses for my English major, a course focused on Asian American literature. The course allowed me to see my ethnic identity as emerging and negotiated, especially after reading Carlos Bulosan's (1946) *America Is in the Heart.* But I could not bring myself to begin writing. Looking back, I can see my writer's block manifested itself in the pressure to restrict my writing to monolingual norms and ideologies.

I was on the verge of tears, realizing I had spent at least five hours in front of my desktop screen and was still facing a blank page, when my mother called out to me that dinner was ready.

"I'll eat later, es que no tengo nada escrito todavía,"[6] I answered.

Hearing my response, my mother quickly came to my room, and though initially she wanted to reprimand me, she soon saw my face of frustration and asked what I was hoping to write about. I told her about the idea I had for the paper and the two texts I was planning to use. I provided summaries to Edith Eaton's (1909) "Leaves from the Mental Portfolio of an Eurasian" and Jhumpa Lahiri's (2003) *Namesake.*

"Suena como a lo que me contaste de Gloria Anzaldúa *Borderlands/La Frontera*"[7] was my mother's response.

I had previously taken a class on critical theory in which we read Anzaldúa, and I had introduced the text to my mother. Though my mother, a university-educated woman, enjoyed reading literature and literary criticism on a regular basis, she had not encountered hybrid border scholarship like Anzaldúa's (2007). Since then, she had quickly become intrigued with the idea of borderlands and multilingualism.

She explained that she could see the idea of "dos culturas"[8] in all of us. I recall her adding, "Es que aquí uno ve y aprende de muchas culturas. Uno no puede ser igual que antes, pero tampoco totalmente diferente."[9] She then suggested I write the ideas I had just shared with her, and she insisted I write them as they came to mind. I remember having English and Spanish words on my screen and my mom reading over them. I recall having the word *diversity* in my first sentence and my mom saying how at various public- and school-related events, she heard the word *diversity*, but many times its use seemed superficial. She said she thought the idea was "pegajosa."[10] I translated the word to "catchy" and all of a sudden had an idea for my first "official" sentence.

I wrote what came to mind, and my first sentence referred to America. But my mom, as my dad always reminded me, said, "América es un continente no un país,"[11] a *conscientização*[12] they attributed to their reading of texts such as Eduardo Galeano's (1997) *Open Veins of Latin America.*

The first line of that final essay reads, *"Diversity, a rather catchy word* in major cities of the U.S. nowadays, results from the movements of people from different countries and cultures to other places, as it does from individuals who are born in a specific place and culture and who have a second culture, *as product of a family heritage"* (emphasis added). Reading this sentence six years later, I still feel proud of it, and though I know I probably would change much of the essay today, the changes would not be ideologically distant from what the sentence expresses.

Recalling narratives like this one is an indication that as a bilingual student and Spanish-speaking Colombian in higher education, all this knowledge was not discounted. The act of translingual practice was productive in this bicultural and translingual context. Translingual practice with my mother allowed me to channel my bilingual, bicultural, and emerging hybrid ethnic identity. Moreover, growing up in a saliently translingual space but still feeling the pressures to conform to monolingual tenets in writing allowed me to perceive the importance of culturally sustaining pedagogies and practices (Paris 2011). Monolingual beliefs can never really capture bilingual production, the making of the translingual and multicultural text itself. These beliefs, in other words, cannot account for how my becoming an academic in writing studies, in addition to "formal" academic training, owes much to the strength of my family's academic literacies and translingual practices.

INTERNATIONALISM AS ETHNICITY: SHAKIL

Working at Pennsylvania State University's graduate writing center as an international graduate student from Bangladesh has allowed me to leverage my literacy history and identity. Specifically, the first has provided me a common ground of translingual practice between myself and the international students and faculty availing themselves of the center, enacting a "difference-in-similarity" (Canagarajah 2013, 9) process even in Standardized Written English products. The second has allowed me to create an identification between myself and international graduate students I work with, affording uptake for my directive tutorial pedagogy.

Mimicry was fundamental to my literacy education in Dhaka,[13] where reproducing the models presented in the school textbook or reciting the *namaz*[14] as we saw our imams do was considered learning. Outside of the classrooms, we also picked up Hindi and US American slang watching satellite channels. Yet the Bangla, English, Hindi, and Arabic currents of my social milieu were never obstacles to be overcome; rather, they were the context for my translingual practice, a social space inscribing multilingualism-as-norm on the monolingual texts I composed or recited for class or for *namaz*.

This translingual practice of language did not change during my undergraduate education in the United States and in subsequent years as a translator and subeditor for a reporting agency in Bangladesh. These experiences, in fact, honed my sense that "learning to write" is *always* a negotiated "social activity that integrates reading, writing, and diverse semiotic resources" (Canagarajah 2013, 128). I learned that writing can be explicated through modeling, and asking people to learn through shamelessly copying someone else's style could be effective pedagogy. Of course my experiences also enabled me to see the rote method of my schooling and Quranic education was really about calisthenics rather than learning. Whoever did not follow the homework instructions was marked down and chided for trying to take unacademic shortcuts.

In my experience as a graduate-center tutor, I have found "directive tutoring" (Shamoon and Burns 1995, 145) works well with the international graduate students who attend the center regularly. Most times the students I work with on the production of academic texts readily accept my suggestions for revision. However, other times, they explain that my suggestions seem to take their arguments in directions they do not wish to go. This difference of opinion often leads us to engage each other in our various Englishes as a part of our negotiations for the student's revision. In such instances, students also often ask pointedly for the rationales for my suggestions and in the process end up making explicit "domain-appropriate abstractions, domain-appropriate linkages to case-specific data . . . which provides opportunities for reflection and critique" (Shamoon and Burns 1995, 147). In other words, they must think rhetorically about how their literacies are situated literacies and also learn that articulating such discourses to outsider audiences enables a better understanding of their arguments.

Arguably, my identity as a South Asian international graduate student factors into the positive uptake of my directive method with international students at the center. Like me, many of them are pursuing their postsecondary education (especially those in the sciences) in English and do not distinguish between the various languages making up their linguistic repertoires. Also, like me, they found themselves categorized as English-as-a-second-language (ESL) writers when they came to the United States (whether at an undergraduate or graduate level), even if they had been writing and reading in English as long as they had been going to school. Thus, our translingual practice, and my Bangladeshi international-graduate-student ethnic identification, seem to make them comfortable in communicating frustrations over being categorized as ESLs but also help them recognize the need to negotiate such positionings as a part of pursuing education in the United States.

I believe the following exchange with an international postdoctoral scholar in music arts, who regularly visited the writing center, can exemplify and extend my argument about this translingual practice and how it ties to ethnicity. "Dr. Cho," from Korea, after working with me a few weeks (during which time we often talked about how multilingualism was the norm in South Asia and English was the medium of instruction for my school), asked me if I would tutor her son for the TOEFL exam and college applications. She explained that she liked my directive method of tutoring, that it would work well with her son. In addition, since I grew up in a multilingual society but pursued higher education in the United States, she thought I would know the type of educational trajectory her son was going toward and would make a good mentor. The fact that I was not white or European was actually seen as a resource for her son's literacy practices and educational development. Otherwise, I think she might have felt I would not really be able to understand the obstacles a Korean student applying to study at a university in the United States might face. Though I declined Dr. Cho's invitation because I wanted to focus on my dissertation, doubtlessly I was proud of being asked to be a tutor and regarded it as a comment on my instructional ability (and a positive comment on the effectiveness of directive tutoring). I also understood that my ethnic identity—as negotiated and shared during our exchanges at the writing center—played a significant role in Dr. Cho's solicitation. In my brown skin, multilingualism, and emerging biculturality, and because of our potential commonalities, Dr. Cho saw an ethnicized English speaker who could best guide her Korean son as he applied to matriculate into US colleges.

My work at the center functions to combine both my international graduate-student identity and my pedagogical repertoire. My particular hyphenated categorization resonates in ways fundamental to the effectiveness and uptake of my translingual practices. When my consultation techniques work, international tutees at the graduate writing center often understand them in ways inextricably connected to their identifications with me as a fellow international and a fellow multilingual writer.

TRANSLANGUAGING, UPTAKE, AND
ETHNIC IDENTIFICATION: JERRY

"I thought you were ABC." I have heard this statement countless times from my international students from China after they have discovered I am in fact not ABC, or American-born Chinese. I do not take offense to the ABC mischaracterization, nor do I take it personally when a Chinese student submits an assignment with my surname spelled as *Li*, the Chinese-ified version of *Lee*. But this mischaracterization is curious for at least two reasons. One, it is a recurring phenomenon and not an isolated experience of misidentification. Second, I have never given any indication of proficiency in Chinese to my students. In fact, 我根本不懂汉语![15] Therefore, I am left wondering, what enables me to "pass" as a person of Chinese descent to others who are "actually" of Chinese descent?

Pennycook's (2012) argument that, in a globalized sociolinguistic ecology, resourceful speakers are able to "pass" as having an affiliation with a particular language background emphasizes the point that our identities, especially our linguistic identities, are not fixed and static categories but are rather emergent and continually reconstituted in different sociolinguistic contexts. Put differently, linguistic subjectivity is less an ontological status than a performative occurrence. However, Pennycook's analysis, along with his anecdote of being mistaken for, and having passed as, a nonnative speaker of English, reifies a positivistic logic of language in which doing, using, or practicing language according to perceptible linguistic and pragmatic features is the primary determinant of one's proficiency in a particular language. We must also take into consideration the role of other extralinguistic factors, such as one's epidermal characteristics, that comprise one's racial or ethnic physical complexion. There are parameters of passing predetermined by one's visibly ethnicized physical features, as affirmed in Donald Rubin's (1992) study of racialized features predetermining an interlocutor's assumptions of one's supposed nativeness in English and Subtirelu's (2015) study of students' pejorative comments on their Asian instructors' accents. In a sense, languaging and translingual practice can only get us so far.

My experiences of having passed, even momentarily, as Chinese expose at least one other limitation to Pennycook's theorization of passing. Passing, in Pennycook's (2012) view, assumes the efficacy of a conscious, deliberate effort of manipulating common language expectations held by a particular interlocutor. In my case, it has not been adept translingual practice that has enabled me to pass as Chinese for my students. The very notion of passing suggests intentionality and effort:

you attempt to pass, and you either are successful or not. What about the moments in which we pass without ourselves realizing that an interlocutor has been "testing" us as a candidate to pass? Perhaps during moments of translingual practice, even if we are not attempting to pass, the very act of shuttling (Canagarajah 2010) across language resources facilitates the possibility of being ethnicized in a particular way.

Another curiosity is having passed in spite of my nonproficiency in Chinese. Admittedly, in my classes, I regularly assign texts by Chinese American authors, from Amy Tan's ubiquitous essay "Mother Tongue" to David Henry Hwang's play *Chinglish*. But these choices are not motivated by a misguided hope of trying to pass as Chinese. In fact, my nonproficiency in Chinese during class discussions, or when I accidentally mispronounce my students' names when taking attendance, would make many conclude I am not Chinese. I am aware, though, that this may also be commentary based on ideologies that read emerging language practices for bilinguals born in the United States as deficiency (Zentella 1997). Yet, that many of my Chinese students continue to see me as ABC has complicated my assumptions regarding the interrelatedness of language proficiency and ethnic identity.

Nonproficiency in the traditional sense does not always confine one to particular ethnic identification, and it does not appear to preclude one from an immediately analogous ethnic group either. It is not unusual for an ABC second-, third-, or fourth-generation person of Chinese heritage born in the United States to be nonproficient in Chinese. In the experiences I have briefly described above, the simplest explanation is that my visible proximity to being Chinese enables my students to situate me within their own ethnic heritage. Yet, it is also not simply a matter of being "approximately" Chinese in terms of physiology. During recent trips to China, I have been addressed by strangers in Chinese, but also, in recent trips to Korea, I have been spoken to in Japanese. If you see someone of East Asian descent in China, it is somewhat fair to assume they are Chinese, but what leads you to conclude otherwise? In other words, what accounts for my being hailed as different ethnicities in expected but also in unexpected ways?

Oftentimes, it is ultimately a consideration of uptake: the ways in which the performative nature of translingual practice leads to intended but also unintended outcomes. Discourses of translanguaging tend to presume choice, including which language resources to draw on in a particular context or even whether to "mesh" language resources or to strive to keep them separate. But considering the performative nature of translanguaging is important as well because uptake is not always a calculated or predictable outcome. As I have tried to suggest, many of us, because of our indistinct usage of language resources, and because of our indeterminate epidermal characteristics, may need to concede to the reality that there is a range of categories to which we can be assigned. The process of ethnicization occurs through the ways in which we make use of our language resources but also, in many cases, the ways our interlocutors choose to take up our usage. It is important to consider the ways in which translingual practice can cause us to become mistakenly located within unexpected ethnic categories, but these considerations must continue to be understood in terms of the reasons we see certain forms of identification as desirable and others as not. This way, translingual practice, understood as a constellation of dynamic communicative practices that traverse and transform conventional linguistic boundaries, is, in addition to a capacity to shift identifications with different cultural groups, an opportunity to critically examine the politics of the very act of shifting identifications.

CONCLUSION

How does our experience comment on the translingual practice/ethnicity connection? Eunjeong performs ethnicity by deploying a Korean word strategically. Her performance of identity helps her develop solidarity with her Korean students and construct an in-group identity they seem to be seeking. Eunjeong's narrative explains how we may have to sometimes perform our own traditionally associated (in-group) ethnicity, as no one can be assumed to be proficient in the languages of their heritage. Heritage too must be performed sometimes for strategic reasons. Eunjeong's strategic translingual practice reminds us that Korean ethnicity, like any ethnicity, is never a static and stable entity in and of itself. Eunjeong's translingual practice brings to light the ability of individuals to help define, through their use of language and other semiotic resources, what it means to be "ethnic."

Sara develops the paradox that our heritage sometimes gives us the resources for developing hybrid identities, contesting the traditional notion that heritage is always associated with purity or homogeneity. It is her family that provides her the heritage to develop a bicultural identity. But a remaining question is, how should we label the new ethnicity she is indexing through her translingual practice? It could be neither "just" Colombian nor New Yorker, Spanish nor English, but something in between that requires a new label or even defies the very process of labeling. Many of us are seeking new labels in the context of the creativity accompanying translingual practice, but Sara's experiences point us to the value of living between the categories the labels themselves signify. Her narrative speaks to the notion that language and identity can be performative, not essential.

Shakil's narrative also represents identities that defy traditional categories at our disposal. He first points out that language contact and translingual practice are very much the norm in Bangladesh, and recognizing their value enabled him to leverage them for his own literacy practices. In addition, Shakil's narrative extends the idea that ethnicities and ethnic identification can to some extent result from an identification-in-difference, such as the positioning of international students in US academia. As a Bangladeshi international student working as a graduate tutor, Shakil, like Sara, also illustrates that "language [can be] inscribed on the body" (García and Wei 2014, 18). Even as he aligns his tutoring practices toward standard tutoring pedagogies, he cannot avoid how others see him, and sometimes these tensions of uptake are invitations for identifications rather than othering.

Similar to the way Shakil's narrative goes beyond merely emphasizing the value and power of translingual practice for identity, Jerry's narrative also suggests potential risks and dangers from semiotic resources beyond language. Ways to perform or index our desired identities are not left to our own devices (another point that suggests the limits of playful metroethnicities). These identities must receive uptake. However, in many cases, we are ascribed identities that do not correspond to the resources at our disposal. The fact that language norms are diverse adds to this risk. The inherent plurality of language norms leads to a wide range of possibilities for uptake in different sociolinguistic contexts. For instance, in some cases, Jerry is unexpectedly ascribed an ABC identity. Jerry's narrative therefore shows that identity is not constructed through language resources alone. Other semiotic resources like body and materiality are also important.

From this point of view, ethnicity is a complex semiotic achievement. It depends on how diverse semiotic resources are orchestrated in relation to dominant ideologies and norms to seek the desired uptake for specific identities and voices. But the reality remains that, in spite of our efforts to index a particular heritage or to even assume a particular ethnicity, sometimes we become ethnicized by others in ways we may not always expect or even comprehend.

The realization that the constitution of ethnic identity through language is an inevitable but also ongoing process, which emerges from all our narratives, is the pedagogical implication we wish to leave for our profession. Voice, identity, or ethnicity is not optional. Whether we like it or not, readers will frequently ascribe an identity to our texts, spoken or written. It is much better to be creative, critical, and proactive to perform our identities in desired and strategic ways. This performance might sometimes involve resisting dominant norms and ideologies to mesh unconventional semiotic resources. Students may also have to account for audience expectations in engaging with their biases and norms intelligently to gain the desired uptake. This is a proficiency that has to be developed through protracted work over time and space, but in the same way that meanings in language are negotiated between two interlocutors, it is important to remember that the ways in which our identities are constituted is also an ongoing, intersubjective process.

Notes

1. In 2004, Vershawn Ashanti Young introduced the term *code meshing* to describe the way students incorporate features of African American Vernacular English, a variety traditionally reserved only for "home" or "nonacademic" spaces, into their academic writing (Young 2004). Unlike expressions such as *code switching* or *code mixing*, which can refer generally to switching between or the mixing of different "codes" (i.e., languages or dialects), Young was referring specifically to the blending of dialects or even registers in a manner that would be prohibited according to traditional conventions of "academic" writing. Suresh Canagarajah (2006), in his article "The Place of World Englishes in Composition," developed code meshing as a mode of languaging that promotes multilingual student writers' multidialectal communicative practices in composition. Canagarajah argues that code meshing treats the communicative act as merging various codes rather than separating them and prioritizing "native" varieties. While the translingual orientation to writing entails more than simply promoting code-meshed discourses, the appropriateness of code meshing is often the focal point of critiques against the translingual paradigm (such as in Lyons 2009, and, more recently, in Matsuda 2013).
2. Ana Zelia Zentella's (1997) *Growing Up Bilingual* and her perspective of moving between various Englishes and Spanishes as code switching and "anthropolitical linguistics" can serve as a good example of how translingual practice does not treat languages and ethnic affiliations as discrete but as emergent and negotiated.
3. *gyopo*—"Korean immigrant"
4. *geurae*—"okay"
5. Even though García and Wei (2014) conceptualize "translanguaging" differently from translingual practice, as they situate it as a sociocognitive practice through an emergent bilingual framework, the multilingual literacy practices they examine and argue for are similar (if not the same) to those we investigate in this chapter.
6. "I don't have anything written yet."
7. "It sounds like what you told me about Gloria Anzaldúa's *Borderlands/La Frontera*."
8. "two cultures"
9. "The thing is that, here, one sees and learns from many cultures. One cannot be the same as before, but also not completely different."
10. Colombian Spanish word for "sticky."
11. "America is a continent, not a country."

12. Paulo Freire's (1971) "consciousness" as stipulated in his book *Pedagogy of the Oppressed.*
13. Dhaka is the capital of Bangladesh. According to the CIA *World Factbook*, it has a population of approximately fifteen million, making it one of the most populated megacities in the world (Central Intelligence Agency 2015).
14. Obligatory ritualized prayer in Islam. In Arabic it is called the *salat.* However, in Bangladesh, as in most of South Asia, it is called *namaz*, a word of Farsi derivation.
15. Wǒ gēnběn bù dǒng hànyù—"I don't even know any Chinese."

References

Anzaldúa, Gloria. 2007. *Borderlands/La Frontera: The New Mestiza.* San Francisco: aunt lute.
Blackledge, Adrian, and Angela Creese. 2008. "Contesting 'Language' as 'Heritage': Negotiation of Identities in Late Modernity." *Applied Linguistics* 29 (4): 533–54. http://dx.doi.org/10.1093/applin/amn024.
Bulosan, Carlos. 1946. *America Is in the Heart: A Personal History.* New York: Harcourt, Brace.
Burke, Lucy, Tony Crowley, and Alan Girvin, eds. 2003. *The Routledge Language and Culture Reader.* New York: Routledge.
Butler, Judith. 1999. *Gender Trouble: Feminism and the Subversion of Identity.* New York: Routledge.
Canagarajah, A. Suresh. 2006. "The Place of World Englishes in Composition: Pluralization Continued." *College Composition and Communication* 57 (4): 586–610.
Canagarajah, A. Suresh. 2010. "A Rhetoric of Shuttling between Languages." In *Cross-Language Relations in Composition*, edited by Bruce Horner, Min-Zhan Lu, and Paul Kei Matsuda, 158–79. Carbondale: Southern Illinois University Press.
Canagarajah, A. Suresh, ed. 2013. *Literacy as Translingual Practice: Between Communities and Classrooms.* New York: Routledge.
Central Intelligence Agency. 2015. "World Factbook: Bangladesh." Central Intelligence Agency. https://www.cia.gov/library/publications/resources/the-world-factbook/geos/print_bg.html.
Cooper, Marilyn M. 2014. "The Being of Language." In *Reworking English in Rhetoric and Composition: Global Interrogations, Local Interventions*, edited by Bruce Horner and Karen Kopelson, 13–30. Carbondale: Southern Illinois University Press.
Dirks, Nicholas B. 2001. *Castes of Mind: Colonialism and the Making of Modern India.* Princeton, NJ: Princeton University Press.
Eaton, Edith. 1909. "Leaves from the Mental Portfolio of an Eurasian." *The Independent ... Devoted to the Consideration of Politics, Social and Economic Tendencies, History, Literature, and the Arts (1848–1921)* 66 (3138): 125.
Freire, Paulo. 1971. *Pedagogy of the Oppressed.* New York: Herder and Herder.
Gal, Susan, and Judith T. Irvine. 1995. "The Boundaries of Languages and Disciplines: How Ideologies Construct Difference." *Social Research* 62 (4): 967–1001.
Galeano, Eduardo. 1997. *Open Veins of Latin America: Five Centuries of the Pillage of a Continent.* New York: Monthly Review.
García, Ofelia, and Joanne Kleifgen. 2010. *Educating Emergent Bilinguals: Policies, Programs, and Practices for English Language Learners.* New York: Teachers College Press.
García, Ofelia, and Li Wei. 2014. *Translanguaging: Language, Bilingualism and Education.* New York: Palgrave Macmillan.
Hall, Jonathan. 2014. "Multilinguality Is the Mainstream." In *Reworking English in Rhetoric and Composition*, edited by Bruce Horner and Karen Kopelson, 31–48. Carbondale: Southern Illinois University Press.

Horner, Bruce, Min-Zhan Lu, Jacqueline Jones Royster, and John Trimbur. 2011. "Language Difference in Writing: Toward a Translingual Approach." *College English* 73 (3): 303–21.

Lahiri, Jhumpa. 2003. *The Namesake.* Boston, MA: Houghton Mifflin.

Lyons, Scott R. 2009. "The Fine Art of Fencing: Nationalism, Hybridity, and the Search for a Native American Writing Pedagogy." *JAC* 29 (1): 77–105.

Maher, John C. 2010. "Metroethnicities and Metrolanguages." In *The Handbook of Language and Globalization*, edited by Nikolas Coupland, 575–91. Oxford: Wiley-Blackwell.

Makoni, Sinfree, and Alastair Pennycook. 2005. "Disinventing and (Re) Constituting Languages." *Critical Inquiry in Language Studies* 2 (1): 447–68.

Matsuda, Paul Kei. 2013. "It's the Wild West Out There: A New Linguistic Frontier in U.S. College Composition." In *Literacy as Translingual Practice: Between Communities and Classrooms*, edited by A. Suresh Canagarajah, 128–38. New York: Routledge.

Paris, Django. 2011. *Language Across Difference: Ethnicity, Communication, and Youth Identities in Changing Urban Schools.* New York: Cambridge University Press.

Pennycook, Alastair. 2010. *Language as a Local Practice.* London: Routledge.

Pennycook, Alastair. 2012. *Language and Mobility: Unexpected Places.* Clevedon, UK: Multilingual Matters.

Pennycook, Alastair, and Emi Otsuji. 2015. *Metrolingualism: Language in the City.* New York: Routledge.

New York City Department of City Planning. 2015. "Population." http://www1.nyc.gov/site/planning/data-maps/nyc-population.page.

Pratt, Mary Louise. 1991. "Arts of the Contact Zone." *Profession*: 33–40.

Rampton, Ben. 1999. "*Deutsch* in Inner London and the Animation of an Instructed Foreign Language." *Journal of Sociolinguistics* 3 (4): 480–504.

Royster, Jacqueline Jones. 1996. "When the First Voice You Hear Is Not Your Own." *College Composition and Communication* 47 (1): 29–40.

Rubin, Donald L. 1992. "Nonlanguage Factors Affecting Undergraduates' Judgments of Nonnative English-Speaking Teaching Assistants." *Research in Higher Education* 33 (4): 511–31.

Said, Edward W. 1978. *Orientalism.* New York: Pantheon.

Shamoon, Linda K., and Deborah H. Burns. 1995. "A Critique of Pure Tutoring." *Writing Center Journal* 15 (2): 134–51.

Spivak, Gayatri Chakravorty. 1993. *Outside in the Teaching Machine.* New York: Routledge.

Subtirelu, Nicholas Close. 2015. "'She Does Have an Accent but . . .': Race and Language Ideology in Students' Evaluations of Mathematics Instructors on RateMyProfessors.com." *Language in Society* 44 (1): 35–62.

Young, Vershawn Ashanti. 2004. "Your Average Nigga." *College Composition and Communication* 55 (4): 693–715.

Zentella, Ana Celia. 1997. *Growing Up Bilingual: Puerto Rican Children in New York.* London: Blackwell.

PART 2

Pedagogical Interventions

3

ENACTING TRANSLINGUAL WRITING PEDAGOGY
Structures and Challenges for Two Courses in Two Countries

William B. Lalicker

TRANSLINGUALISM IN THE GLOBALLY NETWORKED LEARNING ENVIRONMENT

The last several years have seen calls for a new translingual paradigm to reframe composition pedagogy.[1] *Translingualism* is the term I will use for several interrelated traits of student discourses: cross-language relations; transnational, international, or global Englishes; and intercultural rhetoric. Ulla Connor (2011) defines the latter term as "the study of written discourse between and among individuals with different cultural backgrounds" (2); adding the assumption that different cultural backgrounds imply different language backgrounds, my working description of translingual writing courses is those in which a number of native English-speaking (L1) students and nonnative English-speaking (L2) students come together to bring translingual experience (and transcultural rhetorical consciousness) to the classroom; and in which purposefully structured course elements encourage students of differing languages of origin to work together to influence the rhetorical acts and rhetorical consciousness of their counterparts. More specifically, the translingual courses I am discussing include these ingredients:

- The course is English composition, focusing on first-year or more advanced general education nonfictive writing for any student, rather than on ESL/EFL approaches designed mainly for international and L2 speakers.
- The class includes a significant proportion of students whose first languages are English and whose first languages differ from English (or are global Englishes), native English speakers with L2 speakers.

DOI: 10.7330/9781607326205.c003

- The course approaches writing with a kairotic recognition of its translingual situation: course content considers events and contexts and purposes, historical and cultural and linguistic and specific, that condition acts of writing.
- The course includes assignments and activities requiring students from differing language and cultural backgrounds to work together to produce writing through negotiated interactive processes.

Lu and Horner (2016) describe one approach to translingualism as a concern with "difference as the norm of all utterances, conceived of as acts of translation inter and intra languages, media, modality during seeming iterations of dominant conventions as well as deviations from the norm" (208), and that's the underlying emphasis in my translingual writing courses. Translingual writing courses recognize that this concern is not limited to ESL-dominant classrooms; these classes are English composition, typical FYC and post-FYC writing courses, consonant with what Matsuda and Silva (2006) describe as "mediated integration" (246) of L1 and L2 students in a composition course. With Atkinson et al. (2015), I resist "the growing misunderstanding that L2 writing and translingual writing are somehow competing with each other or, worse yet, that one is replacing the other" (383). The translingual courses welcome L1 and L2 students alike and adopt Suresh Canagarajah's (2014) "translingual paradigm" that "does not disregard established norms and conventions as defined for certain contexts by dominant institutions and social groups" but in which "speakers and writers negotiate these norms in relation to their translingual repertoires and practices" (8–9). Translingualism is present, but accidental, in most composition classrooms, as we recognize what Paul Kei Matsuda (2006) identifies as "the myth of linguistic homogeneity" (637); yet translingual courses make translingual rhetorical interaction central to course methods, writing assignments, and kairos-conscious outcomes. Approaching translingual reality in our classrooms purposefully prepares us to access what Alastair Pennycook (2007) calls "transcultural flows" and the resultant rhetorical creativity in the classroom's intercultural mix.

Why do translingual courses matter? A number of composition theorists have provided ample reason; for a succinct argument signed by fifty compositionists, see Bruce Horner et al. (2011). The justification for translingual and intercultural composition courses is that they represent a complete attention to matters of purpose and audience, matters inseparable from cultural context and intercultural negotiation. Translingual writing courses are rhetoric at its core: they focus on communicating effectively to audiences across the boundaries of difference;

they focus attention on how discourse operates so our students leave our courses knowing how to apply principles of written rhetoric in a wide variety of situations for transferability. According to the WPA Outcomes Statement for First-Year Composition (2014), "*Rhetorical knowledge* is the ability to analyze contexts and audiences and then to act on that analysis in comprehending and creating texts. Rhetorical knowledge is the basis of composing. Writers develop rhetorical knowledge by negotiating purpose, audience, context, and conventions as they compose a variety of texts for different situations" (145). In the dialogic, negotiated classroom situation, translingualism has its most profound rhetorical effects, as both L1 and L2 users of English gain rhetorical knowledge that moves beyond the conventions-centric assumptions and valorization of Edited American English that mitigates powerful nonfictive and academic writing.

Translingual writing courses make the acts of composition not just mechanical or grammatical but epistemological, using the exchange of language to broaden knowledge and understanding of the world. If, as Horner et al. (2011) assert, translingual realities require "changes to writing programs in the design of writing curricula" (309), the next step is to incorporate translingual rhetoric into composition pedagogy. These changes to writing programs, if they are to have this fully epistemological effect, must go beyond what Christiane Donahue (2009) notes as a tendency "to focus on the increasingly global nature of U.S. classrooms and U.S. students or students attending U.S. universities—the internationalizing of *our* world. . . . A few scholars have also turned their attention to broader questions about academic writing in other countries and the complicated linguistic relationships that are evolving there" (213). Donahue's incisive critique calls us to design writing programs in which internationalization "'de-naturalizes' our assumptions and stances" as we "resist an import-export model" and replace it with "an equitable exchange one" (232).

If too-common current models of pseudointernationalized English composition involve sending students from the United States to study in China under the auspices of US professors importing a monolithic Standard English, or bringing international students to the United States to learn from US professors that same monolithic Standard English, a new model could be structured around equitable exchange. An equitable-exchange model could incorporate not one course in the United States or abroad but two courses: one in (e.g.) China, one in the United States. As Doreen Starke-Meyerring (2015) suggests, writing programs can "be opened up for mutual inquiry and collaboration in globally networked learning environments (GNLEs), that is, learning environments that rest on robust partnerships extending across institutional, linguistic, national, or other boundaries in order to facilitate faculty and student participation" in emerging global realities (308). A GNLE establishing an equitable-exchange model could incorporate a course-one writing class with both Chinese and US students in an English composition class in China, and the same binational cohort of students could take course two as an English composition class in the United States. An equitable-exchange class could incorporate the engagement of Chinese instructors of English in the US-based writing course, as well as the US writing instructor teaching in China. An equitable exchange also means including US students who represent not a mythical US monoculture but the more representative cultural and linguistic diversity of our domestic student bodies. The US students in course one, studying writing in China, could simultaneously take a course in Chinese culture and Chinese language; the Chinese students in course two, studying English composition in the United States, could take a course in US history. This set of structures for a transnational, translingual set of composition courses describes the design of the program I planned for an exchange between West Chester University in the United States and Guizhou University in China.

That's the way the courses were planned. But the way things actually happened shifted the emphasis to fit with another one of the translingual approaches Lu and Horner (2016) describe, an approach that sees "all communicative practices as mesopolitical acts, actively negotiating and constituting complex relations of power at the dynamic intersection of the social-historical (macro) and the personal (micro) levels" (208).

The design of the program I planned began with a vision positing translingual writing as a transnational practice in which intercultural experience supported rhetorical learning. The challenges to that vision revealed that establishing a translingual or transnational pedagogical framework for writing courses is necessary but is not sufficient in the pursuit of translingual rhetorical learning. On the macro level, material conditions within study-abroad programs, and within (and between) institutions, reframed the intended pedagogical contexts; on the micro level, material conditions in the lives of our students restricted the achievement of translinguality through transnational writing. And now I make a confession: course one didn't happen—though real course design, details of the syllabus, and arrangements with the Chinese university are all represented in this chapter exactly as planned; in all cases, except for the actual teaching of the course, Multicultural Writing and its activities are represented faithfully. What I will describe about course one is thus an idealized vision only imperfectly and hypothetically achieved.[2]

Noting the political and economic interests framing both higher education generally and writing programs more specifically, Starke-Meyerring (2015) asks, "How might we understand the situatedness of writing programs in the struggle over the neoliberal globalization project? What opportunities do emerging GNLEs offer to help us explore and rethink the roles writing programs can play in globalizing higher education? What new questions do they raise for the study of teaching and writing, as well as for WPA work?" (309).

The present study attempts to address these questions, or to provide a cautionary tale. As in a scientific experiment with a "failed" result that nevertheless provides useful information, an analysis of the writing program that was enacted—and not enacted—suggests the terms for successful future action in transnational writing programs.

COURSE ONE: WRH210, MULTICULTURAL WRITING. SITE: GUIZHOU UNIVERSITY, GUIYANG, CHINA. STUDENTS: TWELVE CHINESE, TWELVE FROM THE UNITED STATES

WRH210, Multicultural Writing, is a West Chester University (WCU) general education-option writing course. To redesign the course for a translingual focus, I proposed to teach the course in English during a four-week summer session on the campus of Guizhou University (GZU) in Guiyang City, capital of Guizhou Province, China. GZU has an enrollment of 32,152 (25,053 undergraduates) and is highly internationalized, engaging in partnerships with about fifty universities in at least fourteen countries (Guizhou University 2015). My university has been a partner institution for over five years. The four-week Multicultural Writing course was planned for a summer session in Guiyang, with (ideally) twelve GZU undergraduates and twelve US undergraduates from my own institution. At the same time the twelve WCU students were taking this WCU course on the GZU campus, they would benefit from GZU's enrolling them in a free GZU course in Chinese history and culture with Chinese students and faculty and a WCU course in Chinese language taught by WCU faculty.

Multicultural Writing's catalog description focusing on writing as a multicultural force lends itself to a translingual approach: "This course focuses on understanding the role that writing plays in shaping a multicultural society. Assignments will ask students to write for diverse social contexts and will help students expand their repertoire of genres and writing strategies" (Lalicker 2015b). In my syllabus, I added this detailed description:

> Many of us will find ourselves operating, as citizens and as working people, in diverse social contexts that cross international and intercultural borders; therefore, the genres and writing strategies that we learn should not be limited to those of our own home cultures. . . . In this course you will become familiar with the rhetorical and writing standards of several world cultures, with special emphasis on Chinese and American (English language, Western tradition) styles of writing. Each culture has its own genres, traditions, and assumptions about what is acceptable and effective in the rhetoric underlying that culture's writing, and you'll study those traditions as well as the rhetorical hybridities that make multicultural writing, and intercultural writing, successful—and you'll write essays in several genres to demonstrate your understanding of the rich intellectual and communicative possibilities opened by your receptiveness to the multicultural writing situation. (Lalicker 2015b)

The course included specific objectives honoring the official course description and simultaneously addressing the translingual nature of this course section. The aspect of translingualism focusing on difference as the norm of rhetoric, and on the transformation of conventions, was specified in requirements that students understand "how a transcultural rhetorical consciousness may contribute to creative discovery and successfully hybridized writing in the context of world Englishes" and that students demonstrate "the ability to adjust [their] communication and argument style to write effectively for audiences of a culture other than [their] own" (Lalicker 2015b). The aspect of translingualism focusing on rhetorical knowledge as cultural and audience context was specified in requirements that students understand "how culture influences the ways that discourse communities and individuals communicate in writing" and "how differing cultural traditions on topics such as education, human nature, and social class influence the practice of rhetoric and writing" (Lalicker 2015b). The aspect of translingualism focusing on historical and social conditions for communication was specified in a requirement that students understand "the basic theories and traditions of rhetoric and writing from several cultures: first the great and ancient Chinese traditions; then the classical Greek traditions of Plato and Aristotle that undergird Western rhetoric; plus additional traditions, including indigenous 'native American' traditions, African and postcolonial traditions, and the feminist-borderlands theory of Anzaldúa" (Lalicker 2015b).

To ensure that students with Chinese as their first language and students with English as their first language would engage in an equitable exchange, performing a negotiated generation of texts, a syllabus segment described the intercultural partnering or "tandem" model in the course. As the syllabus said, "The Chinese students possess a lived expertise in Chinese culture and traditions, including rhetorical traditions. The American students similarly possess a lived expertise in American traditions, plus the competency in English writing that comes with practice in a native language. . . . Students will be paired or grouped for joint writing assignments in which Chinese and American students will work together to produce essays. This 'tandem' model of learning is . . . transformative, as a way of gaining understanding and competence in our subject" (Lalicker 2015b). The course assignments were similarly designed to enact translingualism. The introductory-essay assignment asked students, "What makes writing good, in your culture?"; three genre-essays assignments asked students to collaborate as they wrote literacy autobiographies, policy arguments, and review essays in the context of reflection on models of these genres from multiple rhetorical traditions represented by readings from the Western canon, from Chinese thinkers (in English translation), and from other world cultures. Authors included Anzaldúa, Aristotle, Achebe, Douglass, Momaday, Meng Zi, Xun Zi, Lin Zexu, Mo Zi, Sun Zi, Orwell, Seneca, Freire, and Kisautaq Leona Okakok on themes such as language, rhetoric, human nature, and education (Lalicker 2015b). The themes interrogated cultural assumptions; allowed students in the translingual context to consider differences in audience and purpose; highlighted rhetorical structures originating in the language and culture of each reading; and encouraged translingual negotiation as preparation for course two of the planned sequence.

**COURSE TWO: ENG368, BUSINESS & ORGANIZATIONAL
WRITING. SITE: WEST CHESTER UNIVERSITY, WEST
CHESTER, PENNSYLVANIA, UNITED STATES. STUDENTS:
TWELVE CHINESE, THIRTEEN FROM THE UNITED STATES.**

ENG368, Business & Organizational Writing, is a general education-option writing course featuring a focus on business-oriented genres. I taught this transnational version of the course during a five-week summer session on the campus of West Chester University (WCU) in the Philadelphia metropolitan region. WCU has an enrollment of about 17,000 (about 13,700 undergraduates) (West Chester University 2015), the largest enrollment of any campus in the state's only public (state-owned) university system. WCU has been minimally internationalized; administrators aim to increase international enrollment and international exchanges, and about twenty courses per year are taught internationally. Guizhou University is one of WCU's most active partner institutions; a WCU course is taught at GZU, or GZU students come to WCU, nearly every year. I taught Business & Organizational Writing with twelve GZU students, plus an accompanying GZU English professor who attended and added comments in every class session, and thirteen WCU students, at WCU in summer 2011, and planned to do so for the summer of 2015.

GZU administration requested the Business & Organizational Writing course in 2011 and again in 2015. GZU students were also provided a WCU course in US history and culture, plus field trips to some of the many Philadelphia-area sites central to the origin and history of the United States. WCU students registered for the international-partnership section of Business & Organizational Writing in either year without knowing they were taking a course section with a transnational approach: there was no notation in the registration information, so the cohort who took the course in 2011 did so randomly (though in 2015 students might have taken it purposely as part of the planned two-course translingual sequence). No student chose to drop the course when they discovered they were enrolled in this transnational variant with requirements for partnering with international students on writing assignments. The official course description is very broad: "The nature of communication within business and organizations. Theoretical basis and practical application" (Lalicker 2015a). Unlike the Multicultural Writing course, Business & Organizational Writing's catalog description implies that corporate-writing purposes and conventions are at the heart of the course. Chinese university administrators who chose this course for their students likely sought writing practice in pursuit of economic globalization, a translingual provision of functional skills for commerce with Western companies. But the course's attention to the theory behind corporate communication opened the door to a more thoroughgoing and critical attention to rhetoric and translingualism, and the official course objectives on the syllabus required students to demonstrate "an ability to understand principles of discourse communities (including organizational and global cultures) in the context of businesses and organizations, and apply those principles for appropriate style" and understand "the challenges of cross-cultural and intercultural writing in the context of globalized business and organizational communication, and strategies for meeting those challenges" (Lalicker 2015a).

The specific enactment of translingual and transnational principles in the syllabus included the aspect of translingualism, emphasizing difference as the norm of rhetoric as writers work "to understand an audience that necessarily differs from the rhetor" and consider "the challenges we sometimes find in communicating our message to someone who differs from us by gender, by generation, by race, by interest, by economic class, by life experience, by culture or nationality"; writers commonly "switch codes, alter speaking styles, change our level of written formality, to communicate effectively to an audience differing from us" (Lalicker 2015a). Concerning the related aspect of translingualism emphasizing rhetorical knowledge as cultural and audience context, the syllabus noted that "writing—and thinking—that involves crossing the boundaries from one's baseline assumptions about the world, that connects us to differing cultural assumptions, provides the conditions for creative synergy, for new ideas born of new perspectives" and that "businesses and organizations now operate interculturally, transnationally, in globalized contexts. . . . Even the English language itself is now transnationally influenced by the several intersecting 'world Englishes' that allow business communications to occur in a common, but culturally conditioned and necessarily flexible, linguistic space" (Lalicker 2015a). The aspect of translingualism concerned with historical and social conditions for communication required students to learn "from the experiences and knowledge of people from a differing set of linguistic, cultural, historical, rhetorical, social, economic, and other value systems" in order to "find the common ground that leads to effective communication" (Lalicker 2015a).

As in the Multicultural Writing course designed to be taught in China, the Business & Organizational Writing class emphasized an equitable exchange of expertise and a negotiated generation of completed assignment texts: "Students in this special section of ENG368 are part of an international partnership between Guizhou University in China and West Chester University. . . . About half of the students are from GZU, and about half are from WCU; students will be assigned to two- or three-person teams for regular study, for work inside and outside of the classroom"; several assignments would be completed by binational teams who would be given time in class to make arrangements for study sessions and team writing sessions both in class and outside of class so "*zhongguo ren* and *meiguo ren* alike" could "benefit from practice in communicating for business and organizational purposes with their counterparts from the other hemisphere" to achieve "an interculturally enriching reality and functional agility that is the present norm for many businesses, institutions, and disciplines" (Lalicker 2015a).

The Business & Organizational Writing syllabus was written for a student population that, in its US component, took the course without expectation or preparation for engaging with what Min-Zhan Lu (2006) calls "living-English work," the complex translingual negotiations always required of L2 writers but, we may infer, only intermittently recognized by most L1 writers (605). Thus the L1 students in Business & Organizational Writing required an extensive explanation of the translingual context in which the assumption of hegemonic agency for L1 writers was subverted; in which even individually authored writing was subject to translingual team input; and in which team-authored writing both replicated the collaborative-writing model common in corporate communication and foregrounded translingual negotiation of discourse.

The main assignments in the course were (1) the introductory assignment, a memorandum, for which US and Chinese students were paired so each US student interviewed a Chinese student about that student's goals for the course and wrote a memorandum reporting the information, and each Chinese student did the same assignment based on interviews with the paired US student; (2) a customer relations letter (complaint, bill adjustment, collection on unpaid bill, etc.) written as a team project by paired Chinese and US students; (3) a resumé and accompanying job application letter, written individually but with collaborative workshopping by US and Chinese students together; and (4) a problem-solving or policy recommendation report, written by teams of Chinese and US students. Syllabus information framing this translingual engagement required students to work on some assignments in the binational teams and on some assignments individually. But even the individually authored assignments required peer workshops in which the peers included those who began from a differing set of linguistic and rhetorical and cultural baselines. Each team assignment also included a required addendum summarizing the contributions of each team member. Such addenda encouraged reflection and an increased consciousness of translingual contributions and negotiations (Lalicker 2015a).

The schedule of assignments, readings,[3] and activities further suggested the combination of conventions-focused coursework and translingual negotiation. The course goals detailed in the syllabus, for instance, included these requirements: "Understand and respect the priorities, values, and motivations of those who read your business writing from cultural positions differing from your own. . . . Know how your power to cross boundaries as you communicate can lead to more effective problem-solving between individuals and groups, and more efficient work within an organization" (Lalicker 2015a).

The themes, objectives, and activities are the same for this overtly translingual course as they are when I teach the course for the standard cohort of US students. Global contexts, intercultural communication, and awareness of translingualism are featured in every Business & Organizational Writing course I teach, with or without a recruited international student contingent. The necessity of global perspectives in business writing courses is obvious from the inclusion of global content in most business-writing textbooks; and the required textbook, Philip Kolin's (2012) *Successful Writing at Work*, is only typical (chosen for conciseness and relative affordability as much as for its acceptable rhetorical stance). Kolin's (2012) comments on intercultural understanding for successful business writing begin on page 2; the text includes several segments about the translingual negotiation inherent to syntactic and rhetorical decisions by the writer (2–5, 131–51, 235–37).

ENACTING TRANSLINGUALISM: COURSE PLANS, PROGRAM STRUCTURES, AND STUDENT REALITIES

Both course one, Multicultural Writing, projected to be taught at GZU, and course two, Business & Organizational Writing taught at WCU, had the same aim: to destabilize or subvert the simple (or simplistic) comfort of writers writing monolingually or monoculturally and to encourage a complicated, hybridized, negotiated rhetoric. It might be assumed by some critics that the primacy of English as the language of instruction, and as the written language of assignments, advantaged the students for whom English was a first language; but immersion at a Chinese university, plus the tandem assignments, were designed to encourage a decentering of monolingual positions, to inhere a non-English-dominant context, and to require respect for Chinese audiences in negotiating writing acts. The courses were designed for Chinese and US students alike to confront complexities of audience, context, and genre, making clear that conventions alone—with any assumption of monolingualism or Edited American English as a standard for correctness—are insufficient without a complete set of rhetorical considerations.

As noted above, course one didn't happen—though the translingual assumptions and pedagogical practices, plus the activating administrative arrangements between the US university and the Chinese university, are all represented exactly as planned, and as initiated if not fulfilled. And as noted above, Multicultural Writing might be seen as an experiment with a "failed" result that nevertheless provides useful information, the failure of Multicultural Writing to be conducted at Guizhou University revealing a challenge to translingually oriented composition instructors. Multicultural Writing at GZU, if it were to happen, depended on several logistical elements: the willingness of international partner universities; an interested cohort of Chinese students and US students; the provision of the usual student services at GZU; and travel funding. GZU, and to a large degree WCU, provided all these elements except two: the interested cohort of US students and travel funding for them. What makes a US student willing to travel to China for a course? Possible motivating factors include an acquired enthusiasm for the challenges of international travel; an affinity for Chinese culture or language, or for intercultural experience; an assumption that international study is an inherent part of any complete education; and an assurance that curricular requirements (general education writing requirements or major requirements) will be fulfilled by the study-abroad course.

The writing program I envisioned and planned, and of which I was able to enact only half (course two), might be analyzed further to illustrate a number of ways in which it represents the ideals of equitable exchange in translingual writing programs and the ways in which economic globalization in higher education challenged those ideals. One way of considering the planned program might reproduce Christine Tardy's (2015) approach, which follows the Norman Fairclough (2003) model of critical discourse analysis, to unpack the relationship between university strategic plans arguing the universal centrality of globalized higher education and the practical delivery of that transnational educational model; Tardy identifies the frequent contradiction between strategic-plan and university public-relations language about the importance of internationalization and the reservation of a globalized pedagogy for the elite few (245–62). Another way of considering the planned program might reproduce Starke-Meyerring's (2015) macro-level focus on global higher education as a neoliberal project, especially since my program planned to pair course one's Multicultural Writing general education course native to my US university with a course two's Business & Organizational Writing general education writing-emphasis option, a course native to my US university but specifically requested by the Chinese university apparently eager to prepare Chinese students for participation in the globalized neoliberal economic order.

However, the purpose of the present analysis is to identify the writing program's translingual project not just on the macro level of historical and sociopolitical forces but more specifically on the micro level, where local institutional factors and personal decisions by students condition the struggle to enact translingual writing pedagogy. The degree to which the planned writing program was not enacted—and was enacted, and the fact that the translingual and transnational Multicultural Writing course in China didn't happen and the translingual and transnational Business & Organizational Writing course in the United States did happen, depended only partly on the macro-level factors and at least equally on the effect of macro influences on the micro level of the personal, social, and economic situatedness of students.

At my university, few students arrive from their secondary schools with the cultural preparation or sophistication to make them comfortable about traveling to "exotic" (non-English-speaking, non-Western, less industrialized, less touristic) locations. The university's commitment to internationalization has little presence in students' educational consciousnesses, and though Multicultural Writing is a general education option, it's not a requirement; students may take any one of a long list of courses to fulfill the general education and English major requirements for which Multicultural Writing is an option. But the more dominant fact influencing the failure of Multicultural Writing to achieve the minimum required number of WCU students willing to travel to GZU to take it was students' inability to pay the financial premium to travel. Despite our many institutions' almost fetishistic brandishing of *internationalization* as a part of a vision statement, a mission statement, a strategic plan, or a transformative general education focus (insert your preferred academic administrative buzzword here), faculty and administrators ignore the fact that underfunded students, not just unfunded budget lines or unsalaried professors, shut down programs. My public university's combination of low price for state residents and high ratings on the various (if sometimes dubious) best-college lists have made it selective. But the students who are admitted still tend to be working class and middle culture; with summer jobs and loans to pay, they don't have thousands of dollars for a course abroad, and it's tough to get Dad or Grandma to see the value of the trip, even if they have the money. Many institutions (including mine) have a small number of scholarships and awards to help with funding, but it's not enough. A university—or a writing program—may tout an "internationalized" brand or a "global" label, but if material conditions are ignored, the reality of internationalization may be limited to students who are financially privileged or who come preloaded with cultural savvy.

Jenny Stuber (2011) notes, in *Inside the College Gates: How Class and Culture Matter in Higher Education*, that students studying abroad "gain foreign language skills and an appreciation for the art, architecture, food, and customs of another culture"; citing Pierre Bourdieu, she identifies these skills as "forms of cultural capital that are valued by the privileged classes" (13). Stuber quantitatively documents the fact that affluent students are far more likely to study abroad than working-class or first-generation students; upper-middle-class students begin with substantial cultural capital, then increase their privilege through international study, becoming more attractive to employers (65–75). Stuber cites "class differences in students' participation" in study abroad; notes the constraining nature of the jobs that working-class students must hold; and gives the example of one campus where faculty-led study abroad trips cost "upwards of $4,000—with little or no financial assistance": such international study "constitutes perhaps the largest class divide on campus" (82). Less privileged students "enter higher education with different cultural dispositions"—they can't afford study abroad but see it as a mere luxury, not something educationally useful; therefore, higher education leaders should frame study abroad not as a "fun experience" but as "an experience that builds independence, leadership, and academic competencies" (170). Stuber suggests a reframing in which international study programs "would focus more on cooperative work experiences and immersion in another society's institutions. . . . In this regard, off-campus study becomes more than a vacation or an opportunity to party with other young people in a cosmopolitan locale. While the development of such programs would be resource-intensive, they have the advantage of appealing more broadly to students who approach higher education primarily as an educational endeavor" (170). Stuber makes it clear that study-abroad programs are not serving the needs of an economically diverse student body. Those students who most need language skills and appreciation of transnational rhetorical customs aren't getting them.

Starke-Meyerring (2015) applies a similar critique more specifically to writing-abroad programs. She observes (drawing on Dewey, Bruffee, Sorrells, and Scotts) that "globalization in higher education is at the heart of WPA work—it is about how . . . learning environments will be designed, what kind of learning they will facilitate, who gets to participate, who is learning with/from whom, and whose knowledge counts" (308). Of course, internationalization may be supported not only by studying abroad but also by internationalizing curricula and including international students, initiatives my domestically sited but binationally populated Business & Organizational Writing course enacted. Nevertheless, a properly enacted GNLE requires funding for equitable exchange between institutions; if a university touts study abroad as a hallmark of its internationalization, study abroad ought to be available to all who seek its transformative intercultural educational effects. The experience of my attempted establishment of a GNLE with an equitable exchange of

Chinese and US students in transnational learning sites suggests we must change material conditions if all of our students' (domestic and international, economically elite and working class) knowledge counts.

As long as translingual composition is a second-tier resource priority for institutions, or international study remains a luxury compounding privilege for the most affluent demographic among our students, translingual composition won't be a transformative pedagogy; it will hardly exist. Those of us who value translingual composition must address its material conditions if this reframing of academic rhetorical learning is to become far more central to general education—ideally, a requirement (whether achieved through international study, expanded language requirements, or through the internationalization of our domestic classrooms); we must make funding needy students a priority when planning study-abroad programs so the study-abroad cohort is more economically (and racially and culturally) diverse. As Tardy's (2015) research makes clear, frequently there is "a disconnect between university and writing program discourses of internationalization and diversity," a distinction that may suggest (if we are cynical) messages that are "merely cosmetic, a result of marketing research and intentional branding rather than a reflection of institutional values" (259). Tardy (2015) notes that "writing programs on the ground may be doing much more to support global citizenship and promote inclusion for diverse students than universities as a whole. . . . Composition journals and conferences have increasingly embraced international issues. . . . Yet, there have been far fewer discussions of how these issues relate to broader institutional missions and strategies" (259). Both institutions and writing programs are talking the talk on translingualism, but they are not walking the walk of strategic-plan-based funding to enact international, translingual, and diverse study abroad for composition and writing studies.

Translingualism occurs in every composition classroom, to some degree, as students bring varied linguistic, dialectal, and cultural positions to code mesh on our own home campuses, but to extend translingualism to its fully international enactment requires an activist attention to its currently limiting material conditions. These conditions include funding study abroad for a more diverse range of domestic students but should extend to making students coming from abroad welcome and well funded on domestic campuses (rather than serving merely as full-tuition-paying cash generators). As Tardy (2015) says, institutions and writing programs have embraced a discourse of internationalization and translingualism, but we must examine "the ways those discourses might shape writing program decisions and practices, and how we might construct our own program spaces to reflect (and create) the values we want to embrace and embody" (259). Our institutions and programs should create material conditions for a more diverse student body to practice writing abroad and should also include budgetary support for the research, curricular, and faculty-development labor to support the most astute pedagogical approaches to international and translingual course offerings.

Translingual pedagogies (as suggested, for instance, in the context of the two courses here described), if they are to be consonant with a broadly multicultural understanding of how language and culture and written communication interact, cannot be equated with international study by a select segment of the US student population. The challenge before us is not just to recognize the presence of global Englishes or translingualism in writing courses but to design and fully institutionalize—with appropriate material conditions—writing programs that, to invoke Donahue (2009) again, "resist an import-export model" and instead incorporate "an equitable exchange one" (232).

And productive work can be done locally, at the institutional and student level, to encourage equitable exchange and an extension of transnational learning to a more diverse student body. The most honest and straightforward approach would be to prioritize centralized, institution-level, hard-money budget-line funding of transnational programs according to the professed discourses of internationalization as vital to modern higher education: institutions could regularly include funding for needy students to participate in study-abroad programs. But more creative funding approaches can be accessed from the smorgasbord of institutional funding tactics, such as university foundation student awards or scholarships; alumni-named funds or large philanthropy grants for diversifying the study-abroad population; the linking of translingual or writing program administration research projects to the funding of undergraduates participating in such research and programs. And raising funds isn't the only structural challenge. As Stuber (2011) suggests, student understanding of study abroad needs a reframing so all students see the transnational experience as central to intellectual growth and not a party-hardy perquisite for the privileged, and this reframing can start at the program level. If first-year orientation programs, in which first-year composition frequently participates, prepare students for intercultural competence, and if first-year composition courses are common study-abroad offerings, we move transnational learning from a luxury option to a valuable required course central to general education, via translingual writing programs. If we link transnational writing courses with other transnational courses (language courses, history and culture courses, interdisciplinary courses), especially general education courses in demand to fulfill core requirements, within the structure of a coordinated study-abroad menu, students have more reasons to earn credit hours abroad: it makes sense to travel to take two or three courses abroad simultaneously, rather than just one course, for the same travel cost. We should also explore the establishment of cooperative work-study experiences and internships abroad, many of which may draw on and enhance students' writing abilities, as an attractive version of translingual learning. Yet we too seldom collaborate on any of these creative programmatic approaches, these innovative GNLEs, to make transnational courses worthwhile for our students.

The brief history related in this chapter shows how difficult it is to meet the challenge of not just designing but actualizing an appropriate translingual writing program. Fortunately, course two, Business & Organizational Writing, did occur as planned—once. It worked with GZU students and WCU students for a five-week session on the WCU campus in 2011. (The Chinese university withdrew from the 2015 version of course two due to the US university's withdrawal from the 2015 version of course one: an ironic application of the principle of equitable exchange, or equitable nonexchange—a broken GNLE). The Business & Organizational Writing course that did occur (in 2011) brought China to my US students even as it created an intercultural site of learning for students from each university and each country. But the cancellation of the second attempt to teach the course with Chinese students and US students working and writing together in the United States, after the unsuccessful attempt to fund a cohort of US students to take a paired writing course in China, provides a cautionary tale: a translingual writing program without full inclusion will fail. It would be an unfortunate irony if our study-abroad programs ostensibly designed to enable two-way translingual, transnational courses fail because they limit access mostly to a small population of our richest, whitest, most monolingually Edited American English-enacting students. Transnational writing programs can do better than to continue to privilege a relatively homogeneous subset of our diverse US student bodies.

If we value translingualism and internationalization, we must enact it in more complex and inclusive ways by bringing students from the United States and L1 students of multiple cultural positions to translingual contexts, and by bringing international and L2 students to experience the translingual contexts of our domestic classrooms, for the benefit of all. Enacting translingualism in composition-course pedagogy requires us, as instructors and as students, to embrace risks and challenges but also to cultivate more completely the humane and generative engagement with difference at the heart of all community, and at the heart of the most productive rhetorical knowledge.

Notes

1. See, for instance, Canagarajah (2014); Connor (2011); Jay Jordan (2012); Shirley Logan (2010); Lu and Horner (2011); LuMing Mao (2002); Matsuda (2006)); and the collections edited by David Martins (2015) and by Matsuda et al. (2006).
2. Required texts for the Multicultural Writing course were Michael Austin (2010), an anthology of readings; and Harris and Kunka (2011), a grammar reference handbook.
3. The required text for the Business & Organizational Writing course was Kolin (2012), a standard business writing textbook.

References

Atkinson, Dwight, Deborah Crusan, Paul Kei Matsuda, Christina Ortmeier-Hooper, Todd Ruecker, Steve Simpson, and Christine Tardy. 2015. "Clarifying the Relationship between L2 Writing and Translingual Writing: An Open Letter to Writing Studies Editors and Organization Leaders." *College English* 77 (4): 383–86.

Austin, Michael, ed. 2010. *Reading the World: Ideas that Matter.* 2nd ed. New York: Norton.

Canagarajah, Suresh. 2014. *Translingual Practice: Global Englishes and Cosmopolitan Relations.* London: Routledge.

Connor, Ulla. 2011. *Intercultural Rhetoric in the Writing Classroom.* Ann Arbor: University of Michigan Press.

Donahue, Christiane. 2009. "'Internationalization' and Composition Studies: Reorienting the Discourse." *College Composition and Communication* 61 (2): 212–43.

Fairclough, Norman. 2003. *Analyzing Discourse: Textual Analysis for Social Research.* London: Routledge.

Guizhou University. 2015. "About GZU." Accessed May 27, 2015. http://www.gzu.edu.cn /page/main602/about/index.html.

Harris, Muriel, and Jennifer L. Kunka. 2011. *The Writer's FAQs: A Pocket Handbook.* 4th ed. Upper Saddle River, NJ: Pearson.

Horner, Bruce, Min-Zhan Lu, Jacqueline Jones Royster, and John Trimbur. 2011. "Opinion: Language Difference in Writing—Toward a Translingual Approach." *College English* 73 (3): 303–21.

Jordan, Jay. 2012. *Redesigning Composition for Multilingual Realities.* Urbana, IL: NCTE.

Kolin, Philip C. 2012. *Successful Writing at Work. Concise.* 3rd ed. Boston: Wadsworth.

Lalicker, William B. 2015a. "ENG368 Business & Organizational Writing, Introduction and Syllabus. ". Unpublished document. Microsoft Word file.

Lalicker, William B. 2015b. "WRH210 Multicultural Writing, Introduction and Syllabus." Unpublished document). Microsoft Word file.

Logan, Shirley Wilson. 2010. "Ownership of Language and the Teaching of Writing." In *Cross-Language Relations in Composition,* edited by Bruce Horner, Min-Zhan Lu, and Paul Kei Matsuda, 183–88. Carbondale: Southern Illinois University Press.

Lu, Min-Zhan. 2006. "Living-English Work." *College English* 68 (6): 605–18.

Lu, Min-Zhan, and Bruce Horner. 2011. "The Logic of Listening to Global Englishes." In *Code-Meshing as World English*, edited by Vershawn Ashanti Young and Aja Y. Martinez, 99–114. Urbana, IL: NCTE.

Lu, Min-Zhan, and Bruce Horner. 2016. "Introduction: Translingual Work." *College English* 78 (3): 207–18.

Mao, LuMing. 2002. "Re-Clustering Traditional Academic Discourse: Alternating with Confucian Discourse." In *ALT/DIS: Alternative Discourses and the Academy*, edited by Christopher Schroeder, Helen Fox, and Patricia Bizzell, 112–25. Portsmouth, NH: Heinemann.

Martins, David S., ed. 2015. *Transnational Writing Program Administration*. Logan: Utah State University Press.

Matsuda, Paul Kei. 2006. "The Myth of Linguistic Homogeneity in U.S. College Composition." *College English* 68 (6): 637–51.

Matsuda, Paul Kei, Michelle Cox, Jay Jordan, and Christina Ortmeier-Hooper, eds. 2006. *Second-Language Writing in the Composition Classroom: A Critical Sourcebook*. Boston, MA: Bedford/St. Martin's.

Matsuda, Paul Kei, and Tony Silva. 2006. "Cross-Cultural Composition: Mediated Integration of U.S. and International Students." In *Second-Language Writing in the Composition Classroom: A Critical Sourcebook*, edited by Paul Kei Matsuda, Michelle Cox, Jay Jordan, and Christina Ortmeier-Hooper, 246–59. Boston, MA: Bedford/St. Martin's.

Pennycook, Alastair. 2007. *Global Englishes and Transcultural Flows*. London: Routledge.

Starke-Meyerring, Doreen. 2015. "From 'Educating the Other' to Cross-Boundary Knowledge-Making: Globally Networked Learning Environments as Critical Sites of Writing Program Administration." In *Transnational Writing Program Administration*, edited by David S. Martins, 307–31. Logan: Utah State University Press.

Stuber, Jenny L. 2011. *Inside the College Gates: How Class and Culture Matter in Higher Education*. Lanham, MD: Lexington.

Tardy, Christine M. 2015. "Discourses of Internationalization and Diversity in US Universities and Writing Programs." In *Transnational Writing Program Administration*, edited by David S. Martins, 243–62. Logan: Utah State University Press.

West Chester University. 2015. "About the University." *West Chester University Undergraduate Catalog 2015–2016*. Accessed May 30, 2015. http://www.wcupa.edu/president/about WCU.aspx.

"WPA Outcomes Statement for First-Year Composition (Revisions adopted 17 July 2014)." 2014. *WPA: Writing Program Administration* 38 (1): 144–48.

4

WHO OWNS ENGLISH IN SOUTH KOREA?

Patricia Bizzell

The English language is woven into South Korean culture everywhere. Road signs throughout the country are printed in English and Chinese as well as Korean. Shopfronts sport English names, even those not outposts of familiar US franchises such as Dunkin' Donuts and KFC. Endless reruns of US television programs, in English, are shown on Korean television, and the commercials often feature tag lines in English, as in the ad for a restaurant in which a handsome young hipster croons "I love steak!" while forking juicy bites into his mouth (the rest of the commercial is in Korean). When I was there in 2011 teaching at Sogang University, apparently I looked like an English speaker because everywhere I went, at bus stops, in elevators, in supermarket check-out lines, schoolkids approached me to try out their English.

This is not to say large numbers of Koreans are fully bilingual in English and Korean, but then, they do not need to be. Understanding the South Korean linguistic situation is aided by the translingual model of language interaction advanced by Bruce Horner, Min-Zhan Lu, Jacqueline Jones Royster, and John Trimbur. This model highlights the obsolescence of the idea that in order to "have" a language, you must possess near-native fluency in it. You might instead "have" enough of a language to understand pop-music lyrics or action-movie dialogue in that language, or to interact with a native speaker of that language who does not understand your native tongue very well. In other words, English-language norms in South Korea are "heterogeneous, fluid, and negotiable," as Horner et al. explain about the translingual approach generally (Horner et al. 2011, 305).

This is not to say all Koreans have equal power over how English is integrated into Korean culture. But I concur with Mi-Hyon Jeon, who uses Stuart Hall's concept of "postmodern globalization" to explain South Korea's role as an "agentive state" successfully participating in

DOI: 10.7330/9781607326205.c004

the globalization process, including the global spread of English, and adapting it to local conditions (Jeon 2009, 233, 234). Samuel Gerald Collins agrees.

> While generic invocations of imperialism may remind us to eschew cultural chauvinism in the classroom, these tell us little of the cultural practice of English in specific social and historical contexts. . . . After all, hegemonic processes are not just the top-down imposition of beliefs . . . . English is already *part* of "local" culture; those relationships ultimately determine the shape of "world Englishes." (Collins 2005, 427, 418)

Thus, as Jeon argues, globalization should no longer be seen as "an external force which undermines national sovereignty" (Jeon 2009, 234). And as Xiaoye You reports about English in China, "English is no longer a language owned by any particular people or nation" (You 2010, 9); South Korea, I contend, owns English in its own way just as much as any country where it is traditionally the native language.

I've picked up the notion of ownership from You as both metaphor and literalization. Metaphorically, South Korean society owns English in the ways suggested by Jeon and Collins above, pushing back vigorously against the "top-down imposition" of the language by deciding how important the language will—or will not—be in Korean culture. While fluency in English is prestigious, and can be economically advantageous, I found that Koreans are fiercely proud of their Korean language and culture, to the point of viewing negatively the Korean-born who leave the country to live elsewhere. Literally, too, English proficiency is treated as a commercial property in South Korea: people spend a lot of money to attempt to acquire it, and in the process, native-speaker US citizens of European descent are strictly controlled employees who are prodded to deliver the goods. Although, as I will show, there are disturbing elements in this linguistic situation, South Korea can also in some ways model a more enlightened approach to language acquisition and difference in the United States.

ENGLISH IN SOUTH KOREA

English is certainly a language that has entered South Korea from elsewhere, and many Koreans feel so much pressure to learn it that some scholars describe the country as gripped by a "collective neurosis of English fever," as Jin-Kyu Park has it (J.-K. Park 2009, 50). According to one report, Koreans spent the equivalent of $19 billion on English education in 2009, distributed among English-language *hakwans* (after-school for-profit programs), private schools with an English-language curriculum, and schooling abroad in native-English-speaking countries (Lee, Han, and McKerrow 2010, 338). Like the Slovaks in Catherine Prendergast's (2008) study, Koreans are "buying into English" for economic reasons. As of 2010, about 55 percent of job interviews with Korean companies are conducted at least partly in English, and nearly 25 percent spend half or more of the interview time using English (Jambor 2011). Anecdotally, I note that the Korean engineers who worked with my husband at Samsung communicated with their Chinese counterparts in English, and our young friend Hoi-Sung conducted his company's financial business with European clients in English. It seems, then, that English in South Korea might be considered to be another "devil's tongue," as English has been in China, according to Xiaoye You (2010), forced on Koreans by economic imperialism. But in South Korea, as in China, the situation is actually more nuanced.

The cultural meaning of English in Korea is conditioned by the fact that the country was never colonized by an English-speaking power. In the mid-nineteenth century, when Western powers pushed into other Asian countries, the ruling Korean dynasty resisted their incursions and actively persecuted Koreans who adopted Roman Catholic Christianity and Western learning (Collins 2005, 419). In this context, as Collins explains, English "could only be said to represent imperialism" (Collins 2005, 419). However, when Korean ports were forced open, not by a Western power but by Japan in 1876, Western academic and political ideas, Christianity, and the English language became associated with efforts by young Korean progressives to preserve their national independence and protect their indigenous culture. They started the country's first English-language newspaper in 1896 to recruit international support for Korean sovereignty (Collins 2005, 420) and at the same time successfully pushed for the unique Korean alphabet, called *han-gul*, to become the official letter system for the Korean language instead of Chinese characters (Lee, Han, and McKerrow 2010, 346). When Japan annexed Korea in 1910, Korean patriots continued to use English to plead their country's cause abroad. And English gained more positive regard when US-led forces drove Japan out of the country during World War II and then prevented a Communist takeover of the entire peninsula in the Korean War of 1951 to 1953.

Nevertheless, English has never been made an official language of South Korea, as it has in Singapore, for example, and in other non-native-English countries where the language is in wide use. In contrast, the so-called English fever of contemporary South Korea has developed in tandem with expressions of loyalty to Korean. The Ministry of

Education promotes Korean-only materials, and a popular television game show tests contestants' knowledge of the language (J. S.-Y. Park 2009, 53–54). Moreover, Joseph Sung-Yul Park describes an entire genre of self-deprecating Korean jokes about English-language usage called *yumeo* (a Korean pronunciation of the English word *humor*). Perhaps this genre enacts some of the subversive intent of similar humor reported by Prendergast among her reluctant Slovak English-language learners, but in Korean examples, the subversion is often directed not at a foreign overlord but at an overbearing Korean boss. At the very least, *yumeo* seems to suggest that breakdowns in English communication need not be taken all that seriously. My sense is that while remaining intensely proud of their Korean language and culture, South Koreans are comfortable with a degree of linguistic mixing. After all, it's been going on in the peninsula for centuries. Chinese loan words still abound in Korean, and a Korean-English dialect known as *Konglish* is also widely used in the cities, offering coinages such as *eye shopping* for what we in the United States would call *window shopping*.

A Korean graduate student in the English Department at Sogang got into a joking match with me about how similar Koreans are to Jews— both peoples have historically contested homelands, both cultures highly value children and family life, both believe they have the world's most beautiful and elegant native tongue, and both think of themselves as smarter than everyone else! We laughed, but I also got the idea that for some, at least, Koreans' comfort about the presence of English in their culture is bolstered by confidence that their beautiful Korean language is too strong to be displaced anytime soon—unlike the anxiety that seems to motivate many English-only advocates in the United States.

EXPAT ENGLISH TEACHERS IN SOUTH KOREA

Expat teachers from native English-speaking countries teach English in Korean universities and secondary schools, but the largest number work in after-school supplemental programs called *hakwans*. I interviewed twenty-six young expats—thirteen men and thirteen women— from the United States, Canada, Ireland, Australia, England, New Zealand, Scotland, and South Africa (see app. 4.A). Overall, the expats' stories suggest Korean employers do not feel obliged to honor Western sensibilities about race or gender, nor do they promote kinds of language learning that would now be regarded as best practices in Western schools. For better or worse, their power to enforce their preferences on the expat teachers provides further evidence that Koreans own

English in South Korea. It certainly seems that Korean employers firmly control most of the expat teachers (my privileged position at Sogang will be described below).

Other scholars, too, have interviewed expat teachers, and Mi-Hyon Jeon finds that "the superior position of native English teachers [due to their possession of the cultural capital of English] was not always realized in their lived experiences" (Jeon 2009, 237), a delicate way of describing their typically low-level position. For one thing, expat teachers of Asian descent had to deal with what one Korean American expat interviewed by John Song Pae Cho called a "'white men theory' that 'white people speak better English than Korean Americans'" (Cho 2012, 227). Teachers of African descent also were not welcomed in the hakwans. Many recruiting websites state openly that Black people will have a hard time getting hired. I was able to interview only one African American, whom I'll call Kevin (all teachers' names used here are pseudonyms). He tried for two years to get a job with no success, he believes for racial reasons. After his resumé sparked interest from recruiters, they'd never call back once he sent the photograph every application requires. Eventually he told a recruiter up front that he is Black and the man was able to get him a job writing questions for hakwan English-reading selections; his employer did not want to use him in the classroom for fear of parental displeasure, or so Kevin thought. Mexican American Rafael, who looks Hispanic to US eyes, did get a job in the classroom, but as he told me, "We kind of fly under the radar here; the Koreans don't know we aren't white." While the expat teachers I met found these racial attitudes offensive (and I recognize them as part and parcel of an outdated monolingualist ideology identifying race, language, and nation), the young expats had little opportunity to push back against them.

Being North American is also an advantage if you're looking for a hakwan job, as might be inferred from the fact that fifteen of my interviewees are North American, and they are the ones who get more of the most desirable jobs in the greater Seoul area. North American accents (US and Canadian) are favored. Emily, from South Africa, was told her accent would make it harder for her to get a job. Anecdotally, I can report that our favorite expat bar in Seoul showed American football on its big screen every week, reflecting the denizens' interests, while in the bar's second location in Daegu, a regional city, my husband and I found a lively crowd of New Zealanders cheering their rugby team.

Expat teacher Vanessa observes wryly, "I've had really big advantages, being female, being American, blonde hair, blue eyes." Her comment suggests that in addition to racial and pronunciation preferences,

Korean employers also consider gender in their hiring practices. Cho's Korean American teacher interviewees contend that "white female teachers were considered to be the most desirable for English conversation" (Cho 2012, 228), and the expats I interviewed concur: the general opinion is, as Miri told me, "Koreans typically look for young females," and "appearance is huge—if you are older or overweight, they are not interested." Dana believes that "being a youngish girl" helped her get a job, but she's embarrassed by the constant comments about her body made by both male and female Korean coworkers: "'We like your skinny figure,'" "'We like your curvy body.'" According to Kay, "They told me they hired me specifically because I was female and they wanted someone more nurturing and caring than my male colleagues."

Though such remarks might be legally actionable in a US workplace, the expat teachers all report feeling relatively powerless in relation to their Korean employers. Even contractual obligations are often not met. Colleen's complaint is typical: "I'm never paid on time," and she once went unpaid for three months. Kent reports that "we are all walking on egg shells" for fear of getting fired, and he's seen people axed for no reason (or so it seemed to him). Orson calls contracts "toilet paper"; when he protested a work day—not in his contract—that stretched from seven in the morning to ten at night at three different locations, his employer threatened to inform immigration that he had molested a child if he persisted in complaining. One of the Korean American teachers interviewed by John Song Pae Cho actually referred to himself and the other expats as "English prostitutes" (Cho 2012, 233).

The expats' role typically is to provide conversation practice, and no prior teaching experience is required. Most do not teach English grammar; that is done by a Korean coteacher. Eric complains that the students "just want to play games" and that he is "an entertainer, not an educator." Dana concurs: "I feel like Vanna White with my SmartBoard." While Jim, one of the few professional teachers in my sample, notes repetition and drill are necessary in learning a language—something the untrained expats may not realize—he too expresses frustration at curricula he sees as both rigid and disorganized. Meryl, a professional teacher from Australia, describes her school as "massively disorganized." For example, in the kindergarteners' science class, "every week you get a little pack of things they can't do anyway" because they don't have enough English to understand the tasks. Yet she is required to stick with the prescribed curriculum. Meryl prefers hands-on materials, such as different-sized containers for teaching metric measurement, but her school won't buy them. Meryl also laments that there are "massive amounts of errors" in the school-generated English workbooks. She has successfully lobbied for some choice of reading books, the prescribed text being much too hard for the grade level, and she's started a writing program in which the kids actually compose continuous prose; before, writing meant filling words into blanks or picking correct sentences.

Meryl's experience with classroom materials that were clearly beyond the students' abilities suggests the fierce competitiveness among parents to push their children's English acquisition quickly, perhaps to impress their friends by displaying their child's highly advanced workbook. Many teachers report pressure from parents to promote children to higher-level classes, as in these comments from Trevor: "Some parents set expectations that aren't met by the child's ability, and they threaten to pull the child out unless he moves up," but then the children feel lost and frustrated in a class that's too hard for them. Dana reports she was pushed by her employer to falsify placement test results in order to move children up. At the very least, it seems that Korean "English Fever" encourages competitiveness US educators might deplore. Within the economy of Korean "ownership" of English, English proficiency here functions as a commodity parents believe they have purchased. The expat teachers are relatively powerless purveyors of that commodity, even though they believe not all parents are getting what they think they've bought.

The happiest teachers are those who are allowed to design their own course materials or who get to teach content-related courses. Bob loved a middle-school group with whom he read novels such as *Life of Pi* and *Lord of the Flies*, and Hannah cherishes her one experience teaching history to English-proficient sixth graders. Steve and Rafael are pleased that their new employer, a hakwan that teaches a range of academic subjects, has allowed them to start a debate class. Thirteen of the twenty teachers in my sample with no previous teaching experience have found their work rewarding enough that they have obtained ELL teaching certificates or applied to graduate school in education. They generally express warm feelings about their students. Vanessa got "very emotionally attached" to her kindergarteners, and Guy felt like "a big brother" to his young students. Shaynah emphasizes, "The kids were the best part. Their faces are just awesome when they understand something. It's very redeeming." Many agree with Kay and Bob that their students are "really bright" and "trying hard." Maybe too hard—several teachers expressed concern that their students' schedules are too demanding and thus, as Hannah put it, "the kids don't get to be kids." However, I have no intention of criticizing the demands many Korean parents place on their children. My point is that whether or not the Korean system offends the sensibilities of the expat teachers, they have very little control over its expectations, either of the students or of themselves. From their perspective, Koreans are in control.

TEACHING ENGLISH AT SOGANG UNIVERSITY

English proficiency tends to be distributed in Korean society according to economic advantage, a situation not unfamiliar to US educators. English is taught in the public schools, but parents who can afford it send their children to the private-pay hakwans. The more prosperous send their children to schools with a full English curriculum, such as the so-called international school attended by the children of my older expat friends, where students from outside the country were a tiny minority among the Koreans. The most prosperous Koreans send their children abroad to school in native English-speaking countries. English proficiency is expected of those students who make it into top Korean universities. For example, at Korea University, 35–45 percent of classes in all subjects are taught in English, and the percentage is not far behind at Sogang, the Jesuit University in Seoul where I taught for two semesters. My most English-proficient students were those who'd had the opportunity to study abroad, and their English language level is suggested by the fact that the Sogang English Department's course offerings in British and American literature resemble those at most US schools (see www .sogang.ac.kr/english/academic/103_under_0105.html).

In the summer 2011 term, I taught a composition course, the last of three English courses required of all Sogang students. My group of seventeen included some high-achieving students who wanted to get the requirement out of the way and others who were repeating the course after achieving a final grade below B minus (some of these had, technically, passed). Like the expat *hakwan* teachers, I started this course with a prescribed curriculum, in my case featuring a workbook that included a lot of short-answer exercises and one-paragraph written responses to very short academic reading assignments. Unlike the hakwan teachers, I did not feel this curriculum was too advanced for my students—on the contrary, it seemed about right for most of them at first. But the field quickly began to spread out by the second of our five weeks of classes, whether from boredom or resistance to the effort required. With the greater freedom allowed a university professor—perhaps enhanced by the fact that I was a native English speaker from a US college—I took the opportunity to encourage my students to try longer writing assignments, which seemed well within the capabilities of most of them, and

I added oral reports to our task list. These students' fluency in spoken English varied, too; some could contribute comfortably in spontaneous class discussion, while others remained silent unless presenting a formal report, in which case they spoke pretty well.

I assigned general paper topics that allowed the students considerable leeway in choosing their specific topics, something they found unusual. While they seemed to like having choices, the seriousness with which they addressed the assignments varied considerably—again, attitude variations that US teachers will recognize. For example, one assignment asked for a description of "then and now," how something has changed in their own lives or in Korean culture (one objective of the assignment was to give them practice using past and present tense). Here is how Jack, one of the students repeating the course, addressed it (student names are not the actual English names they adopted). He decided to contrast college life with his prior military service, required of all Korean men (I am reproducing all the excerpts here exactly as written).

> When I started my military service, I received 4 clothes and 2 pairs of shoes from a supplier. I had to wear only these clothes during 2 years! It is too small in number. And I can't find any sense of passion on this clothes. And the quality of this clothes is low. It seems that military clothes make me dull. And it gets rid of my personality. I don't like this clothes. But in college, you can wear any clothes. Your clothes look good, and you can show your character through your clothes.

Jack seems to be playing this assignment for laughs, exaggerating his dismay at the military clothing's lack of stylishness, and indeed, he was something of the "class clown" in this summer-school course. Although trying again to pass a requirement, possibly he did not see English proficiency as all that important to his future—or possibly he was pushing back against a requirement that had become onerous to him.

In contrast, here's another paragraph generated by the same assignment, from Mindi, who'd spent a high-school year in Illinois. She decided to talk about changes in how Chusok, a major Korean holiday, is celebrated.

> Among Koreans, it is thought to be their ancestor's distribution that crops grow well and become available for them to harvest. So traditionally this time around, whole relatives gather and perform ancestral rites to appreciate for the year's harvest and pray for next year's. For this ritual, Koreans prepare many kinds of food including dishes of meat, vegetable, and fish and so on. However, Women's sacrifice is what really has been supporting this custom. Who will prepare the food for the ritual? Korean women; mothers and elder daughters do. Now even new syndrome has occurred.

It's named "A holiday syndrome." When it gets nearer and nearer to big holiday such as Chusok, women feels like they are down with some illness-es. Their body aches without a reason. The cause of this syndrome is huge stress ladies get from the thought of doing hard work during the holiday.

I suspect Jack did not share Mindi's educational advantage of a year of English immersion; clearly her writing is more fluent than his. But I also contend that she seems more invested in the exercise. I sense pride in conveying her modern Korean feminist perspective here—a viewpoint rather new to Korea. And for Mindi, English was clearly important to her future plans. She was a Chinese studies major who wanted to improve her English for use in her chosen career, the hotel industry in Shanghai.

In the fall 2011 semester, I taught two literature courses, and I was free to choose the course materials though constrained by the avail-ability of English-language books in Korea. Perhaps I had greater free-dom of choice in these courses because they were considered to be at a higher level than the English composition course I taught in the sum-mer session, although I infer from the student profiles in my summer course that at Sogang, one did not need to complete all three English course requirements before beginning to study literature in English.

This curriculum structure seems to assume a certain degree of fluid-ity and negotiability in English proficiency. I found that in one of my fall 2011 courses, an introduction to literary study course comprised of first-year students, almost all of the nineteen were able to deal quite well with the US textbook I used and the literature we analyzed (poems by Emily Dickinson and Robert Frost, short stories by James Joyce and Eudora Welty). Here's the beginning of Jay's analysis of Frost's poem "Stopping by Woods on a Snowy Evening."

"Whose house this is I think I know. He is in his working place though; He will not see me stopping here to watch his house fill up with bright sunshine." When I was a high school student, studying and staying in the high school more than 12 hours in a day, I longed to escape from that prison, looking outside the school. There was beautiful village near school which was seen from the class where I studied. The outside place of the school seemed really peaceful and lovely. In school, I struggled to survive from the competition for university entrance exams, but in the peaceful village near school, there played children without any concerns and worries. The house wives come and go and other people seemed that they were enjoying their own time. I wished I had belonged to that peaceful world. But I had a thing to do, so I went back to my study put-ting up with inconvenience.

Jay goes on to explain that he had "miles to go" like Frost's speaker and wonders whether either of them will ever get a break from harsh life.

Many Korean students will tell you high school in their country is much harder than college because of the entrance exams Jay mentions. But I want to emphasize that Jay's demeanor in class was anything but hangdog. He seemed quietly confident, indeed more mature than most of the other first-year students. In the essay I have quoted above, I think he was using the practice with English to reflect creatively on his experience—suggesting not only good English fluency but also a comfort level with the language that enabled him to use it for his own purposes.

I also taught an American novel course already entitled in the course catalog Sexuality and Literature. Free to choose my own books, I decided to feature narratives on learning to perform one's gender, that is, to behave in conventionally masculine or feminine ways. Gender-role conventions are changing in South Korea right now, calling the traditional patriarchy into question, and the topic was provocative for my fourteen junior and senior English majors. This course differed very little from what I would have offered my upper-division majors at Holy Cross, my highly selective US Jesuit college: for the Korean students (plus one exchange student from France and another from China), six novels instead of eight or nine, and five-to-seven-page papers rather than ten pagers, though the assignment topics were similar. These students made more errors in English than I usually see among my Holy Cross students, but they wrote well and analyzed literature sensitively. Here's Julie's opening paragraph from a paper on social climbing and gender:

> American dream has been one of the key concepts for understanding American culture, whether past or present, as it is the idea that has constructed the Americans' behaviors, work styles, and relationships. Basically, it is the idea that people can succeed and live happily and affluently through hard work, which was originated in a time where people from European countries started moving in to America for economic and social freedom. As it reflects hopes and lives of Americans from dating back to 1600s to today, it has been used in many different novels as the central theme. In the two major American novels, *The Great Gatsby* and *Bread Givers*, the idea is also at the center, leading main characters dreaming of achieving high status in American society. Of all different hopes and dream for achieving American dream, women are mostly portrayed as wanting to change their lives through marrying up into the group of people from rich backgrounds rather than choosing their loving ones. For instance, in book *Bread Givers*, the issue of marrying up is at the center as the four Jewish American sisters confront problems with their father who strongly believes that his daughters have to marry up to sustain their immigrant lives. The choice of marrying up can also be found from the book *Great Gatsby*, particularly through the character Daisy. By seeing the marrying up issue in the two novels, I would like to find the reasons behind women dreaming of marrying up.

This opening paragraph is not radically different from what I get from my Holy Cross students. In Julie's case, the seriousness with which she undertook literary study reflected her ambition to attend graduate school in the United States. We kept in touch, so I know she went on to earn a Fulbright scholarship to Brown University, where she got a master's in American studies.

In all these courses, I was supposed to be teaching the English language, so in responding to students' papers, I corrected the students' English and explained their errors, concentrating mainly on those that repeated. Old fashioned, I got hard copies of papers from them and hand wrote these comments, but I also used a different color of ink to comment on their ideas and argument structure. In all three classes, the students expressed pleased surprise at the attention I gave to their ideas. In the Korean language, the verb for *taking* a course is *listening* to it, and I gathered they did not expect to have to take so much initiative in designing critical analyses. Most of them seemed to like it, though they also took a workmanlike and determined approach to improving their English. Be it noted that my approach to commenting implied that perfect English fluency was not required before one's ideas could be taken seriously.

In addition to teaching these courses, I also helped launch a writing-across-the-curriculum program at Sogang and a writing center where students could get help with both English- and Korean-language writing (in addition to prioritizing course offerings in English, Sogang has a vibrant Korean-language department and one of the best programs in the world for teaching the language to nonnative speakers). I believe Sogang welcomed me as a visiting professor primarily to take advantage of my expertise in developing these new writing initiatives. At the same time, I did not dictate the terms of their development. A colleague from the Sogang English Department, Yo-An Lee, functioned, in effect, as my manager. This was a collegial arrangement and I was quite grateful for the guidance, but in the nicest possible way, my colleague conveyed that he was in charge. He identified the topics and occasions for my workshops with Sogang faculty, who were new to the idea that those who were teaching subjects other than English or Korean might need to pay attention to how their pedagogy was developing students' ability to write academic discourse in the languages—or not. Professor Lee also helped me plan and conduct workshops for graduate student TAs and writing center tutors. At his request, I was also able to bring two other US experts, Charles Bazerman and Carolyn Miller, to visit Sogang and speak to audiences of faculty, graduate students, and writing tutors.

I hope my input at Sogang was useful. I think it was; certainly, people were cordial when I left and gave me a beautiful piece of Korean pottery as a going-away present. At the same time, it was clear to me that my Korean colleagues were not over awed by visiting US scholars, not in the slightest. They took what was offered and made their own judgments about it—I heard a few faint echoes of disappointment on occasion, but the main point is, they decided. They determined the value of what I and the other visiting scholars contributed. Also, interestingly, although both the writing center and the writing-across-the-curriculum program were engaged in pitched battles for funding while I was there, I was not directly involved in these discussions. I did not have that kind of influential position in university politics.

I am not complaining at all. I loved being at Sogang, and I learned a tremendous amount from my immersion in a linguistic situation far more translingual than any I have encountered so far in my US teaching. I was thrilled to attend the dedication of the writing center a couple of weeks before I left Korea. The importance of writing at Sogang is suggested by the fact that this center is centrally located on campus, in the same building as the Office for Jesuit Mission, and, by the way, equipped with much nicer furnishings and more up-to-date electronics than our modest little writing center at Holy Cross had at that time. But my Sogang experiences convinced me that my Korean students and my Korean colleagues felt quite comfortable setting their own agendas for English. To a greater or lesser degree, they owned it. I, like the hakwan teachers, was employed to assist them in acquiring this commodity.

MULTIPLE LANGUAGES IN SOUTH KOREA AND THE UNITED STATES

I have hoped to show here that South Korean culture presents a linguistic environment in which it is normal to encounter different languages. Koreans are proud of their native language, and they've worked hard to preserve it against inroads, as when, during the Japanese occupation, it was banned from schools and Koreans were even required to adopt Japanese names (see J. S.-Y. Park 2009, 53). Recall that my writing-across-the-curriculum work at Sogang aimed to improve writing pedagogy in Korean as well as in English. At the same time, Koreans seem untroubled by the presence in Korean of loan words, from Chinese based on long tradition, and now, more frequently, from English. In addition, many Koreans are eager to learn English for educational and economic advantage, and I saw great interest in other languages too. Recall that my student Mindi was a Chinese major, studying that language as well as English; another of my older expat friends, from Germany, was tutoring a Korean graduate student in German.

I speculate that my literal and figurative term *ownership* helps explain these Korean attitudes. Figuratively, South Koreans "own" English to the extent that they determine how the language will be integrated into their national culture. Koreans did not decide English would become the valuable international lingua franca—and one student expressed sadness to me that her beautiful Korean tongue had not achieved that status—but in general, I did not sense the kind of anxiety about English overwhelming Korean expressed by English-only advocates in the United States, who seem very fearful that the common language is being undermined. Literally, too, Koreans can imagine control over English as at least partly conveyed by economic advantage. On the one hand, this situation could be seen as unjust, but on the other, it puts English within reach when you can pay for it. Paying for it becomes a practical problem, not one for personal or national breast beating about traditional values being compromised—again, an anxiety that surfaces amid US controversy over language pedagogies.

There seems little reason, then, to take a condescending view of South Korea as a country woefully colonized by invader English. In fact, the South Korean attitudes toward language diversity I have been describing seem quite progressive to me, in comparison to views that prevail in the United States, no matter how much I may deplore Koreans' outmoded reliance on a race-language-nation identity model impacting the hiring of expat English teachers. Attitudes toward language diversity in Europe are even more progressive, witness the Council of Europe's policy of encouraging what they call "plurilingualism." According to the Council's *Guide for the Development of Language Education Policies in Europe,* "An adult European who has completed secondary education" might be expected to know the main national language spoken and written in school; a regional spoken variety of this language; another regional or minority language, spoken and/or written; "one or more foreign languages understood, but not necessarily spoken, to a basic level"; and another "foreign language mastered to a higher level with an ability to speak and write" (Council of Europe 2007, 8).

In sharp contrast, at the US college where I teach, I try to treat the languages my students bring to class as assets (see Bizzell 2014), but I struggle against the English-only attitude that seems to prevail at Holy Cross. Even though the college requires every student to master another language to the "intermediate" level (equivalent to four semesters of college-level study), and even though our study-abroad program is flourishing, languages other than English are rarely used in courses that are not language-learning courses. I wish there were more like the liberation theology class taught in Spanish because so many significant sources are written in Spanish. You can take the course if your Spanish is good enough. But what about integrating different languages into more courses, in which academic-level fluency might not be required, or not of every student? A biology professor told me recently of sending her students to track down foundational articles concerning a line of research the class was studying, and the team who found the article in German professed themselves to be utterly stymied. What, they couldn't muddle through a translation, maybe with the help of a fellow student studying German? Of course they could; they just thought they shouldn't have to because it was a bio class, not a German class. These narrow US attitudes toward linguistic diversity may soon result in our country's being left behind while the rest of the world progresses via economic and cultural exchange. True, English is the global lingua franca right now, but won't we look terribly unsophisticated if that's the only language in which we are prepared to deal?

APPENDIX 4.A

My US Jesuit college's Human Subjects Committee approved the design of my research into the experiences and opinions of the expat English teachers in Seoul, which I modeled on Catherine Prendergast's method with her Slovak interviewees (see Prendergast 2008, 19 ff.). I prepared a consent form each interviewee and I signed, with one copy for me and one for the interviewee. I let the person know that I intended to publish this research and that I might quote their words, paraphrase them, or bundle the responses with those of others to indicate trends, but that I would not use their real name. I stated that to the best of my knowledge, the interviewee incurred no risks by participating in my project. I have contact information for my interviewees and will let them know when this book including my chapter is published.

I prepared a set of twenty-four questions, provided to each interviewee, that asked about their educational and work background before coming to South Korea, teaching experiences in South Korea, views of English use in South Korea, life in the Seoul expat community, and experiences with Korean culture. While these questions indicated my general areas of interest, we did not proceed through them in lock-step fashion. Some interviews stuck more closely to this script than others, but in general, the questions served as guidelines for me to ensure that all my interviewees were asked for similar sorts of information. Most interviewees talked freely with little prompting from me.

I met my interviewees through my husband. He had preceded me to South Korea and had formed a friendship network among the young expat teachers who frequented a popular bar and grill in our Seoul neighborhood. Conversations with the expats made me realize they had much information regarding the spread of English worldwide, valuable because those who are teaching it have received little scholarly attention. I began by asking the expats I had met whether they would be willing to be interviewed; once my interview project got under way, word of it spread in the community, some people asked to be interviewed, and others accepted invitations from me in order for me to get a balance of men and women among the respondents and represent diverse countries of origin. I spoke with fifteen US citizens, four Canadians, two Irish, and one person each from Australia, England, New Zealand, Scotland, and South Africa. Thirteen were men and thirteen were women. Their ages ranged from twenty-two to forty; most were in their late twenties and early thirties. All had experience teaching in hakwans, and a few also had experience doing similar work in the public schools; two had moved on to adjunct positions teaching English at the university level. One had entered hakwan management.

I interviewed each person for one to two hours in a restaurant or coffee shop in our Seoul neighborhood. I took extensive notes during the interview and also requested a current cv. I was able to type up these notes within forty-eight hours of each interview and to e-mail any clarification queries that were needed. Tape recording the interviews did not prove feasible given the ambient noise in our interview locations.

References

Bizzell, Patricia. 2014. "Toward 'Transcultural Literacy' at a Liberal Arts College." In *Reworking English in Rhetoric and Composition: Global Interrogations, Local Interventions*, edited by Bruce Horner and Karen Kopelson, 131–49. Carbondale: Southern Illinois University Press.

Cho, John Song Pae. 2012. "Global Fatigue: Transnational Markets, Linguistic Capital, and Korean-American Male English Teachers in South Korea." *Journal of Sociolinguistics* 16 (2): 218–37.

Collins, Samuel Gerald. 2005. "'Who's This *Tong-il?*': English, Culture, and Ambivalence in South Korea." *Changing English* 12 (3): 417–29.

Council of Europe, Language Policy Division. 2007. *From Linguistic Diversity to Plurilingual Education: Guide for the Development of Language Education Policies in Europe (Executive Version)*. . www.coe.int/t/dg4/linguistic/Guide_niveau3_EN.asp#TopOfPage.

Horner, Bruce, Min-Zhan Lu, Jacqueline Jones Royster, and John Trimbur. 2011. "Language Difference in Writing: Toward a Translingual Approach." *College English* 73 (3): 303–21.

Jambor, Paul Z. 2011. "English Language Necessity: What It Means for Korea and Non-English Speaking Countries." ERIC document No. ED528279. http://files.eric.ed.gov /fulltext/ED528279.pdf.

Jeon, Mi-Hyon. 2009. "Globalization and Native English Speakers in English Programme in Korea (EPIK)." *Language, Culture and Curriculum* 22 (3): 231–43.

Lee, Jong-hwa, Min-wha Han, and Raymie E. McKerrow. 2010. "English or Perish: How Contemporary South Korea Received, Accommodated, and Internalized English and American Modernity." *Language and Intercultural Communication* 10 (4): 337–57.

Park, Jin-Kyu. 2009. "'English Fever' in South Korea: Its History and Symptoms." *English Today* 25 (1): 50–57.

Park, Joseph Sung-Yul. 2009. *The Local Construction of a Global Language: Ideologies of English in South Korea.* Berlin: Mouton de Gruyter.

Prendergast, Catherine. 2008. *Buying into English: Language and Investment in the New Capitalist World.* Pittsburgh, PA: University of Pittsburgh Press.

You, Xiaoye. 2010. *Writing in the Devil's Tongue: A History of English Composition in China.* Carbondale: Southern Illinois University Press.

5
TEACHING TRANSLINGUAL AGENCY IN ITERATION
Rewriting Difference

Bruce Horner

Three different responses to language difference in writing in the field of composition studies are presented in "Language Difference in Writing: Toward a Translingual Approach" (Horner et al. 2011). There is, first, an eradicationist approach directed at stamping out whatever might be identified as different from what is identified as the norm, a.k.a. standard. Second, there is an accommodationist approach that argues for tolerance of differences not identifiable as error insofar as writers are granted the "right" to "their own" language. And then there is the translingual approach, toward which the authors of "Language Difference" argue their readers should work.

But as the authors acknowledge, the translingual approach remains at best emergent, whereas the eradicationist and accommodationist approaches are prevalent. One possible consequence of the emergent status of a translingual approach is that it is easy to conflate with an accommodationist approach, especially insofar as a translingual approach shares with an accommodationist approach an opposition to the eradicationist approach. This opposition is also quite understandable since tolerance seems clearly preferable to, well, the intolerance the eradicationist approach is aligned with. Moreover, there are enough warnings in "Language Difference" about the importance of such tolerance, and against discrimination on the basis of perceived or claimed differences in language, that it seems fair to align the argument for a translingual approach with an accommodationist argument. Further, it's not hard to see that those teacher-scholars who have been making arguments for a translingual approach have in their past work made the case for expanding the range of language practices teachers should

DOI: 10.7330/9781607326205.c005

consider and even accommodate—I'm thinking here, for example, of Min-Zhan Lu's (1994) "Professing Multiculturalism," which argues for the acceptability of a student's deployment of the phrase *can able to* to express a condition of having both the ability and the permission to do something: for example, ideally, students "could able to" use phrases like *can able to* in their writing without being marked down for failing to conform to conventional uses of *can* and *able to*—an argument cited in work frequently identified as advancing a translingual approach (see, for example, Canagarajah 2006).

All that said, I would like to use this chapter in part to articulate a distinction between what I identify as a translingual approach and an accommodationist approach. I'll do so by identifying one of the key differences between them, namely, that a translingual approach takes difference in language not as an option writers may choose to pursue or not, nor as a feature marking some writing but not others, but as an inevitable feature of all writing, whatever forms that writing might take. So, for a translingual approach, the issue is not whether to eradicate or accommodate differences in language but instead what kinds of differences to make through writing, how, and why. In the perspective I'm advancing, a translingual approach treats languages as the ongoing, always-emerging product of practices. Hence, even those utterances that appear merely to reiterate conventional linguistic forms are renewing those forms and thus producing difference by their iteration of these forms in a different spatial and temporal location.[1]

This means that our usual ways of understanding language difference by reference to specific glossal features are inadequate, though not immaterial, to a translingual approach to language difference in writing. Both eradicationist and accommodationist approaches perpetuate monolingualist tenets by a focus on just such features, a focus that treats language, languages, and language varieties outside time, with accommodationist approaches merely multiplying the number of thus abstracted languages to be permitted. In contrast, a translingual approach defines context, writers, readers, and languages as always emergent and in co-constitutive relation to one another. While in one sense this approach might seem to represent a reversion to conventional rhetorical approaches to writing in its emphasis on context (or more frequently audience), a translingual approach differs from conventional rhetorical approaches by its insistence on not only the interdependent relation of context, writers, readers, and languages to one another but also on their emergent, rather than stable, character: utterances as always transforming all of these and their relations to one another rather than positing stable writers and readers (and their identities) drawing on likewise stable language resources to bridge divides and to accommodate equally stable contexts. The challenge of imagining a pedagogical approach that would not simply perpetuate monolingualist tenets, even in efforts to break with them, is exacerbated by the dominant's provision of alternatives that operate nonetheless within the dominant's framework for understanding language, language relations, and language users (see Horner 2016). For example, pedagogical strategies that might, in fact, break from that monolingualist framework might well resemble, at least superficially, those we are predisposed to think of as conventionally monolingualist—strategies leading to students writing what we are disposed to identify as monolingual texts from a translingual approach—and vice versa.

The complex relationship between dominant language ideologies and local language practices in writing thus has complicated implications for pedagogy: what might seem to encourage conventional writing and understandings of writing might in fact break from these, and what might seem to encourage breaks from these might in fact reproduce them. Here I explore these complexities by describing a few of my own attempts at breaking with dominant frameworks for approaching language difference in writing, focusing on the strengths and limitations of two seemingly obvious strategies by which to address language difference: considerations of mixed-language writing and translation. By mixed-language writing, I refer to engaging students in considerations of texts that explicitly mix languages and address issues of language difference. For example, I've asked students to consider both the issue of language difference Haunani-Kay Trask (1987) raises in "From a Native Daughter" and also Trask's use of different languages and genres within that text.

A pedagogy directed at expanding the range of allowable linguistic practices might well introduce students to writing like Trask's that stretches that range by mixing languages and might encourage students to at least experiment with producing writing that similarly stretches the range of acceptable practice by mixing languages, genres, language varieties, and modes (all understood as stable and discrete). However, without dismissing the potential value of introducing students to such writing, such an approach, despite its strengths, is limited in accepting dominant definitions of what counts as difference in language, so its pedagogical energy risks leading students to accept and experiment with producing writing the dominant has already defined for us as language difference rather than calling those definitions into question.

What this approach comes to valorize can seem merely the flip side of what the dominant claims to valorize, or demand: glossal, modal, genre conformity is replaced with glossal, modal, genre difference. Such an argument in fact aligns quite nicely with dominant culture's valuing of at least some writing by at least some writers precisely for breaking with convention in recognizable ways as evidence of, say, those writers' genius and individuality and its disparagement of writing that is "merely conventional," a.k.a. timid and tame.

The complex relations between what the dominant identifies as "different" in language and what might actually constitute language difference in writing was brought home to me a while ago by my first-year composition students' responses to two texts—Walker Percy's "The Loss of the Creature" (Percy 1954) and Trask's "From a Native Daughter" (Trask 1987). I began the course by having students work through ways to make sense of Percy's essay, thinking this experience would prepare them to deal with what I presumed they would find to be the more challenging work of making useful meaning of Trask's essay, given its obvious breaks from conventions of language and genre. Percy's essay, after all, is a text by a dead white American male—the epitome of what I expected students to take as the cultural norm—and written in what I was predisposed to think of as conventional American English. Trask's essay, on the other hand, mixes English with Hawaiian language, deploys songs and what seem like chants into the text, and was written by a living native Hawaiian activist woman—the antithesis of what I anticipated my students would take to be the cultural norm, especially for a text assigned in a college course. I expected my students to resist Trask as an unwelcome deviation from the trajectory of "normal" writing represented by Percy.

In fact, however, my students had the reverse reaction. Percy, they complained from the start, was inarticulate, never came to a straightforward point, and used terms to make an argument, if he had one at all, that they found alien and alienating. Trask, on the other hand, they found to be making a clear and straightforward argument. On first reading Trask, they expressed relief, and even gratitude, that her writing was not like Percy's. It may bear mentioning that, to my knowledge, none of my students responded in this way out of any particular sympathy with Trask's argument or identification with her as, say, fellow native Hawaiians or native peoples—they all gave every indication of being lower- to middle-class white long-term residents of the surrounding southern Midwest area of the United States who heretofore had not given much consideration to the issues Trask's argument raises (at least not in the terms or from the perspective she raises them). But for them, what counted was the difficulty of making sense of Percy, given his style of argumentation (a style they did not recognize as a way of arguing), and the ease of making sense of Trask, given her style of argumentation, an ease they especially welcomed given their own conditions of having many demands on their time (from work, other teachers, and family members).

I did not conclude from this experience that there is no need to require students to read texts like Trask's—that is, texts from marginalized groups expressing marginalized positions and using different language practices. There is obvious and demonstrable value in having students engage in what the dominant encourages them to dismiss as marginal on the basis of the social identities of the writers. But I did conclude that a translingual pedagogy must approach language difference differently: not only in terms of the social identities and positions of writers, and not only in terms of the forms of language (and writing technologies) deployed, but also in terms of the inevitable difference effected by the location of the written utterances in both time and space and the transformation of writers, readers, contexts, and language effected through utterances, terms that define difference in writing as always emergent and contingent. In the case of Trask's writing "From a Native Daughter," for example, Trask, as a scholar, is rewriting—reproducing and revising—the meaning and practice of academic writing. The mixing of languages and genres in which she engages are neither novel nor conventional but both. However, at least some readers are predisposed to see her deployment of such practices as evidence of her difference from a "norm" of sameness in language, genre, and so forth. But, depending on the temporal spatial location of the activation of her utterances by readers, the significance of her utterances varies. In the FYC course I've described, Trask's utterance, following Percy's, had a very different valence than it might have in other locations, for other readers.

What I do conclude, therefore, from the experience of that course is that I need to focus my attention and that of my students on what seems different as well as "the same," in writing by both canonical and noncanonical writers—Percy and Trask and Thoreau and Kuhn and Anzaldúa, for example—rather than presuming those writers whom the dominant identifies as the cultural and linguistic norm—Percy, Thoreau, Kuhn—are homogeneous in their language practices, whereas the other writers—writers of color, women, "foreigners"—are by definition at a discrete remove from that norm. As I've already reported, students' own responses to these writers fail to correspond to such designations. And as my students and I have discovered, close examination of the texts of these writers also fails to support the validity of those designations of difference and sameness. For example, Henry David Thoreau's (1995) *Walden* mixes languages and defies generic category. And Thoreau's argument, like that of Thomas Kuhn (in his essay "The Historical Structure of Scientific Discovery" [Kuhn 1962]) as well as Trask's, encourages investigation of the relation between language practices and knowledge (an investigation highly appropriate as a point of departure for students taking a course on college composition). The question my students and I consider, then, is not whether to allow or take up language practices that dominant monolingualist culture encourages us to think of as "different" and why. As students' responses suggest, there is no clear sense of what counts as different, or the same, in confronting actual texts. Instead, we ask what differences specific language practices—whether seemingly conventional or not—might make to the positioning of writers and readers and to contexts, knowledge, language, and the relation of all these to one another. (These include, of course, the language practices of rewriting that reading itself participates in.) So, for example, rather than asking whether it's acceptable for Trask to insert phrases from Hawaiian into her text, or for Thoreau to use *I*, we look at the potential effect of Trask's footnotes and other conventional scholarly references, and of Thoreau's use of Latin and insertions of poetry into his prose, and at what different meanings Thoreau seems to be giving to *economy* and Trask is giving to *language*. And of course, we consider what these meanings might imply for students' own writing—what they might develop, and not, in their writing as they respond to the practices of these (other) writers. Thus, I don't use texts like Trask's in teaching composition as a means of adding to the range of allowable language practices (a.k.a. the students' language repertoires) in what would then reinforce an "additive" model of multilingualism retaining the key tenets of monolingualist ideology's identification of languages as discrete from one another and tied indelibly to the identities of particular groups of language users. Instead, I use Trask's, and all other writers', texts to help my students and I rethink what differences might be made through and in all writing practices, whether marked by the dominant as conventional writing or as unconventional, by treating all these as emergent practices located in time as well as space.

To address and break from monolingualist ideology's tenets more explicitly, I have also begun engaging students in double translation—that is, having students experiment with translating words and phrases identifiable as English into language marked as not English, and then back. Conventionally, the concern of translation is to find the equivalence in two languages: such as, for *education, éducation*. Such an approach to translation assumes both the discrete character of languages and the internal uniformity of each and aims at achieving, through a particular ("correct") translation, an exact transfer of meaning from one linguistic medium to the other so the linguistic medium itself remains transparent, invisible. And such an approach thus appears to demand the equivalent of native-speaker fluency in two languages so as to achieve such transparency. Thus, a focus on translation runs the risk of reinforcing, rather than countering, monolingualist notions of language and language relations.

To work against such notions, I ask students instead to produce several viable yet different translations of a single common word or phrase in English related to their work as students, consulting not only ordinary dictionaries in English to consider variant meanings but also the *Oxford English Dictionary* to build on the range of meanings over time and their etymological relation to terms in other languages. In addition, I ask them to consult a translation dictionary that provides multiple ways of translating the term into a language other than English. Specifically, the assignment reads:

> Writ[e] a draft essay in which you consider the differences that might result from a change in choice of words, or vocabulary. You might think of this as an investigation of translation: what's involved in the re-writing of a term, or phrase, by substituting a different term or phrase (including possibly "rewording" by rearrangement of a phrase), even terms from a different language.
>
> Start by selecting a term or phrase related to your work (Should it be called "work"? Something else?) here at the University of Louisville that seems to you to be commonly used and yet susceptible to different definitions and interpretations. Here are some examples for you to consider using: *student, study, education, learning, teaching, professor, revision, writing, discovery, scholar, reading, academic, assignment, test.*
>
> To consider alternatives, consult three types of dictionaries: 1) the ordinary kind of dictionary that would provide you with some current definitions and close synonyms of the term you've chosen to explore; 2) the *Oxford English Dictionary . . .*, which gives a history of the origins, different versions, uses, and meanings of the term over time; and 3) a translation dictionary that offers multiple ways of translating the term you've chosen into a language other than English (ideally, this would be a language with which you have some familiarity).
>
> In your draft essay, describe the different possible definitions, meanings, and ways of translating the term you've found. Then explain why writers might choose one or another definition, or term, to name what they all might seem to refer to, however loosely (this can include a "foreign" term, since it's common for writers to "borrow" terms from another language

to identify a concept or phenomenon they're trying to describe). Explain the basis for selecting at least three possibilities, including one that would involve use of a term from a language other than English. (Feel free to consult with others more familiar than yourself with that language for help, but be sure to acknowledge that help in your essay). Explain as well which of these you yourself would select, and why, especially given . . . the relationship between word choice, thinking, and living.[2]

There are several features of such an assignment that distinguish its aim as translingual (at least as I'm defining that term). First, it assumes a diversity of terms and meanings within any language, as well as, obviously, a diversity of possible ways of translating any one term into another language rather than treating languages as equivalent to stable "codes" (and, hence, treating translation as a matter of correct decoding/recoding). Second, in asking students to consult various translations within a language (English included) for a specific term and to "feel free to consult with others more familiar than yourself with that [other] language," it works against the monolingualist tenet of native-speaker fluency and expertise by positing all languages as complex, indeterminate assemblages of possibilities and all language use and meaning determination as collaborative rather than algorithmic. Third, by asking students to explain their choices in translation in terms of "the relationship between word choice, thinking, and living," the assignment posits linguistic decisions in composing as always located in (physical and social) time and space, rather than outside these, in co-constitutive relationship to context, self, and purpose. Fourth, in asking them to not only "explain the basis for selecting at least three possibilities" for translating a term but also to "explain as well which of these you yourself would select, and why," it posits the students themselves as active contributors to language understood as always-emergent practice. Finally, and more generally, by having students consider multiple terms to use to refer to the same phenomenon within as well as across languages, it treats translation, and thus language difference and the difficulties and pleasures of such difference, as the inevitable norm of all writing. Conventional translation is thus treated not as a discrete practice but as a more intense version of the challenges all writers face (see Pennycook 2008).

It will be readily apparent that though the pedagogical strategies I have described follow from tenets of what I think of as a translingual approach, they do not present students with something called *a translingual approach* for them to consider, select, resist, or oppose. Instead, they operate from, assume, and imply a translingual language ideology. Some might therefore object that I am not teaching a translingual approach at all, or that at best a translingual approach remains part of a "hidden" curriculum I am surreptitiously imposing on students who might otherwise choose to adopt a monolingualist approach. To which I answer that, first, the ideology of monolingualism likewise does not announce itself as a language ideology for students to choose (or not) but, rather, inheres in conventional composition pedagogical practices in the United States (and elsewhere) (see Horner and Trimbur 2002); and second, that, as Pierre Bourdieu observes of all language ideology, it

> has nothing in common with an explicitly professed, deliberate and revocable belief, or with an intentional act of accepting a "norm". It is inscribed, in a practical state, in dispositions which are impalpably inculcated, through a long and slow process of acquisition, by the sanctions of the linguistic market. (Bourdieu 1991, 51)

Thus, to attempt to teach a translingual approach as a choice is to fail to understand its character as an ideology (like monolingualism) and therefore to underestimate what is entailed in encouraging the former and breaking with the latter. Finally, in keeping with a translingual understanding of language as located only in practice, to attempt to transmit a translingual approach to students is to treat as fixed what a translingual approach would insist is always and necessarily subject to reworking—here, ironically, the meaning and practice of being translingual (see Lu and Horner 2016).

Others might object that the kinds of changes the strategies I have described might effect are in fact quite minimal and fail to address the urgent needs of student writers who have been condemned on the basis of their language practices precisely because these practices are recognizably different from what is believed to be the norm. There are, after all, differences in the scale of consequences for different kinds of language difference that the strategies I've described fail to address. The politics of the pedagogy I've described, in other words, might well seem to be "discreet" to the point of being invisible, if not inconsequential.[3] But without discounting the need to defend student (as well as other) writers against prejudicial treatment on the (putative) basis of language difference, I argue that a less discreet—say, explicit—pedagogical focus on the legitimacy of those kinds of language differences is likely to be less consequential, ultimately, insofar as it (1) tends to reinforce the reification of monolingualist definitions of language and language relations and language users, and (2) mistakes and conflates the politics to be pursued in and through the material social practices of coursework with the politics of the material social practices of legal defenses of language rights at the level of state policy and law.

This is not to say that the subject of language and language relations, including language policies, is not suitable for composition courses. On the contrary, it seems appropriate, if not inevitable, that language and language relations should emerge explicitly as the subject of course investigation in first-year (and "advanced") composition courses. In the course in which the strategies described above were deployed, language difference and its relation to identity, legitimacy, and knowledge were key points of investigation and debate. (Elsewhere, Patricia Bizzell has described a course that focuses explicitly on investigating different perspectives on English and other languages [Bizzell 2014]). But from my perspective, the work of such courses should be not to settle on the correct perspective students are to advance in their writing in light of investigating the facts of languages and the history of their relations. Rather, the course work should aim at developing specific dispositions toward language in contest with other, dominant language dispositions—dispositions that have consequences for language and language practices as these are continually rewritten by students and their teachers. In its effects on language dispositions, a pedagogy that enacts the tenets of translingual ideology can be a consequential approach to language and language relations.

Notes

1. For a fuller explication of this perspective, see Lu and Horner 2013.
2. The assignment builds on ideas introduced in the chapter "Vocabulary" in Lu and Horner's (2008) textbook *Writing Conventions*.
3. For an account of such a discreet politics in writing pedagogy, see James Seitz (1993).

References

Bizzell, Patricia. 2014. "Toward 'Transcultural Literacy' at a Liberal Arts College." In *Reworking English in Rhetoric and Composition: Global Interrogations, Local Interventions,* edited by Bruce Horner and Karen Kopelson, 131–49. Carbondale: Southern Illinois University Press.

Bourdieu, Pierre. 1991. *Language and Symbolic Power,* edited by John B. Thompson. Translated by Gino Raymond and Matthew Adamson. Cambridge, MA: Harvard University Press.

Canagarajah, A. Suresh. 2006. "The Place of World Englishes in Composition: Pluralization Continued." *College Composition and Communication* 57 (4): 586–619.

Horner, Bruce. 2016. *Rewriting Composition: Terms of Exchange.* Carbondale: Southern Illinois University Press.

Horner, Bruce, Min-Zhan Lu, Jacqueline Jones Royster, and John Trimbur. 2011. "Language Difference in Writing: Toward a Translingual Approach." *College English* 73 (3): 303–21.

Horner, Bruce, and John Trimbur. 2002. "English Only and U.S. College Composition." *College Composition and Communication* 53 (4): 594–630.

Kuhn, Thomas S. 1962. "Historical Structure of Scientific Discovery." *Science* 136 (3518): 760–64.

Lu, Min-Zhan. 1994. "Professing Multiculturalism: The Politics of Style in the Contact Zone." *College Composition and Communication* 45 (4): 442–58.

Lu, Min-Zhan, and Bruce Horner. 2008. *Writing Conventions.* New York: Penguin Academics.

Lu, Min-Zhan, and Bruce Horner. 2013. "Translingual Literacy, Language Difference, and Matters of Agency." *College English* 75 (6): 586–611.

Lu, Min-Zhan, and Bruce Horner. 2016. "Translingual Work." *College English* 78 (3): 207–18.

Pennycook, Alastair. 2008. "English as a Language Always in Translation." *European Journal of English Studies* 12 (1): 33–47.

Percy, Walker. 1954. "The Loss of the Creature." In *The Message in the Bottle: How Queer Man Is, How Queer Language Is, and What One Has to Do with the Other* , 46–63. New York: Farrar, Straus and Giroux.

Seitz, James E. 1993. "Eluding Righteous Discourse: A Discreet Politics for New Writing Curricula." *WPA: Journal of the Council of Writing Program Administrators*16 (3): 7–14.

Thoreau, Henry David. (1854) 1995. *Walden; or, Life in the Woods.* Boston, MA: Ticknor.

Trask, Haunani-Kay. 1987. "From a Native Daughter." In *The American Indian and the Problem of History,* edited by Calvin Martin, 171–79. Oxford: Oxford University Press.

PART 3

Institutional/Programmatic Interventions

6

DISRUPTING MONOLINGUAL IDEOLOGIES IN A COMMUNITY COLLEGE
A Translingual Studio Approach

Katie Malcolm

A translingual approach proclaims that writers can, do, and must negotiate standardized rules in light of the contexts of specific instances of writing. Against the common argument that students must learn "the standards" to meet demands by the dominant, a translingual approach recognizes that, to survive and thrive as active writers, students must understand how such demands are contingent and negotiable. (Horner et al. 2011, 305)

At the 2015 Conference on College Composition and Communication, the word *translingual* appeared in the main title of eleven panels representing four-year institutions—a clear sign that translingual theories and practices are inspiring changes in a number of these schools, doubtlessly to the benefit of their multilingual students. In a parallel movement, community colleges have also undertaken recent institutional changes to improve education for multilingual students by implementing acceleration programs, some of which allow them to skip over a number of previously required "remedial"[1] courses. In the January 2015 publication of the *Community College Review*, Shanna Smith Jaggars, Michelle Hodara, Sung-Woo Cho, and Di Xu assess this trend of accelerated learning in community colleges, focusing on two nationally recognized writing programs: the Community College of Baltimore County's (CCBC) accelerated learning program (ALP), developed by Peter Adams; and Katie Hern's reading/writing acceleration, which has grown into the California Acceleration Project (CAP). In addition to offering students an alternative to the daunting ladder of remedial courses required at many two-year schools, Jaggars et al. note that both

DOI: 10.7330/9781607326205.c006

programs offer students practice with actual academic reading and writing instead of the decontextualized grammar skills that are a staple of
most remedial writing courses (Jaggars et al. 2015, 21). Noting the success of both ALP and CAP, Jaggars et al. posit, "The broad majority of
students can benefit from what we might term 'supported acceleration':
compressing or shortening the student's sequence while providing
academic and affective supports that help him or her succeed in that
more rigorous environment" (Jaggars et al. 2015, 21). Just as translingual pedagogies are currently celebrated in writing programs at many
four-year institutions, accelerated learning has been championed in
many two-year colleges—yet these two approaches are not always mutually informed.

Particularly in my own area in the Pacific Northwest, CAP and ALP
have become two prominent models for helping students move more
quickly through their remedial-writing requirements. CAP's model
condenses two developmental English courses into one four-credit academic reading/writing course, offered in either a single semester or
stretched out over two (Hern 2011, 3). ALP fosters "supported acceleration" by allowing students who have tested into CCBC's developmental English course, English 052, to take a smaller version of English 052
(with a class size of ten students) *and* a traditional English 101 course
during the same semester (Gabriel and Gallagher n.d.b). According
to ALP's website, the same instructor teaches both the 052 and 101
sections, and (unlike CAP) ALP's English 101 course combines students with different placements into one college-level environment;
students who placed into English 101 are also in class with the accelerating students. Emphasizing that the support class, English 052, does
not focus on a "discrete set of writing skills" but rather "assignments
and learning skills that will help support the students' success in their
ongoing English 101 assignments," Jaggars et al.'s review validates ALP
developers' perspective on the program: that focusing on the actual
struggles students face in English 101—such as juggling work and
school successfully, understanding assignments, and finding money
to buy books—helps students succeed more consistently than does an
isolated focus on academic writing conventions (Adams et al. 2009,
62–63). Uniquely, ALP appeals not only to the instructors and students
who have firsthand experience with this, but also to fiscally concerned
administrators. A video on the ALP website argues that ALP "doubles
the [students'] success rate; cuts the attrition rate in half; does it in
half the time; at slightly less cost per successful student" (Gabriel and
Gallagher n.d.a). Similarly, Hern's CAP, which also promotes academic

reading and writing practice over decontextualized skills, contains few, if any, additional costs to the college (Hern 2011, 3–4; Jaggars et al. 2015, 9). Given the success rate and minimal cost, it's no surprise other versions of ALP and CAP have been adopted by community colleges across the country—and as a result, multilingual students who otherwise may have been cordoned off into remedial ESL or developmental English tracks are given access to college-level, transfer-credit-bearing English courses.

Although eliminating the remedial course requirements that lead to high attrition and fail rates is a crucial step toward college access and success, in this chapter I argue that translingual considerations— promoting the recognition and negotiation of students' multiple languages and discourses (rather than the suppression or elimination of these discourses)—are of paramount importance in acceleration programs' attempts to help students "survive and thrive as active writers," as Bruce Horner, Min-Zhan Lu, Jacqueline Jones Royster, and John Trimbur put it (Horner et al. 2011, 305). These translingual considerations include institutional practices that examine, critique, and resist the monolingualist ideologies that deem certain students in need of remediation from the outset and also incorporate this key understanding of "language differences and fluidities as resources to be preserved, developed, utilized" into the accelerated classroom (Horner et al. 2011, 304). Lu and Horner describe a translingual approach as one recognizing that language difference is not simply a product of "mistakes" made by members of nondominant groups but that "difference is an inevitable product of all language acts"—an inherent outcome of the very acts of reading and writing within specific (temporal-spatial) contexts of power (Lu and Horner 2013, 585). Pedagogical practices that help students recognize their language differences as iterative assets for disseminating and creating knowledge can be key to fostering the retention and success of students who have learned to see their own writing as encumbered by "errors."

By challenging the view that students who place into remedial courses have linguistic differences that create insurmountable barriers to successful college writing, acceleration programs such as ALP and CAP offer a unique opportunity for the widespread development of translingual pedagogies and practices. Indeed, without explicit attention to translingual ideologies, it may be all too easy for instructors and institutions to unintentionally reinforce one or both of the two monolingualist responses to language difference Horner et al. warn against: an imposition of "standards" (eradicating difference) or of "code-switching" (hiding difference in the public contexts in which many students aspire to participate) (Horner et al. 2011, 306). Translingual approaches can be particularly crucial to acceleration programs such as ALP in which the courses designed to support the accelerating students (e.g., English 052) were formerly remedial courses institutionally positioned to help students (re)produce seemingly fixed, monolingual reading and writing practices. Indeed, the institutional history of these courses could contribute to a view of acceleration programs as vehicles to help students hide or eradicate language differences more efficiently. Given the pervasive monolingualist frameworks in which these courses have operated until now, it is easy to see how students, faculty members, and administrators could conceive of acceleration programs as opportunities for students to more quickly and efficiently learn to omit or switch from fixed "problems" into equally fixed "standards" instead of learning to see both of these as negotiable and in flux (Horner et al. 2011, 205). This monolingualist view of acceleration may be compounded by arguments to administration that, in order to secure funding, position students and courses as budget-saving commodities.

In what follows I describe an acceleration program that used third-space theory from research on writing studios (Grego and Thompson 2008) to intentionally disrupt monolingual ideologies and advocate translingual practices at both the institutional and classroom levels. On an institutional level, this program allowed students to take a college-level, first-year writing class—English 101—and, similar to ALP, a tandem class that would offer support. Unlike ALP, however, this support class would be a completely new, college-credit-bearing course: English 100, Critical Literacy for College. Rather than using the existing developmental English or ESL courses on the books, English 100 intentionally combined students from various linguistic backgrounds, placement tracks, and English 101 sections. In this context, in which difference—across cultures, home languages, years of practice reading/ writing English, prior experiences in college, and current English 101 sections—would be one of the only recognizable norms, the need to utilize (rather than eradicate) all these differences as reading and writing resources was readily apparent to the students and other English faculty members. On a classroom level, the focus of English 100 also gave students a chance to see their discourse practices as negotiations—including negotiations among what they were learning in English 100, the linguistic conventions promoted in English 101 sections and throughout the college, and different academic spaces—particularly in the blended face-to-face and online hybrid sections.

NEGOTIATING INSTITUTIONAL SPACES

The English 101+100 acceleration program was developed at an urban, state-funded community college, which I'll refer to as UCC, and located in one of the most racially, ethnically, and linguistically diverse neighborhoods in the Pacific Northwest. Currently, UCC has three distinct "English" programs: an international English program (IEP) for students studying abroad; ESL, primarily for immigrants and generation 1.5 students; and an adult basic education (ABE) track with remedial courses intended for "native" English speakers. Prior to 2013, each program contained five or more noncredit courses guided by the well-intentioned, monolingualist desire to help students reproduce a presumably standardized "English" grammar that would supposedly help them find meaningful employment or transfer to a four-year institution.

Although many UCC students on the IEP and ESL tracks shared hopes of transferring to a four-year university at this time, their institutional designation as "non-native English speakers" required them to be in tracks separate from the university-transfer track housing the college-level composition courses and ABE tracks. In addition, "non-native English speakers" at UCC were (and, unfortunately, still are in some cases) not given a choice to take classes with "native English speakers" unless they scored high enough on the COMPASS, a multiple-choice, writing and reading placement exam largely focused on students' ability to identify decontextualized grammar conventions. As the UCC Student Assessment Services [unidentified to maintain anonymity] website explains to incoming students,

- Native English speakers take the Standard COMPASS Reading and Writing and the COMPASS Math.
- Non-native English speakers should begin testing with the ESL/COMPASS Grammar/Usage, Reading, Listening, and the COMPASS Math. The test software will move examinees earning high scores in Grammar/Usage and Reading, into the Standard COMPASS Writing and Reading for placement into English courses.

"Non-native speakers" begin this high-stakes test at a disadvantage they can only overcome if they perform successfully on this exam. Although ideally the separate ESL courses would be helpful for students who are hoping to gain additional practice with academic reading/writing, this is not necessarily the case—in a section called "Attitude" on the same website, students are given the following advice: "Realize that your placement on this test will determine at what level you begin your college experience. If you expect to rush through the test, you could place into pre-college (developmental) work which will require quarters of your time and energy and drain your college funds or financial aid which pays for only 45 credit hours." Although this warning applies to all test takers, it is particularly salient for students who must begin the exam at the deficit ESL level and can only hope to gain access to the courses that will not "drain [their] college funds" by performing on the test as a "native" English speaker would.

The cautionary "Attitude" note on UCC's website provides an ironic institutional recognition of how COMPASS can be used to direct students into pathways that delay their time to (and chances for) graduation. For not only do these noncredit courses isolate seemingly multi- and monolingual students into different remedial tracks, but data from UCC's recent Title III grant revealed that—at least in the case of the developmental English track—these courses operated as more of a barrier than a path; for example, only 48 percent of students who placed into English 096—a course only two rungs below English 101 in the UCC course sequence—entered English 101 within two years. Although deeply troubling, these figures are not surprising given the extensive research on the detriments of noncredit courses in which students focus on mastering decontextualized "skills," sometimes doing little to no academic reading or writing (see, for example, Adams et al. 2009; Bartholomae 1993; Rose 1988; Shor 2001). Prior to 2013, UCC students who placed into the lowest developmental English track were required to work on basic grammar skills in an English 086 lab, then move into two separate reading and writing courses (English 094 and 095), subsequently working on paragraphs in English 096, and then focusing on five-paragraph essays in English 098—all before finally entering English 101. Not only did this sequence perpetuate a monolingualist conception of reading and writing practice in which students must master one imagined, predetermined English skill before beginning to work on another, but it also required students to take at least four semesters of classes that did not offer graduation credits and, in many cases, created obstacles for obtaining financial aid.

In this setting, celebrated acceleration programs such as CAP and ALP, which have allowed students from Baltimore to California to successfully circumvent their noncredit course and placement requirements, were tempting for us to try to implement at UCC. Given the focus of the Title III grant on the high fail rates of students in our developmental courses, we knew ALP or CAP would be relatively easy to sell to our administrators and would allow us to immediately begin helping students escape UCC's remedial trenches. Yet we were also motivated to create a deep disruption in the monolingualist institutional practices that especially marginalized our multilingual students in nearly every UCC English, IEP, and ESL classroom.

Using Title III grant funding, my fellow English faculty member Holly Gilman and I began to develop an acceleration program that would not only work to decrease the long pipeline of UCC's developmental English courses but would also steer us away from the monolingualist ideologies underpinning most of UCC's institutional policies on English requirements. For this purpose, a program that condensed our existing developmental courses into one class, or even placed students in English 101 and a section of developmental English, would not suffice. Although ALP's and CAP's explicit focus on academic reading and writing practices would certainly shift the conversation about remediation at UCC in a better direction, it would not be enough. As long as students remained in a UCC course that, for decades prior, had assessed writing primarily on "grammatical correctness," we were concerned that we would find opposition—from administrators, fellow faculty members, and perhaps even the students themselves—to implementing a curriculum in which language differences were positioned as both norms and resources for students to use in their academic reading and writing endeavors. Instead of attempting to work within our current institutional sequence, we drew from the Studio approach advocated by Rhonda Grego and Nancy Thompson, which would allow us to use thirdspace theory to directly challenge UCC's monolingualist ideologies—both institutionally, and in our classroom practices(Grego and Thompson 2008).

As we began writing curriculum for English 100, Holly and I focused on Grego and Thompson's use of Homi Bhaba's theory of the "thirdspace" as an "imaginary space that exists 'in-between [the] political polarities' of the right and left through which traditional and oppressive power relations [hegemony] are maintained" (Grego and Thompson 2008, 75). The language produced within this thirdspace does not fit into the ubiquitous linguistic "scripts" of the powerful and powerless (e.g., administrator and teacher, teacher and student, "native" and "non-native" English speaker); instead, it forms new scripts that would help us intentionally replace monolingualist institutional and pedagogical practices with translingual approaches. UCC's acceleration program began with a focus on students who placed into English 098, the first course in the UCC English sequence, which combined students from the developmental English, IEP, and ESL tracks. Through a pilot, the first twenty-five English 098-designated students who volunteered were able to enroll in one section of English 100 and whichever sections of English 101 fit their schedules. Unlike English 098, English 100 would carry college-transfer credit and, due to administrative negotiations and a desire to make the course a more permanent fixture in the program, it would also carry the same number of credit hours as English 101. English 100 students would not all be in the same section of English 101—a typical English 100 class would have students from seven or more English 101 classrooms. With the unmistakable presence of so many differences, learning to recognize, articulate, and negotiate the linguistic demands of "college writing" in its many forms was a task students, other faculty members, and administrators understood we would have to confront in English 100.

TRANSLINGUAL PRACTICES IN ENGLISH 100

Because English 100 was comprised of students from different English 101 classes, Holly and I could more easily make the case that English 100 could not look like English 098 or 101 classes. In fact, it made the most sense (to our administrators, fellow faculty, students, and us) to devote English 100 class activities and assignments to helping students explore and negotiate the ideologies underpinning their varying tasks in English 101. As students constructed, deconstructed, and reconstructed their English 101 assignments, lectures, and readings for one another, students began to identify the values inherent in these and how they might use them to different ends. The institutional thirdspace of English 100 allowed us to effectively explore translingual reading and writing practices, even while, in many cases, their English 101 classes encouraged monolingualist approaches—for example, directing students to put a thesis statement in the last sentence of the first paragraph or requiring them to decipher how to earn the full points devoted to an abstract "grammar" portion of an essay grade.

As a thirdspace, English 100 offered a unique vantage point for students to explore what was happening in different English 101 classes—when, why, and how to strategically approach their requirements. It became clear to students that because we were not teaching English 101, English 100 instructors could not "explain what this 101 assignment is asking for" (as many asked us to do at the outset), but we could ask students to explore how *they* were interpreting a 101 assignment's requirements, what the purpose of the assignment might be, how they were being assessed, what particular ways of reading/writing/thinking they hoped to gain practice with as they worked on the assignment, and whether there were any particular requirements they might want to negotiate, why, and how. Students offered one another feedback on their English 101 essays using a translingual approach that asked them to not "correct" but rather to underline words or phrases in a peer's essays they thought might be used differently (for different ends) and then to discuss possible alternatives—and the consequences of these—with their group members. After their instructors graded an English 101 essay, we asked students to choose one convention mentioned in the feedback (e.g., verb tense) and then write a reflective essay for English 100 exploring the evolution and varying uses of that particular convention in different contexts. These translingual approaches were institutionally legitimized as students earned college credit for their work with them in English 100, work we assessed on a credit/no credit basis through the students' participation and completion of these reflective essays.

Our first quarter of the pilot was a success; English 101+100 students passed English 101 at a higher rate—and with higher grades—than those who had placed into English 101. However, the larger twenty-five-student class size (later twenty) of English 100 made it impossible for instructors to shift all the monolingualist assumptions that inevitably made their way into the students' small-group discussions. For example, even after we established the translingual guidelines for peer review described above, many students still resorted to crossing out words on each other's essays, explaining "this is what it should be" when looking at a classmate's essay. This occurrence seemed to happen more often when "native" speakers were working with "nonnative" speakers' essays, reflecting UCC's institutional hierarchy that positioned one above the other.

Therefore, when one of our deans asked us to consider designing a hybrid English 100 section, Holly and I agreed with the hope that asking students to discuss their English 101 work online would not only offer them practice in writing in a different institutional space but also give English 100 instructors more opportunities to intervene in monolingualist conversations about "corrections" through the text of their online discussions. We also hoped students who were terrified of writing English 101 essays but often composed online (through Facebook, Twitter, blogs, etc.) would find more comfortable ways to engage in academic writing tasks and students who were less familiar with online writing—now a staple of college communication—might gain fruitful practice in a supportive, low-stakes space.

Our five-credit (quarter system) hybrid class was scheduled to meet five days a week, as most English 101 classes did, but on Tuesdays and Thursdays students would participate in asynchronous, online, small-group discussions the English 100 instructors could then use to facilitate in-class discussions when we met face to face on Mondays, Wednesdays, and Fridays. To draw attention to the multitude of contexts in which they were working, when students shared an English 101 reading or an essay they were working on—anything from a prompt and some brainstorming to a final revision—they had to post a cover letter addressed to their group members explaining various components of the assignment (what it was asking for, when it was due, how it related to other work in the class, and what students needed to do to get full points on the assignment) and what they hoped their group members' feedback would address. At first, many students found writing the cover letter challenging; due to the abstract categories often used to assess their English 101 essays (e.g., "thesis" and "MLA format"), they weren't always sure what exactly they needed to do to receive an A grade on an essay. And, due to the many deadlines they juggled with their other classes and lives outside of school, students sometimes were not certain about when an assignment might be due. In these cases, English 100 instructors required students to talk with their English 101 instructors to find some answers (which had the added benefit of pushing English 101 instructors to be more explicit about their expectations). Below is text from a typical online cover letter:

> Dear literacy group members,
>
>   This time I am going to share with you my latest essay for English 101 class. Which is about Ethiopian American immigrants. The type is cause and effect. It is like introduction for research paper in English 102 class. I just started my essay so it's my very first draft. As usual hope my essay will be improved and fixed with your help.
>
>   In this essay our instructor wants us to explore the question WHY? And we are also required to use at least two credible out side source to support our position. The citation has to be within the context. As of it is my last essay it's really important to get good grade. I want you guys to suggest me about some of the things that I have to be fixed.
>
>> 1.   Does my thesis statement reveal the over all idea?
>> 2.   Did I quote correctly?
>> 3.   Do I need to add more details? In Which body paragraph?
>
>   I believe all of your feedback will be helpful.

To encourage the translingual approaches to feedback used in the face-to-face English 100 classes, students earned points for their feedback posts if they responded to their group members in a way that met three requirements: (1) to directly address the author's questions/concerns stated in the cover letter (which meant considering and negotiating what was being asked of them as readers); (2) to meet a minimum word count (which the students and I negotiated); and (3) to include a quote from the text they were responding to. The latter was imposed to encourage close and careful reading of their peers' texts; to emphasize that students' texts were just as worthy of this careful reading as a text they would quote from in an English 101 essay; and to offer students more practice using quotes—an outcome of UCC's English 101 curriculum and often the college writing practice that was most unfamiliar to students. Below is the text from one of these feedback exchanges, with the students' names removed:

> Hi [X], this is [Y]. First, thank you for sharing your essay with us. You said that your essay is cause and effect essay, but in body paragraph, it seems more likely to be compare and contrast essay at some points. Your thesis statement did reveal the idea that you mentioned in body paragraph You also quote correctly in from your research which relate to the essay.
>
> In your third paragraph, you said that your friend face difficulty from the language. The American judge the language ability of your friend and critics on it, so what did your friend do to solve the problem, or your friend just escape from quit the job?
>
> In your fifth paragraph, you said many American doesn't hired or employed the Ethiopian immigrants, and give the chances to the higher education American. Maybe you can talk about something like . . . why did they do that? not only races right there.
>
> Your thesis reveal the idea for body paragraph, but you didn't mention much about your thesis in body paragraph. For example, you said "Both refugees and winners of the diversity visa lottery of these groups encountered the problem of adopting to the United States in terms of language, school, work, and cultural." You talk about five of these issue, but what about the lottery? It's a little bit confuse at this point.
>
> Thank you for sharing this essay, your essay is great overall. I hope you can improve and get high score for your final essay. Good luck!

In response to this feedback post, the author wrote:

> Hello [Y],
>
> Thank you for the feedback, I found it so help full. In your feedback you said that, "you didn't mention much about your thesis in your body paragraph." I know I didn't mentioned. I am still working

on that. I need to use one more source, which is different from the one I used so I hope I will get supporting points. I will add some examples and details to the body paragraph

And a second feedback post for the author's essay, from a different group member:

> Hi [X], I think you are off to a great start on this essay. Most of the quotes that you have included are in MLA format and nicely add to what you are trying to point out. The only exception was your first quote in your second paragraph. I was not sure if you were paraphrasing here or quoting. Your thesis nicely states your position on how immigrating causes a lot of change and difficulty in a person's life, and that affects all the immigrants (in this case Ethiopians). One thing that would make your thesis stronger is if you first explained what the "diversity visa lottery" is and how that works. I would also like to hear more about the importance of the soccer games and Ekub. Another idea to expand on is why the number of Ethiopian immigrants changed, such as what happened that caused these effects? I think this would help keep your paper in a cause and effect style.
>
> I like how you talked about the difficult subject of how some people are unkind to immigrants. In my eyes immigrants have made this country, and if we are so proud of it we should be happy to share it. Although not everyone feels that way, I hope you meet more that do. I think it is really important how you bring up confidence. It can be really hard to try to learn something new and without confidence the process is much harder. My father does not like to talk many people in English and I know that has kept him from improving his English. And I am too embarrassed to practice my Spanish with other, so I have not improved either. Confidence gives you that extra push to try harder. That is why I am glad I have a class like English 100 were we can improve in a safe space.

Although a number of concessions to monolingualist assumptions are evident in this exchange (e.g., the first student's focus on "correct" quoting in response to the author's question "Did I quote correctly?"), at least two instances of negotiation deserve attention from a translingual perspective. First, students who may otherwise have been focusing on subject-verb agreement in English 098 are instead engaging in a dialogue about academic writing, even trying to articulate and challenge some of the English 101 "conventions," as in the first response's second sentence: "You said your essay is cause and effect essay, but in body paragraph, it seems more likely to be compare and contrast essay at some points." This conversation led the English 100 students and me to a follow-up discussion when we met in our next face-to-face class—how do English 101 instructors describe these various essay genres (compare/ contrast, cause/effect, etc.)? Which features might be present in an essay that fulfills their instructors' expectations—with an understanding that different instructors have different expectations, and even the same instructor might have different expectations across different assignments?[2] Which features might students want to confront or challenge and why? And why might English 101 teachers even assign these essay genres to begin with if students will not be using them outside of English 101—that is, which ways of reading/writing/thinking might be transferable, to where, and how? Of course, the students had better answers to all of these questions than I did—answers that showed they were clearly negotiating what they were learning in English 101 with what they already knew and were learning in English 100 and UCC broadly.

The thirdspace of English 100 also paved the way for the second feature worth mentioning in this exchange: the students' willingness to read and work with their peers' texts in ways that challenge the monolingualist approaches they have been taught to police in themselves and others in nearly every other previous writing class. Indeed, the third post in the above exchange calls attention to the need for confidence in order to improve one's linguistic practice—which is difficult to achieve when students are focused on mastering decontextualized writing conventions and genres. The student draws upon her own and her father's experiences with language to illustrate her point that the author's argument about confidence in his essay is persuasive. And although all three students' posts contain what punctilious teachers might consider numerous linguistic errors, the students work through these as they read and respond to one another in thoughtful ways. Alternatively to the monolingualist practices of reading student writing used most often in English 101, the credit-bearing thirdspace of English 100 sanctioned these translingual reading/writing practices as an alternate academic approach.

Due to students' extensive experience with monolingualist approaches to reading and writing, this particular translingual approach was one English 100 instructors had to attend to intentionally and recursively throughout the quarter. Particularly during the first weeks of class, when students had recently taken either the COMPASS or a course heavily focused on following fixed standards, most students' online cover letters unsurprisingly asked their peers to help them with "grammar."

However, the fact that students were now articulating these expectations and desires in writing through online discussion posts offered English 100 instructors an opportunity to work with these monolingualist approaches as a written text of the class. We asked students to reread their cover letters and ask, "Did your questions help you achieve your goals for this essay? Are there other kinds of feedback you could have asked for that could have been more helpful?" Through this reflection, students developed increasingly productive conversations about their reading and writing practices; they began to engage with one another and their texts primarily by exploring questions about the writers' arguments, offering them new perspectives. In the exchange above, the first post responds to the author by asking him to explore the actual causes of racial discrimination he writes about: "In your fifth paragraph, you said many American doesn't hired or employed the Ethiopian immigrants, and give the chances to the higher education American. Maybe you can talk about something like . . . why did they do that? not only races right there." The last comment in particular, "not only races right there," offers a rich example for translingual negotiation in English 100, which students mined in their next face-to-face class meeting by discussing several ways to interpret it and which interpretation might be the most useful for the author to address in his essay.

To highlight these resistant ways of reading, writing, and thinking, at the end of the quarter I asked students to look back at their early posts and discuss what had changed in the ways they discussed their work together. Many students noted how limited they were at first in their ways of reading, as is evident in the following post, offered to a classmate's first draft in week three:

> Remember we had peer review on thursday i think and i was one of the people who read your paper. have to say that your paper was solid but your paper had some grammar. In your paper i was able to correct some of your errors but wasn't able to correct your whole paper . . . While reading your paper i see that some words you have that you put an extra "s" when it is not meant to be there like "homeworks" it should be homework. Instead of "toys/games" maybe you can write it as toys and games. I mean some of the things you can add a word or subtract a letter that shouldn't be there to make sense. If you know what i mean.

This post negotiates the requirement that students quote from their peers' texts by taking a monolingualist approach, quoting only single words for the author to "correct" rather than quoting in order to share a different perspective on what the author has written. In a response to the same group member's essay several weeks later, the same student wrote:

Hi [Group Member]. Well, I did say i wanted to read more of your paper. Looks like my hope came true! . . . What you got right now i can say is readable, but with your personal story it pulls the reader into your paper more. From citation/quotes from your authors there are many places where you can put them. For example, "Once trust is built, and the two feel as if they are committed fully to each other, then this can lead to marriage." This if you got a quote from them you can place it here that further describes what you mean . . . So, basically you can add in quotes to places that feel like you are not describing enough and a quote can just do that. Giving the reader two perspectives that relate to each other in some sense.

The last two sentences in particular show the student articulating a conceptual framework for quoting and creating connections between texts by "add[ing] in quotes to places that feel like you are not describing enough. . . . Giving the reader two perspectives that relate to each other in some sense." Elaborating on this with his group members in class, the student took a translingual approach to negotiate what his English 101 teacher had told him about when to use quotations with his own experiences of using quotes successfully.

FROM "ENGLISH ONLY" TO "WHICH 'ENGLISH'?"

"I have to work on my English essay."
"Which English? 101 or 100?"
—overheard among students in an English 100 class

Teaching students to recognize, critique, and contribute to the varying forms of "English" at UCC would have been far more difficult to do if our English 100 students had not been in different English 101 sections collaboratively exploring the idiosyncrasies of their 101 coursework. The institutional thirdspace of English 100 allowed students to critically examine the various ways UCC defined "writing"; how they could look to one another and themselves as writing resources; and how they might negotiate the use of these resources as they interpreted their (and their classmates') English 101 instructors' expectations. Likewise, the hybrid component of the class allowed students to conceptualize and practice academic reading and writing in different spaces through online discussions of classroom writing and in-class discussions of online posts. Although English 100 instructors might offer a perspective on a question raised in class, ultimately the students contributed to and created knowledge about what it meant to write in a college-level English course at UCC. In addition, these students shifted UCC's institutional designation of academic "English" as they read and wrote in English 100 online discussions.

Given the socioeconomic status of our students, English 100 instructors had legitimate concerns about their access to a computer outside of school or how strange and unfamiliar writing within an online learning management system (LMS) might be. Some English 100 students had no idea they had signed up for a blended online and face-to-face class and only had access to a computer on campus. For these students, the Tuesday and Thursday class times set aside to work online proved invaluable; they spent the hour they would have spent in the physical classroom in the campus computer lab, working with a writing center tutor, or at a local public library, practicing everything from logging in to developing strategies for carefully reading long essays on a computer screen. One English 100 student who had immigrated to the United States only a few years earlier and was inexperienced even with e-mail sought out help from her teenaged daughters so she could work within our LMS. At the end of the quarter, this student reported that learning to feel more confident when reading and responding to online messages was a major accomplishment. Although institutionally labeled as a student in need of "remediation," she successfully navigated the rocky terrain of her academic reading and writing work across unfamiliar college courses and media, all while working translingually through an additional language and discourses.

All of this is not to say English 100 was fully successful in disrupting the pervasive monolingualist ideologies inherent in the English placement practices and courses at UCC. In spite of increased retention and pass rates, UCC faculty members remained skeptical of our acceleration program's value, clinging to the COMPASS test's definition of writing proficiency. And indeed, as we witnessed in English 100, many of our students were encouraged to apply monolingualist frameworks to "rhetorical modes" assignments that asked students to adhere to preformed genres like "compare and contrast," "cause and effect," and "definition" essays in English 101. For this reason, English 100 instructors resisted the common Studio practice of corresponding with 101 teachers about the students' progress, goals, and concerns (e.g., Tassoni and Lewiecki-Wilson 2005, 83–88). Omitting this instructor-to-instructor communication allowed English 100 students to choose whether or not their 101 instructors would know they were in the acceleration program and thus potentially treat them differently from other English 101 students. As an added benefit, by not talking to the 101 teachers, we persuaded students to initiate conversations with their English 101 instructors themselves rather than rely on us to do it for them. However, the fact that students needed to grapple with whether or not to disclose to their English 101 teachers that they were institutionally labeled as "remedial" shows the depths to which monolingualist ideologies still prevail. English 100 successfully blended students from a variety of linguistic backgrounds and UCC pathways, and yet, at the time this is being written, isolated ESL and IEP programs remain, as does the COMPASS placement mechanism. And although English 101+100 helped eliminate one noncredit course for students, the pipeline continues to contain a sequence of two noncredit classes.

In spite of how small the acceleration project's ripples have been, the success of English 101+100 and similar programs has inspired UCC and its sister campuses to engage in a district-wide upheaval of their varying developmental course sequences—a restructuring that aims to shorten the developmental sequence to a maximum of two courses at all three campuses. In addition, two important changes have been made to the former English sequence. First, all three pathways (ABE, ESL, and IEP) are now under the umbrella of "college transfer" instead of only the ABE track for "native" English speakers, a move that institutionally affirms that many multilingual students can and do transfer to four-year institutions after completing their UCC coursework. Second, English 100+101 is offered as an alternative to English 098 for any student who chooses it. Rather than simply directing students into English 098, UCC advisors must talk with students about which option they might prefer, calling attention to the discrepancies in UCC's monolingualist placement methods.

Indeed, this is perhaps the acceleration program's biggest contribution to UCC and its sister colleges: it has disrupted the monolingualist narrative of English proficiency and development by (1) challenging the logic of decades-old placement practices, (2) affirming students' abilities to read and write successfully across various academic spaces and contexts, and (3) doing so in a highly complex space where "productive conflict" is the learning medium (Rodby and Fox 2000, 96–98). The thirdspace position and pedagogy of English 100 allowed us to subtly shift away from UCC's English-only practices and focus instead on questions surrounding which "English"? (why? when? where? for what/whom?, and so forth). And as English 101+100 students successfully negotiated the demands of two classes presenting very different approaches to "English," they demonstrated how, when given permission to do so, students can adeptly recognize when, where, how, and why to reuse, misuse, and create new forms of language.

Notes

1. Terms like *remedial, developmental,* and *ESL* are used as identifying labels in many two-year colleges; with acknowledgement of the many problems inherent in these terms, I use them throughout this chapter to identify specific courses and institutional practices.

2. Lea and Street's (1998) research on instructors' views of their assignments and student writing demonstrates how often this can be the case. Following this research, Lea and Street advocate an "academic literacies" approach, foregrounding academic reading and writing activities as multiple, varied, and social, shaped by relations of power, identities, and institutions. As with Horner et al.'s (2011) translingual approach, Lea and Street's "academic literacies" perspective regards student texts not in terms of fixed deficits but in terms of varied meaning-making processes operating within and in response to these complex relationships.

References

Adams, Peter, Sarah Gearhart, Robert Miller, and Anne Roberts. 2009. "The Accelerated Learning Program: Throwing Open the Gates." *Journal of Basic Writing* 28 (2): 50–69.

Bartholomae, David. 1993. "The Tidy House: Basic Writing in the American Curriculum." *Journal of Basic Writing* 12 (1): 4–21.

Gabriel, Susan, and Jamey Gallagher. n.d.a. "Video 4." Accelerated Learning Program. Accessed May 31, 2015. http://alp-deved.org/powerpoint-on-alp/.

Gabriel, Susan, and Jamey Gallagher. n.d.b. "What is ALP?" Accelerated Learning Program. Accessed May 31, 2015. http://alp-deved.org/what-is-alp-exactly/.

Grego, Rhonda, and Nancy Thompson. 2008. *Teaching/Writing in Thirdspaces: The Studio Approach.* Carbondale: Southern Illinois University Press.

Hern, Katie. 2011. *Accelerated English at Chabot College: A Synthesis of Key Findings.* California Acceleration Project. Accessed May 31, 2015. http://cap.3csn.org/files/2012/02/Chabot-Accelerated-English-Synthesis1.pdf.

Horner, Bruce, Min-Zhan Lu, Jacqueline Jones Royster, and John Trimbur. 2011. "Opinion: Language Difference in Writing: Toward a Translingual Approach." *College English* 73 (3): 303–21.

Jaggars, Shanna Smith, Michelle Hodara, Sung-Woo Cho, and Di Xu. 2015. "Three Accelerated Developmental Education Programs: Features, Student Outcomes, and Implications." *Community College Review* 43 (1): 3–26.

Lea, Mary, and Brian Street. 1998. "Student Writing in Higher Education: An Academic Literacies Approach." *Studies in Higher Education* 23 (2): 157–72.

Lu, Min-Zhan, and Bruce Horner. 2013. "Translingual Literacy, Language Difference, and Matters of Agency." *College English* 75 (6): 582–607.

Rodby, Judith, and Tom Fox. 2000. "Basic Work and Material Acts: The Ironies, Discrepancies, and Disjunctures of Basic Writing and Mainstreaming." *Journal of Basic Writing* 19 (1): 84–99.

Rose, Mike. 1988. "Narrowing the Mind and the Page: Remedial Writers and Cognitive Reductionism." *College Composition and Communication* 39 (3): 267–302.

Shor, Ira. 2001. "Errors and Economics: Inequality Breeds Remediation." In *Mainstreaming Basic Writers: Politics and Pedagogies of Access,* edited by Gerri McNenny, 29–54. Mahwah, NJ: Erlbaum.

Tassoni, John, and Cynthia Lewiecki-Wilson. 2005. "Not Just Anywhere, Anywhen: Mapping Change through Studio Work." *Journal of Basic Writing* 24 (1): 68–92.

7

WRITING ASSESSMENT AS THE CONDITIONS FOR TRANSLINGUAL APPROACHES
An Argument for Fairer Assessments

Asao B. Inoue

How does a writing teacher or program create the conditions for translingual pedagogies to be most successful and effective in classrooms? In order for translingual approaches to language to function effectively in writing classrooms, the program must find ways to cultivate a degree of fair conditions that agree with the basic assumptions translingual approaches hold. One important way programs and classrooms create these conditions for teaching and learning is through their writing assessments. In this chapter, I discuss two necessary translingual imperatives central to translingual pedagogies. These imperatives require conditions that are created through writing assessments, and they amount to a high degree of fairness within writing-assessment ecologies. In the second and third sections of this chapter, I illustrate how the kind of fairness in writing assessments I call for can be seen in two examples, directed self-placement (DSP) and labor-based grading contracts. I end with a list of five ways DSP and labor-based grading contract systems can encourage effective conditions for translingual pedagogies.

TRANSLINGUAL APPROACHES REQUIRE FAIRER ASSESSMENT ECOLOGIES

Translingual approaches understand language is not static and see variation in language use by individuals and groups as both naturally occurring and a strength in the writing classroom. They provide ways to critically engage with language (Horner et al. 2011, 303–4). Horner et al. explain that "this approach sees difference in language not as a barrier

DOI: 10.7330/9781607326205.c007

to overcome or as a problem to manage, but as a resource for producing meaning in writing, speaking, reading, and listening" (303). Thus, translingual approaches to language attempt to use difference and diversity in language practices as the materials for comparing and questioning all language norms and practices, not to find out what is correct or incorrect but to understand decisions and their consequences, to see hegemonic beliefs about language for what they are, not as correct ways to judge expression but as beliefs associated with an historically situated, white, middle-class, monolingual norm. Furthermore, translingual approaches understand difference in language practices as the norm— in fact, difference *is* the norm (Lu and Horner 2013, 584).

These assumptions have clear consequences for the assessment of writing in placement decisions and in classroom evaluation. In order for such assumptions to be meaningful and educative for students, writing assessments must honor and value in tangible ways students' language practices and histories and not punish students for producing language difference (from a hegemonic norm). One can hear implications for how writing is judged and graded in Horner and his colleagues' summation of the approach.

> In short, a translingual approach argues for (1) honoring the power of all language users to shape language to specific ends; (2) recognizing the linguistic heterogeneity of all users of language both within the United States and globally; and (3) directly confronting English monolingualist expectations by researching and teaching how writers can work with and against, not simply within, those expectations. Viewing differences not as a problem but as a resource, the translingual approach promises to revitalize the teaching of writing and language. By addressing how language norms are actually heterogeneous, fluid, and negotiable, a translingual approach directly counters demands that writers must conform to fixed, uniform standards. (Horner et al. 2011, 305)

So, translingual pedagogies do at least two broad pedagogical things: (1) honor in real ways students' language use by recognizing linguistic heterogeneity and (2) do not demand students simply conform to monolingualist expectations, or to a single classroom standard. Both these pedagogical imperatives are operationalized in writing-assessment practices we design. This means the conditions assessment ecologies create must construct linguistic differences as something other than a problem, must avoid a single standard by which all are ranked, and must offer dialogue and negotiation of all languaging. A classroom cannot view language difference (from a hegemonic norm) as a resource for learning while at the same time penalizing students for practicing that difference. Thus, the ecologies created by our writing assessments are the conditions in which translingual pedagogies will succeed or fail.

For translingual pedagogies to work effectively, then, students need power in the program. Writing assessments are one of the primary ways students exercise power or submit to it. They cannot feel pushed around by assessments, placement mechanisms, and grades if they are to feel the system is fair. Assessments must feel fair. I'm avoiding saying that they must *be* fair since I believe that statement is inaccurate. It assumes fairness is something a writing assessment is or can be inherently. It denies degrees of fairness and the way fairness is felt unevenly in student populations—that fairness is mostly a felt sense. Many of the things that construct fairness in any assessment ecology are the same things that construct the validity of decisions from assessments, that is, student participation and agreement on key decisions in assessments (Inoue 2007, 41). Beyond the absence of a single standard by which to evaluate instances of writing, the degree of fairness through participation in decision making boils down to cultivating institutional conditions that allow students to have more control of key aspects of their movement in the program (i.e., placement) and in the products of the assessment of their writing (e.g., grading mechanisms in classrooms).

In fact, as I read it, translingualism itself is a call for new and better ways to conceive of and practice the assessment of student writing in college and secondary classrooms. I've argued in another place (Inoue 2015) that writing assessments, particularly classroom assessments, are ecologies, or complex systems that are "more than" the elements and aspects that constitute them and are interconnected wholes in which the elements that constitute a writing-assessment ecology are diverse and consubstantial. This means students' roles in how they are assessed, placed in courses, or graded determine the products or consequences of the assessment as a system. The more students are engaged and control the ecology, the fairer it is. In short, students' development and awareness of their writing practices depend on students' control of writing assessment in all the ways *control* can mean in a program.

To say control is an aspect of fairness is to say that what we control we often find fairer than what we have no say in or control over. So as I see it, translingual approaches are not just about finding a way to acknowledge and work with the natural diversity and dynamic ways language organically functions and exists in the world, but they are also a call to create fairer ways of assessing student writing, fairer ways to see and judge, which are also ways that allow students to control more within assessment ecologies. For instance, every writing classroom offers a variety of Englishes, and a teacher may say she respects and cares about linguistic diversity (and mean it), may even hold up instances of translingual writing as laudable classroom examples to learn from, but if her assessment practices end up ranking student performances against a norm, a standard, if the point is to move away from those translingual examples to a preferred form of English without students' negotiating such movement in their own writing, then it's clear to me it's not the good intentions of the teacher (her beliefs about language) that are the problem but the presence of grades and their inherent nature as ranking in the assessment ecology. The use of a single standard and grades creates conditions that pull against the teacher's translingual beliefs about language. Translingual approaches resist a standard, which means they do not use a single standard but negotiate and share control over standards with students. Ironically, the absence of a standard opens the classroom up to negotiating multiple ways of valuing student writing. The absence of a standard creates the conditions for more student agency and control in the ecology—that is, more fairness.

Up to this point, there are a least two facets of translinguality I've been working around that amount to providing more agency and control, or fairness, in assessment ecologies. These two facets articulate in more specific ways the conditions writing-assessment ecologies might design in order for translingual pedagogies to work effectively. First, assessment practices must honor, acknowledge, and meaningfully value all language performances in tangible ways students are aware of and have a hand in. This condition comes mostly from how we assess students and their writing. Ranking and grading students or their writing will always work against ideal translingual pedagogical conditions since by their nature, these processes must have a standard to which all are compared. Put simply, grades and any kind of ranking of students or their writing must be absent for translingual pedagogies to be effective. This doesn't mean we don't have things to say about our students' writing, that teachers don't judge students or their drafts. It means all judgments are situated within larger networks of judgment (students in the classroom), just like any instance of language. The consequences or products of judgment are negotiated with students, just like essays and the documents being judged. This assessment condition allows students to have agency and take seriously their language and judgment practices.

The second facet is related to the first but has been implicit up to this point. Assessment practices and processes should allow teachers and students to focus most of their attention and efforts on language as always emerging from or through laboring, working, or performing and not on what is produced. The emphasis, then, is on languaging and judging as labors, not on ranking products. If language and its judgment are labor, they are also inherently paradoxical. What is produced (the product of drafting or judging) is always a variant, illustrating that difference and variation are the norm. Thus, judgment itself is also fluid since it too is an instance of language and negotiation. Just as instances of language are always emerging from practices, so too are instances of judgment, including the teacher's. To illustrate this facet, consider feedback from peers and the teacher on a draft. In a classroom with a standard that students are held to, a classroom that focuses on a draft graded by quality, the discussion about the draft or the feedback on that draft will always point students toward the teacher's notions about the standard, the rubric. Not only does this subordinate all students' feedback, making it dangerous to listen to seriously, but it tacitly coerces students to follow the orders of the teacher (or hear her comments as orders), not negotiate meaning or decisions, regardless of how the teacher couches her comments. In a classroom that focuses on labor, working, and performing, this paradigm changes. The point of assessment is to discuss and negotiate what the student has *done* in her *drafting* and how she might labor forward. Quality is still the center of the discussion, but now the teacher's judgements can more easily sit next to students' feedback since they can more easily be understood as paradoxical, not hierarchical. And of course, the absence of grades on drafts is crucial for this condition to occur. This facet takes seriously students' roles in shaping language, meaning, and judgments of language by listening carefully to students and accounting for the ever-changing and diverse nature of language and instances of judgment. This facet says the condition of fairness is achieved through laboring together with language.

Lu and Horner offer a way to understand what I'm getting at in both facets of translinguality. They explain that translingual approaches work against monolingual approaches that "us[e] recognizable differences in language as justification for prejudicial treatment of these groups by denying the mesopolitics of all communicative practice" (Lu and Horner 2016, 213). To put this bluntly, using unproblematic observations of difference from a standard in language practices is unfair and constructs conditions that are unfavorable. Their statement is a subtle call to create conditions for translinguality through assessment practices by paying explicit attention to the mesopolitics in assessment ecologies, the differences in judgment and products of language laboring.

Part of the mesopolitics of writing assessment is in how teachers and students judge language together (or not) and how they situate the act of judging in the classroom or program. It's in the conditions created by what we believe about language and how it is judged. Lu and Horner recount Louis-Jean Calvet's (2006) discussion of language as only an abstraction. Calvet says we get our notions or beliefs about language by a perceived "regularity of a certain number of facts, of features, in the products of speakers and in their *practices*," which ultimately become "*representations*—what people think about languages and the way they are spoken—representations that act on practices and are one of the factors of change" (Calvet quoted in Lu and Horner 2016, 213). What Calvet is speaking of is assessment, writ large. Our representations of language, our beliefs about language, help us judge instances of it. They are our biases. And if Calvet is correct (and I think he is), then in order for our assessment ecologies to be the effective conditions for translingual pedagogies, our representations of language must agree with at least the two facets of translinguality I'm calling *the conditions operationalized by our assessment ecologies.*

Over the last ten years, I've found ways to construct such conditions through two kinds of writing assessments: directed self-placement (DSP) and labor-based grading contracts. Both create the conditions for the effective use of translingual pedagogies by creating a higher degree of fairness (student agency and control within assessment ecologies) in the classroom or program.

CONDITIONS OF FAIRNESS IN DIRECTED SELF-PLACEMENT

As the DSP literature discusses (Royer and Gilles 1998, 2003), typically students are given material on the program and its courses, such as Fresno State's DSP, a program I directed for a time.[1] Students are asked to reflect upon their experiences and needs, then make a choice with the help of an advisor. At the University of Washington Tacoma, our DSP process leads students through program goals, descriptions of the course options, profiles of typical students who enroll in each option, and annotated student samples that exemplify what is expected of students in the first weeks of each course. It then asks each student to write a short reflection on what they've just reviewed. The process ends with the student declaring a choice.[2] Both schools serve mostly multilingual students of color and working-class students who come to their first-year writing courses speaking and writing variations of the local Standardized English. UW Tacoma's DSP is more structured than Fresno State's but exhibits the same features that create conditions for successful translingual approaches in classrooms. Most DSPs like these emphasize respect for and listening to students and student negotiation and control of the assessment process. These conditions help programs honor linguistic heterogeneity and resist a single, monolingual standard.

At UW Tacoma, the three course options students may choose from each meet the same program goals. The only difference is time. The stretch option offers students more time in the academic year, giving them another quarter to complete their composition requirement, while the stretch plus provides more time in each quarter by the use of an additional writing studio (taken simultaneously) to help students focus on sentence-level issues and provide another set of readers for their writing. The key, however, in any choice in the DSP at UW Tacoma is our learning goals (not outcomes) of the program.[3] Our goals are practices we ask students to engage in and reflect upon. They are not static "standards" students must measure up to in order to pass the requirement. They are labor and process oriented, not product oriented, although they assume products. For instance, one goal that might seem to be counter to translingual approaches to language is the one concerning editing and proofing of language. The program has articulated it as "proof and edit one's drafts in self-conscious ways, ways that allow the writer to consider future proofing and editing practices as rhetorical in nature and as a part of the writing process." The learning goal is not a standard all students must meet, nor do we expect students to meet any particular standards of editing and proofing (e.g., no more than X number of errors per page). Instead, the learning goal asks the student to practice particular labors of editing and proofing that require some contextualized rhetorical thinking. Students may not fully understand what this learning goal means when they first encounter it in the DSP process, but they come to understand it as a set of practices they are coming to develop in courses, even in the studio that could easily be seen as a space of remediation.

Coming to develop is an important aspect of all our learning goals. They are all articulated as practices, focusing teachers' and students' attentions on language use (and the students who use language) "as always emergent, in process (a state of becoming)" (Lu and Horner 2013, 587). This attention to language in our program goals agrees with Horner et al.'s observation that a translingual approach "calls for *more*, not less, conscious and critical attention to how writers deploy diction, syntax, and style, as well as form, register, and media" (Horner et al. 2011, 304). Conscious and critical attention to language means an attention to the processes and labors of reading and writing practices, which include editing practices. As I'll describe below, classroom grading practices can either reinforce or contradict this labor/process quality of any learning goals.

The DSP process also respects students' previous experiences and knowledge about themselves by allowing them to use that knowledge to help make a writing-course placement. The program demonstrates that it not only values their knowledge and language experiences but also trusts them to make a good decision for themselves. Allowing students to decide on their course placements gives students a choice and more agency at the key entry moment in their educational paths at the university. Choice is an important condition for translingual pedagogies because translingual pedagogies are often about articulating language decisions in writing, about understanding and working through language choices, about honoring language heterogeneity. If a student doesn't have much choice in what writing course she will take—if she's placed by a test—it is harder for a writing teacher to expect the same student to make conscious choices in class and in her writing, harder for the student and teacher to interrogate those choices as anything other than signs of deficit. In short, it is harder for the class to honor the student's language decisions in her writing since they could be seen by the student as the very things held against her in her placement in the very course that asks her to see her language choices as choices and not error, as textual markers of practices that can be interrogated and negotiated. The conditions DSP creates through placement are ones that tell students they are respected and have the responsibility of choices with consequences.

Key to respect and feeling their choices are real choices is whether the students feel they are actually heard when making the decision on a course. DSP introduces students to the program by listening to them and letting them decide on the first important decision about them as writers (course placement). Translingual pedagogies, it seems, also rely on listening first to students, reading deeply and compassionately their writing not to find error but to understand choices and decisions on the students' terms, then letting students decide what to do through dialogue and rigorous interrogation. Thus, DSP in my two examples (i.e., Fresno State and UW Tacoma) does not stop students teachers feel might be better served in another course. Instead, in the first week of the quarter or semester, students discuss the possible consequences and expectations of extra work that may be involved in a course choice. Like translingual assumptions about all valuing of language in the world—that the acceptability, use, and value of language are always negotiated—this discussion is the beginning of an ongoing set of negotiations between teacher and student. The DSP is the first formal negotiation, but the grading contract instigates another set of ongoing negotiations with students. Negotiating their choices and grades reinforces a respect for students' knowledge and decisions. I don't pretend to believe all negotiations in the program are on equal ground, but the fact that a student has the ability to negotiate the terms of entry into a course and accept the consequences tells the student that she has quite a bit of control and responsibility over her education and learning, which feels fairer than being placed by a test. Writing placement in this way can set up the larger conditions for student learning in classrooms that agree with translingual approaches to language because, and this is the key, DSP works from explicit principles about honoring linguistic heterogeneity and the negotiability of language practices (not imposed standards).

CONDITIONS OF FAIRNESS IN LABOR-BASED GRADING CONTRACTS

Placement, of course, is just the entry point into a student's writing experiences at a university. The courses themselves must continue to build conditions that provide for translingual approaches. Over the years, I've found grading contracts that calculate grades by labor (not quality of writing) to foster a higher degree of fairness by embodying the two facets of translinguality I've discussed above better than conventional grading. These conditions are possible because a labor-based grading contract focuses students' and teachers' attention on what students are doing and why they are doing it in classrooms, in homework, and in reading and writing practices. Let me be clear: grading contracts are not translingual by nature, but labor-based contracts can provide conditions for such pedagogies if used in particular ways. I've discussed labor-based contracts in several places (Inoue 2012; 2014a; 2014b), so I won't say a lot about them here. I will say the grading contracts used at Fresno State, and those we are currently implementing at UW Tacoma, are based on the amount of labor done by the students. The main elements that make up the labor are how much work students do in any given assignment (e.g., time spent or number of words produced), not on the so-called quality of writing and whether students participate in class or not.[4] There are no grades produced on individual assignments or work, and only when students don't do labor asked of them is a mark placed in the gradebook (labor is either done fully or not done—no other distinctions are made). The default grade for everyone in the contract is a B course grade (3.3 at UW Tacoma), so labor requirements, which are negotiated with students, tend to be high.

Labor-based grading contracts can usually respect students' hard work and effort better than conventional grading, so they create conditions that offer higher degrees of fairness likely difficult to establish with normal grading. When a student works hard and long on something, she is rewarded, even though feedback on that work may be critical or ask for changes. In conventional grading, this isn't possible, as feedback tends to have to justify the grade placed on a draft. Yet even in systems that delay grades until later drafts or in a portfolio system, the student has less room (if any) to negotiate the judgment of her writing in drafts. The teacher is using a standard to judge and give feedback, which determines a grade, so negotiations can only be about how the student can achieve the standard assumed. And if there is no standard assumed, no prompting toward what accomplishes the higher grade, then students get confused ("What do you want in revisions?"). This is not respecting language differences in multilingual or monolingual writers, and any dialogue or feedback on drafts is not a negotiation in the expectations for or judgments about writing translingual approaches to writing ask for. Since draft quality will eventually be graded by the teacher, the student-teacher relationship is dictated by what the teacher judges in drafts and a student's acquiescence to those judgments, not by a negotiation between the teacher and student on decisions and meaning. This means the conditions are structured in the assessment ecology so students listen to teachers, but teachers have less need to listen to students. It operationally says the teacher's language use and practices are more important than the students'. Students must comply if they want a higher grade. Any inquiry into language difference is about how to come up to the teacher's English, so language instances and their judgments are hierarchized in the classroom, the teacher's being at the top. Conversely, by grading labor only and focusing on negotiating meaning and decisions, grading contracts allow teachers and students to ask not whether a piece of writing is "conventional," since judgments along those lines will not matter to the grade, but rather "what kind of discourse the essay might be contributing to sedimenting, how, and why," "foregrounding student agency and responsibility" (Lu and Horner 2013, 594, 595). In short, the discussions around writing and in feedback are negotiations about (the) who the writer is becoming and how the draft is evolving.

It should be noted that labor-based grading contracts simply separate the calculation of course grades from the discussions of writing expectations, quality, and content we have all the time in all courses. So the conditions created are ones that foster discussions of student writing that are in many ways more critical and compassionate, more able to embrace failure and miscues as spaces of learning, and more able to respect language diversity and student contributions to feedback and assessment processes. In addition, they address directly students' feelings about the labor required of them through, for instance, frequent reflection activities and conferencing. In my own classes, much of the subject of many conferences deals with how labor was experienced and what effects it had on drafts or accomplishments.[5] Because there are no grades to rank performances, students and teacher can discuss language practices as simply what is, as occurrences that help everyone by providing interesting instances of language use. For the teacher, feedback can inquire, resisting the need to tell students what to do. For students, reading feedback can be about engaging in inquiry and understanding the nature of language difference and how they and their drafts are evolving, not figuring out what the teacher wants.

The absence of grades allows students to listen more carefully to feedback, but it also allows teachers to read more compassionately and critically their students' writing. It allows students to listen more carefully to feedback because students are not beholden to a teacher as grader. Their revisions of drafts are not contingent on taking all the advice of a teacher and ignoring their colleagues. In fact, students are not reading teacher feedback to understand how the grade is justified. In addition, students can listen to each other and take advantage of more of the linguistic resources in the classroom. The second thing (i.e., teachers reading more compassionately and critically) happens because teachers are not providing feedback that attempts to rationalize a grade or mark. Teachers can say, as Elbow argues about the importance of liking student writing, that the draft is "terrible, but I like it" (Elbow 1993, 201). This relationship between more productive feedback and the absence of grades is prevalent in the literature on grading student writing (Allison, Bryant, and Hourigan 1997; Danielewicz and Elbow 2009; Inoue 2004; Zak and Weaver 1998), but most teachers likely understand this from experience.

But one might ask, could these classrooms simply be creating conditions that give away higher-than-normal grades to less-than-deserving students, or could the conditions that contracts create erode student motivation? Why try hard when all you really have to do is do the work, but maybe not very well, in order to get the grade? I could make a number of arguments for the reasons grading contracts do not contribute to grade inflation or decrease student motivation, but I've made them empirically in other places (Inoue 2012, 2014a). Instead, I'll simply say contracts foster the kinds of conditions necessary for translingual approaches to language by encouraging and structuring into classroom assessments the two facets I've discussed above, which amount to a fairer assessment ecology. These conditions offer alternative ways for students to be motivated in a classroom, ways that may be connected more closely to noncognitive dimensions of student learning like metacognition, persistence, grit, and engagement. Why? Because once grades are no longer the kind of judgment each writing task hinges on, students and teacher must find other things to care about, other motivations, other ways to judge and make judgments, other purposes for feedback. I have found that fair assessment conditions often lead students to be more motivated, not less. Beyond freedom to fail and make their own decisions in drafts, control through negotiation of the contract at the opening of the semester/quarter and renegotiation at midpoint are key. Ira Shor (1996; 2009) has discussed the benefits of a democratic negotiation in grading contracts, so I'll say little about its advantages.

When students negotiate the terms of their own assessment, when they feel respected and heard in these negotiations, when they experience more control over assessment in the classroom, they usually respond by working harder, longer, more carefully. Why? Because, I believe, our human response to respect and faith in us is to give respect and faith back. It is a compassionate response to compassion. This is not a blanket tolerance for student writing or the conflicting judgments on writing in classrooms. It is not a less rigorous course. To be compassionate means one engages in a rigorous investigation into languaging and asks that same rigor of others. It means the conditions may be uncomfortable because students are working harder and longer, but they feel safe. We need more compassion in our grading practices because students and teacher are already in an uneven power relationship, leaving many students with little ability to disagree or argue with a teacher. It's incumbent on us to be mindful of these uneven power relations. In labor-based contract-graded classrooms, we ask students to do work with few (if any) conditions placed on the quality of that work but a lot of conditions placed on *how you do work* and *how much of it is done*. If you respect someone and you have assurances that they respect you back, you'll do just about anything they ask of you. This deep level of respect and faith in students is at the heart of translingual approaches to language, which say to students, "You use language differently than me. Let me listen to you because I respect you and can learn from you so we can do our mutual work, then you'll do the same with me. Let's negotiate this work and the judgments of your writing together."

WRITING ASSESSMENT AS CONDITIONS
FOR TRANSLINGUAL PEDAGOGIES

Clearly, the conditions for translingual approaches to language are not formed by good words teachers say or good discussions they have with their students about things like "what we value" or the problematics of error. Good conditions do not come solely from good intentions. Translingual conditions, like all conditions for learning, are created through writing-assessment ecologies. And like all writing assessments, they must feel fair to everyone. The bottom line is that the key to creating conditions in which translingual approaches to language can be effective in writing classrooms is in the way fairness is constructed in writing assessments. Higher degrees of fairness in assessment ecologies tend to be those that offer more student agency and control, which I've illustrated in my discussions of DSP and labor-based grading contracts. At the most fundamental level, the conditions of fairness begin and end with listening compassionately and carefully to students and their uses of language without the need to penalize anyone's ways with words, instead making sense of the potential emergent in each instance of language, rigorously investigating with students their languaging. Programs can incorporate necessary negotiation processes with students, providing ways to give them power to inquire, question, and affect their choices about their writing and themselves as students. Finally, fair conditions, as I've defined them in this chapter and as translingual approaches emphasize, give students more control over their course placements and the judgments on their writing, honor linguistic heterogeneity, and do not norm students to a single standard.

To conclude, there are at least five ways DSP and grading contracts create particular conditions of fairness that make translingual pedagogies more effective.

- DSP and labor-based grading contracts *respect* students. DSP works with students' knowledge of their histories and competencies in order to help them make a course choice, respecting their human need to be *listened* to and have meaningful control over decisions that affect them. Labor-based contracts respect students by respecting and rewarding their hard work, labor, and persistence first. Contracts eliminate individual grades on assignments but can calculate final course grades by other, arguably fairer, measures equally important to learning, such as labor, which might be a more direct indicator of noncognitive dimensions of students the field is now acknowledging and promoting as important to learning to write (e.g., the *Framework for Success in Postsecondary Writing* [Council of Writing Program Administrators, National Council of Teachers of English, and

National Writing Project 2011]). Fairness is constructed by respecting students' choices and labor.

- The absence of conventional placement tests (or scores) and grades on individual written products in classrooms allows for truer *negotiations* with students. DSP processes depend on students using their own knowledge, getting information on courses, and talking through a choice with advisors or teachers. Labor-based contracts remove grades so discussions of "error" and other language choices are negotiations about meaning and consequences that do not risk students' course grades. In addition, the absence of grades eliminates the need to define "error" beforehand and encourages organic discussions that require teacher and student to *listen* closely to each other, mutually respecting language choices and judgments of language. This respect creates conditions that allow students to articulate how error and language choices have consequences in various readers' interactions with a text, such as in the cases of Min-Zhan Lu's (1994) "can able to" student example and Suresh Canagarajah's (2009) student, Buthainah. Fairness is created by replacing ranking and grades with listening to and negotiating important decisions with students.

- Labor-based contracts provide classroom conditions that favor formative judgments of writing and *negotiations* of those judgments. Since there are no grades, grades do not need justifying. The primary purpose for feedback can be about inquiring and negotiating how readers (including the teacher) make sense of and value drafts, not about fixing problems or making a draft better in order to get a better grade. Fairness is created by mutual interrogation and negotiating judgments.

- DSP and labor-based contracts encourage conditions that allow students more *control* over what course they take and the judgment of their writing in courses. When students self-place, by definition they have more control in the process. In classrooms, contracts are always agreements between parties, thus grading contracts can offer students time to discuss, negotiate, and revise the contract at two points in the semester/quarter. By starting the semester with contract negotiations, the assessment conditions and roles are made explicit. By revisiting the contract at midpoint, students and teacher have a chance to assess how well the contract is working for everyone and how fair it is, and if need be, they can revise it. Fairness is constructed by student participation and control over how course grades are determined.

- DSP and labor-based contracts construct "failure" in *fairer* ways by embracing language diversity as a resource, not as a deficit. DSP allows students to experience course placement as a choice, not as a consequence of some linguistic inadequacy. Labor-based contracts depend on negotiated labor requirements, not quality requirements, which are comparisons to an a priori, hegemonic standard. These conditions help students engage with language more critically. Failure to meet what are claimed to be SWE norms does not harm students' progress but helps their development as writers by encouraging, noticing, and using nondominant language practices in more critical ways, as places to interrogate and negotiate rather than places that must be revised in order to be "most effective," "clear," or "persuasive." These discussions focus on hegemonic English norms as having particular class, racial, economic, and historical origins, as well as being idiosyncratic in readers; on student's language choices as having a range of consequences for various audiences that do not share the same expectations or language practices; on cultural, linguistic, and other differences in the judgment of language that affect what "effective, clear, and persuasive" means to particular readers; and on the emergent and evolving quality of writers and their writing. Fairness comes from not ranking but from considering language performances on more critical terms that embrace failure as places of negotiation, discussion, and potential.

Notes

1.   One can find all the material on Fresno State's DSP program on its website, which includes descriptions of each course, typical profiles of students who might take each course, and an FAQ for students making decisions (Fresno State Department of English 2015).
2.   One can find all the material and the step-by-step DSP process on UW Tacoma's University Writing Program's (2016) website.
3.   I am convinced by Chris Gallagher's (2012) argument against outcomes as too specific and limiting in capturing all that students learn and accomplish in writing programs. I make a similar argument in another place (Inoue 2015).
4.   I realize that even when a teacher accepts a writing assignment based only on the number of words produced and whether those words address a prompt in any way is, in fact, judging quality to a certain degree, but a discussion of this nuance and why it is safer in labor-based grading contract classrooms is outside this discussion.
5.   In my own classrooms, we use labor journals, labor logs, and Twitter to capture our labor each week in order to then reflect upon that information. So our reflections and discussions of the labor of reading and writing can be quite specific and detailed.

References

Allison, Elizabet, Lizbeth Bryant, and Maureen Hourigan, eds. 1997. *Grading in the Post-Process Classroom: From Theory to Practice.* Portsmouth, NH: Boynton/Cook.

Calvet, Louis-Jean. 2006. *Toward an Ecology of World Languages.* Boston: Polity.

Canagarajah, Suresh. 2009. "Multilingual Strategies of Negotiating English: From Conversation to Writing." *JAC* 29 (1–2): 17–48.

Council of Writing Program Administrators, National Council of Teachers of English, and National Writing Project. 2011. *Framework for Success in Postsecondary Writing.* Accessed 1 Sep. 2015. http://www.nwp.org/img/resources/framework_for_success.pdf.

Danielewicz, Jane, and Peter Elbow. 2009. "A Unilateral Grading Contract to Improve Learning and Teaching." *College Composition and Communication* 61 (2): 244–68.

Elbow, Peter. 1993. "Ranking, Evaluating, and Liking: Sorting Out Three Forms of Judgment." *College English* 55 (2): 187–206.

Fresno State Department of English. 2015. "About the First Year Program." 4 Sep. http://www.fresnostate.edu/artshum/english/firstyear/index.html.

Gallagher, Chris. 2012. "The Trouble with Outcomes: Pragmatic Inquiry and Educational Aims." *College English* 75 (1): 42–60.

Horner, Bruce, Min-Zhan Lu, Jacqueline Jones Royster, and John Trimbur. 2011. "Language Difference in Writing: Toward A Translingual Approach." *College English* 73 (3): 303–21.

Inoue, Asao B. 2004. "Community-Based Assessment Pedagogy." *Assessing Writing* 9 (3): 208–38.

Inoue, Asao B. 2007. "Articulating Sophistic Rhetoric as a Validity Heuristic for Writing Assessment." *Journal of Writing Assessment* 3 (1): 31–54.

Inoue, Asao B. 2012. "Grading Contracts: Assessing Their Effectiveness on Differential Racial Formations." In *Race and Writing Assessment*, edited by Asao B. Inoue and Mya Poe, 79–94. New York: Peter Lang.

Inoue, Asao B. 2014a. "A Grade-Less Writing Course That Focuses on Labor and Assessing." In *First-Year Composition: From Theory to Practice*, edited by Debra Coxwell-Teague and Ronald F. Lunsford, 71–110. West Lafayette, IN: Parlor.

Inoue, Asao B. 2014b. "Theorizing Failure in Writing Assessments." *Research in the Teaching of English* 48 (3): 329–51.

Inoue, Asao B. 2015. *Antiracist Writing Assessment Ecologies: Teaching and Assessing for a Socially Just Future*. West Lafayette, IN: Parlor.

Lu, Min-Zhan. 1994. "Professing Multiculturalism: The Politics of Style in the Contact Zone." *College Composition and Communication* 45 (4): 442–58.

Lu, Min-Zhan, and Bruce Horner. 2013. "Translingual Literacy, Language Difference, and Matters of Agency." *College English* 75 (6): 582–607.

Lu, Min-Zhan, and Bruce Horner. 2016. "Introduction: Translingual Work." *College English* 78 (3): 207–18.

Royer, Daniel J., and Roger Gilles. 1998. "Directed Self-Placement: An Attitude of Orientation." *College Composition and Communication* 50 (1): 54–70.

Royer, Daniel J., and Roger Gilles, eds. 2003. *Directed Self-Placement: Principles and Practices*. Cresskill, NJ: Hampton.

Shor, Ira. 1996. *When Students Have Power: Negotiating Authority in a Critical Pedagogy*. Chicago, IL: University of Chicago Press.

Shor, Ira. 2009. "Critical Pedagogy Is Too Big to Fail." *Journal of Basic Writing* 28 (2): 6–27.

University Writing Program. 2016. University of Washington Tacoma. http://www.tacoma.uw.edu/uwp.

Zak, Frances, and Christopher C. Weaver, eds. 1998. *The Theory and Practice of Grading Writing: Problems and Possibilities*. Albany: SUNY Press.

8

SEIZING AN OPPORTUNITY FOR TRANSLINGUAL FYC AT THE UNIVERSITY OF MAINE
Provocative Complexities, Unexpected Consequences

Dylan B. Dryer and Paige Mitchell

Maine's dwindling, aging, and thinly spread population relies on a great many roads and bridges, all of which must be maintained in a hard climate. Meanwhile, mill closures and the collapse of coastal fish stocks have diminished state revenue—perfect storms of demography and geography that have meant steadily declining state budget allocations for public higher education. But our bleak financial situation is only a local variation on a national theme, so our first-year writing program's efforts to negotiate local effects of those budgetary decisions—specifically, our university's decision to aggressively recruit international undergraduate tuition dollars to offset those declining allocations—may be instructive. In describing efforts to sustain translingual FYC sections at our rural land-grant campus, we aim to contribute to three conversations in the developing discourse constituting translingual writing: what it is and isn't; what workaday examples might look like (see Matsuda 2014); and how the networks of documents and administrative structures that constitute writing programs provide important sites for constructive intervention (Shuck 2006; Tardy 2015).

By a translingual FYC classroom, we mean specifically a classroom in which students engage and compose writing about what "English" has been and can be, one that draws explicit attention to the ways in which all language users' decisions contribute to the ongoing production of what gets called a *language*, asks students to learn how to practice a "disposition of openness and inquiry . . . toward language and language differences" with each other (Horner et al. 2011, 311) and invites—though does not require—students to experiment with vocabularies, genres,

DOI: 10.7330/9781607326205.c008

registers, or languages deemed "authorized" for school writing. As some content knowledge (e.g., the concept of diachronic language change, archaic or marginalized Englishes, etc.) facilitates these outcomes, we choose readings that introduce these topics, but our translingual classrooms (recruitment for which is described below) share a program-wide commitment to using students' writing as the main text of the course. Believing all students (and the social institutions in which they participate) benefit by rethinking language as something we do together rather than know individually (Horner, NeCamp, and Donahue 2011, 288), our translingual approach to writing program administration is committed in the long term to scaling these premises across the entire program and, where possible, upward into the curriculum, a commitment that requires us to attend carefully to institutional spaces and curricular practices (assignments, comments, and assessment practices) that best foster the conditions in which this kind of thinking and writing about language can happen. For this reason, we adopt a *documentary* orientation to writing program administration (see White, Elliot, and Peckham 2015, 158–59), one that draws our attention to everyday genres that encode monolingual assumptions along with other cultural and institutional conventions. Critically engaging the wording in boundary documents *about* language practice is one way to incrementally change dispositions toward language use.[1]

Drawing on student work from nine translingual sections of UMaine's English 101 (college composition) spanning fall 2012 to fall 2015, as well as programmatic assessment of this work, we describe some of the complications that arose as we planned, taught, and assessed initial versions of the course. It's our hope that forewarning will forearm others engaged in the "figh[t] to make the material conditions of teaching, learning, and writing adequate for the kind of deliberative and creative disposition transcultural literacy aims to inculcate" (Lu 2009, 293).

HISTORICAL/NATIONAL CONTEXT AND NARRATIVE

Susan Miller finds composition complicit with an "entrenched national ideological function for 'English' as a set of unrealized ideals—a content and linguistic execution that ordinary citizens aspire to but never attain" (Miller 1991, 178). For Miller, "never attain" is the essential point; indeed, if approximating the "seeming regularities" (Lu and Horner 2013, 588) of something repeatedly—if imprecisely—defined as college writing has long been the aim of FYC, BW, and ESL instruction in the United States, this instruction has never managed to reach this goal with any regularity or replicability, decade to decade, campus to site, or even section to section. Stephen North's curtain call for decades of FYC curricula that have tried and failed to "work the necessary transformation" suggests language variation persists, no matter how well-meaning and innovatively designed these curricula have been (North 2011, 203–4). One way of reading such litanies is to say, in effect, that it's time to accept it can't be done and give it up as a bad job (see, e.g., Petraglia 1995).

But before concluding it can't be done and giving it up as a bad job, we might remember this critique depends on what's meant by *it*. A translingual orientation to language offers a significant alternative to previous curricula because it finally reframes the base unit of language itself—less *known* or *owned* than *done* and *enacted* (Lu and Horner 2013). Yet as most readers know, US composition as it is taught to new graduate students, presented in flagship journals, framed in degree requirements, and prioritized in new-job descriptions has broadly turned away from technical problems of producing meaning at the word-and-phrase level and toward the sociopolitical operation of whole texts in social contexts.[2] We call attention to the well-known story of the so-called social turn to highlight one of its unanticipated consequences: the almost complete capture of the practicum and of graduate training in rhetoric and composition by "sociocultural" approaches has almost completely displaced training in the study of English *as a language* (see Atkinson et al. 2015; Aull 2015, 27–32; Haswell 2010, 112–13; Matsuda 2012; Tardy 2015). This displacement, we believe, helps explain a puzzling pattern in programmatic efforts to assess our students' work, to which we'll return in closing.

IMMEDIATE/LOCAL CONTEXT AND NARRATIVE

"Updated U.S. Census figures," announced an article by Kevin Miller in the *Bangor Daily News* a few years ago, "show that Maine is the whitest and oldest state in the nation" (May 13, 2009). These two demographic indicators are obviously interrelated; to put them in sharper perspective, the reporter noted, Maine public-school enrollments have dwindled steadily by about three thousand students a year since the 1970s, no small figure in a state that graduated only about thirteen thousand public high-school seniors in 2013. UMaine has also watched these trends anxiously, as in-state enrollments constitute about 80 percent of the undergraduate population.

Taking into consideration the remoteness, ruralness, and whiteness (even during the summer) of UMaine's flagship campus in Orono (some 150 miles north of Portland), the Office of International Programs has worked hard to recruit citizens of other countries as undergraduates—a resource-intensive process involving substantial upfront investments in travel and staffing for this office. These efforts notwithstanding, strong forms of language diversity had never been sufficient to trigger the elsewhere ubiquitous separate-but-equal L2 FYC courses. This is the most important piece of institutional context to remember in the discussion that follows: no precedent to overturn, no inertia in hiring and staffing, nobody personally or politically invested in such courses, and thus no invocations of "how we've always done it has worked fine."

Instead, the language needs of this relatively small population have historically been met by the Intensive English Institute (IEI), a program housed on campus but reliant on what it collects in tuition. Prospective students with TOEFL scores below the UMaine threshold can apply to IEI, where they purchase a series of noncredit eight-week courses. As their scores improve, they are allowed to experiment with one to two credit-bearing courses and, if successful, pursue full matriculation. Inasmuch as these courses are necessarily aligned to a construct of "English" as framed by TOEFL, they have been poorly aligned with our English 101 course, which emphasizes semester-long recursive assignment sequences, holistic portfolio assessment, and "difficult" readings. In fact, IEI had a long history of advising its alumni to wait until they were seniors to take ENG 101.[3]

Several of these intensively recruited seniors had nonetheless reported to the director of international programs that they were struggling in 101; the director, in turn, asked after a no-credit-bearing course (ENG 001, Writing Workshop) that we had eliminated from rotation but not yet officially removed from the course catalog. Resolute on non-credit-bearing writing classes, our workgroup was nonetheless trapped in the conceptual model of a separate-but-equal special section of ENG 101 until we read the Tanita Saenkhum and Paul Matsuda (2010) CompPile.org research bibliography on writing program administration and second language writing. Guided by their recommendations, we envisioned a multilingual (ML) section of English 101 to be populated half by international students (referred, but not compelled by, international programs and the institute) and half by native speakers (referred, but not compelled by other 101 instructors) based on students' professional or personal interest in language difference—majoring in international studies or business or education, for example, or who had multilingual friends or family. Old and white Maine may be, but there is significant language variation nonetheless, even by traditional definitions of language. For example, there is a substantial Somali resettlement population in Lewiston-Auburn (Huisman 2011); moreover, according to a recent study conducted by UMaine's Center for Franco-American Studies, roughly one-third of Maine culturally identifies as French, French-Canadian, or Franco-American, many of whom learned French as a first language (Peters 2013; Potholm et al. 2013; Quintal 1996).[4]

With only one section to manage, we set the course cap for the pilot section at zero, provided an explanatory note in UMaine's course-management system, and asked the 101 teaching corps to incorporate this announcement in their course descriptions:

> *The Translingual Section.* Section 505, which meets MWF 9–9:50 in NV 327, is our "translingual" section of ENG 101. Half the seats are reserved for multilingual students; half are reserved for native speakers of English who have a personal or professional interest in language (journalism, international business or engineering, social work, education, etc.). The logic of the section is twofold: first, we assume that monolingual native speakers of English and multilingual speakers of English have much to learn from each other; second, the rapidly globalizing workplace needs people who can negotiate in productive ways across multiple languages.

In short, the course was built from a consensus perspective. It proved strikingly uncontroversial to our colleagues and—since we were not proposing a *new* course and were managing enrollment for a special section in ways associate deans found familiar—surprisingly easy to implement.

Institutional and discursive realities then set in. Every semester, we find that once the course cap is lifted, students anxious to fill degree requirements enroll without reading, or without caring about, the course note. Even after four years, most L1[5] students still seem unaware of the nature of the section. (In fact, upon encountering an unusual [for Maine] concentration of overt ethnic and linguistic diversity on the first day of class, many are concerned that they might be in the wrong classroom.) Though our department chair has begun circulating the above course description to advisors and admissions officers, we have yet to receive any inquiries from the interested L1 students we'd imagined. Word *has* caught on among our ML student populations, who promote the course to their own peer groups and IEI cohorts. International program advisors bring their matriculating students to the writing center, where they learn about its resources and the translingual section, and we have recently begun to offer multiple sections.

As the discursive framing of the section passed beyond our immediate control, the perhaps-familiar prefix caused the word *multilingual* to turn into *multicultural* in the official course catalog, an error that has proven difficult to eradicate from department discourse and that continues to

surface in interdepartmental correspondence. This "typo," we now realize, is a striking metonym for widespread misperceptions about what it
means to study language in the United States. Nearly all students come
into the class expecting to learn about different cultures or even to learn
new languages. Classroom practices, like course readings, assignment
sequencing, peer review, and commenting on papers have required
adjusting as we have better understood just how deeply ingrained is the
assumption that engaging language issues means learning about languages and therefore appreciating other cultures. In the next sections,
we describe several sites where we have intervened in these assumptions,
starting with the reading list.

COURSE READINGS

Our first reading/writing sequence was "Language and the Self" from the
FYC textbook *Writing Conventions* (Lu and Horner 2008, 429–32). One
assignment in that sequence asks students to interpret a series of letters
and prayers from Sandra Cisneros's (2008) short story "Little Miracles,
Kept Promises" in light of James Baldwin's (2008) linkage of language
and identity in "If Black English Isn't a Language, Then Tell Me, What
Is?" Where the ML students consistently engaged the politics of language
in both readings (one wrote "Cisneros is trying to draw a picture of their
status in the community and their essential or emotional needs. However,
that made me curious to analyze what difficulties could stand in the way
of speakers of an 'other' language"), their L1 counterparts tended to
mobilize fairly conventional "English-paper" genres—mainly explaining
and then agreeing or disagreeing with the assigned texts (e.g., "Cisneros
and Baldwin are closely related to each other through their strong
opinions on controversial topics"). (All student writing quoted here is
included with the permission of the writers. Names are pseudonyms.)

Intrigued by the ML students' projects, we were initially content to
attribute their insights to a broader frame of reference and a lived experience of these issues. Yet we underestimated the extent to which their
assessors would be unprepared to encounter those frames of reference.
To our dismay, at our final portfolio review (about which more below),
reviewers consistently found the ML portfolios "unclear" and dismissed
complex lines of reasoning on the grounds of "mechanics" compared
to L1 portfolios, whose conventional, even facile, agree/disagree arguments passed easily.

In response, we made adjustments at both program and section levels. At the program level, we made translingual work more central to *all*

sections of ENG 101. For example, the fall 2013 master sequence used by all new incoming teaching assistants included reading and writing about code switching and code meshing. That many of the instructors in "regular" sections of ENG 101 were discussing these concepts with their own students somewhat mitigated the instinctive impulse to perceive the portfolios emerging from the translingual section(s) as likely sites of linguistic imperfection. Meanwhile, a workgroup this past semester also adjusted our assessment rubric (app. 9.A) to guide readers to interpret unconventional prose decisions more agentively: "Do portfolio texts *holistically* suggest the ability to sufficiently *negotiate* conventional mechanics and usage to avoid misleading or confusing readers *and/or to further the writer's purposes?*"

We also made adjustments to the curriculum at the section level: first, the readings in the initial sequence were not representative of global Englishes. (One early student course evaluation even asked for reading selections outside of an "American context.") We adapted William Lalicker's (2013) syllabus for Written Rhetoric 210: Multicultural Writing, a course offered to students from Guizhou University (China) and West Chester University (United States), and the translingual sections now use the anthology *Reading the World: Ideas that Matter*, which provides a repertoire of readings from diverse time periods as well as locations (Austin 2010). Second, portfolio reviewers' responses to ML portfolios suggested to us that a better aim of the translingual section would be to prepare *all* students to make informed choices about whether and how to include translingual rhetorical moves. Subsequent revisions to the course readings ask students to work first on rhetorical theory before explicitly engaging ideas about translingualism. With a working frame of reference, we find, students' understandings of its key insights tend to be less reductive. For example, with a concept like available means of persuasion, students are more prepared to see what it might mean for all writing to involve work on and with "language, language practices, users, conventions, and contexts" (Lu and Horner 2013, 586).

We've come to believe that offering students the space and the means to make this realization themselves is essential not only for their ownership of translingual insights into their and their colleagues' writing but also for their ability to make more deliberate claims on their readers. For example, and consistent with the *multicultural* misnomer we described above, ML students' writing from early iterations of the course tended to equate translingual with a dispensation to discuss their cultural perspectives, perhaps with a smattering of translated "mothertongue" idioms. In other words, little discussion that would significantly problematize what Matsuda has criticized as the "tour guide" mentality (Matsuda 2014, 483). When students have a language to describe the ways writers try to shape their audiences and purposes, they are less likely to work across languages for "show" and more likely to do it more purposefully as a way to marshal an alternative yet essential line of evidence or to invoke a particular kind of relevant expertise.

For example, Zhaozhe differentiated the "graceful sentences using classical examples or events to support main idea, sounds, rhyme and noble meaning" expected of his Chinese compositions from the "ideas, how strong you support it, the reason to claim it, and direct to the point" approach he found expected when he composed in English. Likening these differences to the different grains used to make pastas around the world and their various colors and shapes, Zhaozhe experimented with some Kaplanesque drawings of "Chinese" and "American" rhetorical styles, explaining that his curved and dashed lines that arrived, eventually, at a star representing his "point" represented his attempts to negotiate American essay expectations from an existing repertoire of styles. Yet he refused to essentialize these styles, locating them instead in cultural and material conditions, observing, for instance, that a Chinese convention of "implying" one's thesis rather than stating it explicitly has emerged because "the topic is fixed in Chinese literature" and his audience could easily assume that shared purpose.

ASSIGNMENT SEQUENCING

Assignment redesign is our preferred way to respond to obstacles and miscalculations. For example, initial assignment sequences for the translingual section made too much of language variation for its own sake. While we find that most students accept the premise that all writing is translingual, current sequences accept that some students are more willing than others to experiment with form. Accordingly, the course has refocused on what we think of as translingual *reading* practices intended to foster patient and flexible habits of mind. We remain committed to using "difficult texts" in all FYC courses, but for this classroom, we create extra space for collaborative reading practices. For example, students scan Ruth Benedict's "The Individual and the Pattern of Culture" together in class first to see what they notice. Inevitably, one student notes it was written more than eighty years ago, which enables us to discuss possible difficulties this might pose for readers and strategies they can adopt.

In initial sections of the course, ML and L1 students tended to self-segregate in their seating, limiting opportunities for negotiative communication strategies. We now ask ML and L1 students to interview each other, and subsequent assignments have these same pairs continuing in-class and out-of-class work together, a modification that has positively impacted the level of interest and interaction in the room. With an understanding ally nearby, students feel more able to ask sincere but seemingly "uncomfortable" or "impolite" questions about unfamiliar cultures. Likewise, our L1 students' frequent difficulties in considering perspectives outside of a US context have been mitigated by early assignments[6] that ask students to consider how cultural perspectives influence authors' choices in composing and how their own cultural perspectives influence their reading practices. We also negotiate a writing contract that represents a collaborative agreement on what kinds of writing conventions the class will focus on and how. The contract is revisited and renegotiated throughout the semester as largely an oral agreement that centers the way the class discusses how they will negotiate our rubric conventions, their writing strategies, and so forth. The contract involves a series of reflective questions on how/why the students write; their comments are collected, and the class discusses commonalities and divergences in order to reach a collaborative decision about what to attend to that day. This routine is one of the major differences from the "mainstream" sections of FYC and helps keep language decisions and negotiations in the foreground by giving all students a structured opportunity to talk through differences in their composing decisions that still might have allowed them to achieve similar writing conventions.

PEER-REVIEW PRACTICES

It has proven necessary to devote more attention than was previously envisioned to reconstructing tacit dispositions that undergird "native" and multilingual interactions. The writing contract described above buffers this tendency somewhat, but left to their own devices, the L1 students still tend to engage the ML students as charity cases: humored for their creative turns of phrase perhaps but primarily as needy but deserving cases to be helped in their worthy aspirations toward *good* English. Many L1 students still find it difficult to envision alternatives to these roles; for their part, many ML students expect this treatment, some prefer it, and most have grown so accustomed to it they have difficulty conceptualizing what an English classroom or English writing would look like without such copyediting. Consequently, prior to any peer review, we discuss our contract for *where* and *how* and *when* to focus attention on *what* (such as perspective, exploration of the complexities of their perspectives on course readings, potential connections to other texts, etc.) in each other's drafts.

In other words, it takes time and consistent investment, as Mary Jo Reiff and Anis Bawarshi might put it, "to delay and, as much as possible, interrupt the[se] habitual uptakes" (Reiff and Bawarshi 2011, 331). As they gain trust in this contract, they begin to develop inquiries they are less sure of and whose results are harder to control. Decades of scholarship and research across BW, FYC, and ESL divides predict anxiety here. Students in our UMaine translingual sections are no exception, and the five-paragraph theme remains an inviting strategy for disposing of prompts. We find some students take the entire semester to develop a willingness to explore their own perspectives; others develop a disposition of patience with others' risk taking but do not extend such risks to their own writing. In the next section, we provide some representative examples of coursework from a recent translingual section, as well as some recommendations for how teachers might engage with drafts of papers they are likely to see from a sequence like the one we've provided.

RESPONDING TO STUDENT TEXTS

Our students are mostly intrigued by readings like Canagarajah's "The Place of World Englishes in Composition: Pluralization Continued" and are gratified to find a published authority affirming their suspicion that "Standard Written English . . . is not native to any community" (Canagarajah 2006, 595). While many L1 writers remain reluctant to move alternative Englishes outside scare quotes (perhaps because of tendencies observed in peer review, as discussed above), they are often pleased to take risks with informal phrasings, humor, sarcasm, or experiments with form (like structuring their essays as dialogue) that push back at the felt sense of what an essay can be. Lilly, for instance, was delighted to begin her portfolio essays with experimental, meta introductions (e.g., "The hardest part of starting any essay is coming up with a good, strong, and solid beginning. Unfortunately, I can't think of one. So, I'll just say Hi and Welcome to Essay number two"), which she credited with solving a long struggle with academic writer's block. Such moves not only worked short term for Lilly, but they also supplied her colleagues with an alternative vision of what might constitute an essay (especially conventional notions of how writers are "supposed" to start one and the presumed expectations of her readers), alternatives that contribute incrementally to the ongoing transformation of the genre itself.

Our most recent sequence (app. 9.B) also features several assignments that ask students to examine the speech communities they move among. Useful comments on draft responses to these prompts ask them to inquire into how communication works in each community and to collect concrete examples of these communicative practices with an eye toward the pragmatic accommodations made by all participants. So when Lilly noted she was both a friend and a novice social worker, it was productive to ask her questions like, what kinds of vocabularies do you use with each group? Are there similarities or differences in these communicative strategies? How do your examples demonstrate your translingual abilities and thinking? Such questions prompt students to develop descriptions and reason through how these practices function and also to document both conventional and field-sourced texts for evidence. Lilly reports:

> As a social work major, I've become increasingly aware of . . . all the places where my speech communities overlap themselves. For example, if a friend needs advice from the social worker in me, but is also a coworker while we're at work, then I have two jobs interchanging. I have my future job and need to help others, especially if I understand enough to make an informed suggestion I can present to them, but I also have to communicate with them as a coworker when customers appear without superimposing one over the other.

We continue to struggle to push students like Lilly to see her (admittedly adroit) shuttling among social-work responsibilities and peer dynamics as also involving moments of strain and potential conflict—how the interpretive lens of social worker is changing the way she interacts with her friend or even changing what she hears as a request for advice. This struggle is partially because there's nothing magic about the contents of any assigned reading in an FYC class (even translingual scholarship), so students' initial drafts tend to dutifully affirm translingual premises, recount a bruising grammatical experience with a past teacher, and express hope for "translingual Englishes" to overtake SWE—immediately. In other words, students still must be pushed to specify examples, to critically engage with implications, and to make connections among their experiences, linguistic patterns, and habits of mind and social interactions, just as they would with any other assigned reading. Thus, when Lilly argues "I believe I am a translingual thinker," her first impulse is, predictably, to point to interactions that awakened her to cultural differences to be celebrated: foreign-exchange programs, cultural festivals, second language learning, and so forth. But when pressed to anchor these practices in the everyday, Lilly realized she could cite her "competence in multiple registers, discourses, and languages" by describing opportunities that "opened up [her] modes of communication: business speech communication in Job Corps, the vitality of proper visuals in resumes . . . modulating [her] voice when speaking to an animal . . .and how to interpret emoticons for the online community." As she explains, "Now this may sound an awful lot like I just described myself just living my life, and you'd be 100% right to think that, as that's exactly what translingual thinking is."

Just as we have learned to delay and defer the introduction of translingualism for a more productive engagement, we have also learned to be responsive to a fuller range of complex feelings about these ideas. Students have legitimately complex feelings about SWE, after all. As Shayn noted,

> The power of language can affect someone's identity by forcing them to write in standard written English and taking their motivation away. . . . whereas a technical writer such as myself values the importance of SWE. Being a technical writer not having the freedom to write however I want in a way takes away my power but it gives me and other technical writers a single identity and style. There is no room for your own voice just the facts. When working with language there is a chain of power. Someone who writes in SWE basically has the power to tell others how to write.

Acknowledging ambivalence and contradictory pulls from SWE can also be a means by which students realize how, why, and for what purposes they use it. After all, Shayn is *also* examining the pros and cons of variations in English. If we are still working on better ways to help students like Shayn and Lilly move beyond a simple reinterpretation of their experiences as translingual, these students consistently do work toward an awareness of language differences and how they structure interaction among communities.

This is not to say all ML students take immediately to cross-language experimentation, yet having more obvious resources nearer to hand, it seems, they are more likely to ground their cross-language work in empirical examples. Raquel, a trilingual Serbian, was interested by Lu and Horner's contention that "word choice affects the attitudes and thinking of people who adopt them" (2008, 100) and pointed to Serbian conceptions of family as another example of how her primary language shapes her thinking.

> Serbian language has a very rich vocabulary that indicated different family ties that is not seen in English language. Words like *strina* (your father's brother's wife), *tetka* (your mother's sister), *ujina* (your mother's brother's wife) represent different family relationships whereas in English they are only represented with a word aunt. Somebody who is not born in Serbia

might have hard time conceptualizing why . . . we would not just make it simpler by only using word *tetka* (aunt).

As Raquel explains, "This straightness of my point that if you want to understand how we think and why we use many different words to explain family relationship you have to incorporate yourself in Serbian culture." We find Raquel's work compelling both for its mild critique of English's relative poverty of words for kinship relations and for her insistence on her coinage "this straightness of my point." Fending off a peer's suggestion of "to get straight to the point," Raquel explained that she was not intending to get straight or quickly to her point because she had many more to make but that instead she wanted her audience to understand her reasoning she detailed *along the pathway* she took to form this specific example.

Here, our job is primarily to hold back (and if necessary help hold peers back) from the temptation to help Raquel "clean up" purposeful language choices like "the straightness of my point" (choices she made so as to earn the right to showcase bits of Serbian in a conventional English essay). Instead, we asked Raquel to keep exploring and explaining and reworking her reasoning. These kinds of questions prompted her to explore further effects on how she might further work "academic English writing" with Serbian, in part by considering Serbian's fraught relationship with Turkish. As Raquel explains, "There are so many words that people use everyday, *jastuk* (pillow), *avlija* (backyard), *opanak* (a type of shoes) words that most of them do not even know came from Turkish language." Her point, however, proves to be a concern for what she sees as facile uptake of English words driving a wedge "between generations." Watch how Raquel "Serbianizes" the spellings of the loan words *sorry, casual, fancy,* and *event* to preserve their liminal status.

> Few nights ago, while walking around the town I heard two girls talking, one was saying "sori, nisam znala da je moja odeca previse kezual za tvoj fensi ivent" (sorry I didn't know my outfit was too casual for your fancy event). I understood what she was saying, and her friend did too, but I wondered if older people would as well.

ML students' uptake of opportunities for translingual work has had the effect of helping many of them realize that their knowledge and experiences are resources. By buffering the incessant clamor for an *American essay style,* we help them feel easier about listening to their own ideas and letting them develop on paper. Like Zhaozhe, they also experiment with meshing their cultural writing styles with what they're learning in a US academy, many reporting that they surprise themselves with what they discover.

Such approaches foreground alternative dispositions that make space for students and instructors to understand perspectives from beyond the boundaries patrolled by SWE profiles of regularities. As described in the next section, we have tracked raters' receptions of portfolios produced by the translingual sections as a way to help us pinpoint next steps in teacher training. We'll now take up some of those receptions in more detail as a way to illustrate the benefits of a documentary investigation into local attempts to cross BW/ESL/FYC divides.

ATTENDING TO DOCUMENTS

If we initially affirmed that translingualism is a *disposition* toward language use and variety, we also emphasize that dispositions are *produced* (incrementally and sedimented over time). They are difficult to change, but since they are accretive, they are changeable. To return to the programmatic mission we outlined in our introduction, we emphasize that the work of sustaining institutional spaces and curricular practices most conducive to the translingual dispositions we hope to foster means attending carefully to *documents*. Since documents are translocal and tie the national to the local and the past to the present, we must attend to the ways documents "enact" intentions tangential or counter to our efforts. In the next section, we attend to a set of "ephemeral" documents (rater comments on the portfolios of students from the translingual sections) to both report on and to model a productive attention to these kinds of texts.

As alluded to above, all UMaine ENG 101 students submit a portfolio containing two academic essays and a critical reflection in which they discuss the work of the two academic essays and demonstrate their ability to critically reflect on the academic writing abilities they have developed. These portfolios are assessed by two other instructors of ENG 101, who must agree the portfolio demonstrates the ability to meet the program outcomes described on our Portfolio Assessment Rubric (app. 9.B); a third reader resolves any disagreements.

Raters have so far evaluated 96 portfolios from the translingual sections, completing 205 Portfolio Assessment Rubrics (or PARs, as they are known locally) and writing nearly 514 comments along the way. Although we have no controlled studies of our own to support our conviction that raters' beliefs about language difference are strongly mediated by the language available to them for uptake in these crucial documents, other investigations bear us out (see Hall and Sheyholislami 2013; Kim 2015). We have classified these rater comments in order to

Table 8.1

Comments on passing portfolios	Praise	Minimal appraisal	Describes ability	Describes inability (specific)	Describes inability (nonspecific)	Off-rubric appraisal
114 L1 rubrics	58%	24%	74%	25%	7%	16%
72 ML rubrics	37%	31%	42%	43%	14%	26%

Comments on passing portfolios	Praise	Minimal appraisal	Describes ability	Describes inability (specific)	Describes inability (nonspecific)	Off-rubric appraisal
7 L1 rubrics	14%	—	29%	71%	29%	14%
12 ML rubrics	16%	—	50%	58%	58%	50%

Praise. Portfolio reviewers commend all students for exceeding expectations, and the proportions of praise for L1 and ML students are fairly close, though ML students whose portfolios are passed are somewhat less likely to be applauded for their work.

Minimal appraisal. Given the pace of the reading (three days to read ~750 portfolios at least twice), readers understandably keep their comments terse. We find this tendency slightly more present in reviews of ML portfolios; even passing L1 portfolios are more likely to receive some explanation of a word like adequate. It is the custom to provide more extended commentary to students whose portfolios do not pass review, and it is encouraging that none of the nineteen failing portfolios were failed without substantial explanation.

Ability/Inability. Unless raters are attempting to soften a fail decision, they are far more likely to comment on what an ML student is unable to do than on L1 portfolios—even on rubrics that endorse a pass decision. Moreover, we find raters much more able to locate their critiques of L1 portfolios in specific language from the rubric ("lines of inquiry are supported by assertions rather than textual evidence"), whereas their evaluations of ML portfolios are twice as likely to be diffuse ("weak at times," "lines of inquiry unrevealed"). Because, as we note above in our discussion of Lilly and Raquel, ML students are much more likely to focus on integrating an international perspective and/or to offer evidence from their personal experience, their portfolios often attract critiques of their "inability" to manage academic "evidence" or to pursue a line of inquiry without "overwriting" or going on "tangents."

Appraisal outside rubric criteria. Though the rubric and our calibration sessions help mitigate this phenomenon, raters still sometimes mobilize private scoring schemas or break the frame of the assessment construct by speculating about the author of the portfolio ("s/he doesn't seem to understand [one of the course readings]"), offering advice ("I'm just wondering if they would rather choose a different topic for essay two"), or critiquing without making a specific appraisal ("student's examination of texts is interesting although I'm not sure as to what extent it would be considered critical analysis at times"). As another example, although our rubric deliberately avoids the descriptor clear in order to interfere with raters' susceptibility to superficially fluent prose style, ML portfolios are nonetheless much more at risk from rogue critiques. Meanwhile, raters still find ways to argue for weaker L1 portfolios on the strength of "clear controlling purposes," even while acknowledging that "analysis of course texts is limited." No ML portfolio has so far benefited from this kind of special pleading, suggesting that our (almost exclusively L1) raters remain more comfortable passing a portfolio that features front-loaded organizational schemes typical of Western schooling even when they are relatively deficient in the critical analysis and substantiated lines of reasoning our rubric emphasizes.

investigate any inconsistencies between assessors' reception of L1 and ML portfolios. (Each percentage is of the total in that row; thus, 58 percent of the 114 L1 rubrics feature some kind of praise. We do not count multiple instances of the same comment; for instance, a rater who writes "adequate" for each of the three categories is counted as a single instance of "minimal appraisal").

We have known since Alister Cumming's 1990 exploratory comparison of novice and expert ESL raters that novice raters tend to evaluate student work on tacit criteria from their habituated reading practices. Cumming's finding has been refined into useful taxonomies of rater behavior in subsequent work (see Eckes 2008; Wolfe, Kao, and Ranney 1998), and his central finding is worth revisiting: novice raters did not, he found, "seem to have developed a very thorough 'situational model' for evaluating student compositions" (Cumming 1990, 43). Some applied a perplexing "'text-based' editing strategy" to arrive at "rapid judgements of quality based on often inexplicit criteria" (perplexing, that is, because such edits could have served no purpose to the authors of the papers or to Cumming as the researcher); the others "avoided considering textual features altogether, searching only for 'situational' impressions of the students who may have composed the texts" (44). Their expert colleagues, Cumming found, "integrated their interpretations and judgements of situational and textual features of the compositions simultaneously" and deployed "complex, interactive mental processes" in arriving at their appraisals (43–44).

It's possible to see in these two novice orientations to multilingual students' essays a compressed microhistory of composition's relationship to language variation generally: *either* student writing is conceived of as a site in need of word-and-phrase level monitoring and correction *or*—to the extent that language-level concerns have been excluded from the recent history of the field in its turn toward whole-text, sociorhetorical reception of student writing—as reconstructions of imagined student writers (Dryer 2012; Faigley 1989; Wiseman 2012). Translingual pedagogies like the one we've described here ask us to attend to the word-and-phrase levels of meaning as students work across language relations. If the prior response to language difference was to attempt to eradicate it until the student could "pass" for native (or simply went away), and the contemporary response is more or less to ignore it (see Matsuda, Saenkhum, and Accardi 2013), graduate students and other FYC instructors might benefit from more declarative knowledge about language so as to enable their students to enact the translingual work our assignments are increasingly pushing them toward.[7] Students in our translingual sections have found that this approach indeed "calls for more, not less, conscious and critical attention to how writers deploy diction, syntax, and style, as well as form, register, and media" (Horner, NeCamp, and Donahue 2011, 304); most instructors, however, are not as prepared as they could be to pay that sort of attention. Thus instructors, like their students, continue to benefit from essential distinctions, like the one between grammar and usage. Meanwhile—and especially if they themselves are L1 instructors of English—they should learn to apply insights from EAP researchers who have identified sentence-level conventions in academic genres, to infuse their assignment sequencing with current understandings of second language acquisition, and to read with an array of useful distinctions among code meshing, code mixing, code switching, and even code glossing in mind.

For at UMaine, the essay is unlikely to lose pedagogical and assessment primacy in the foreseeable future; under these conditions, students working translingually will manifest their choices most strikingly at the level of word and phrase and might benefit from instructors better prepared to help them deploy linguistic resources to foreground those choices as deliberate and from assessors better prepared to name, and thus better see, ML students' skilled deployment of unconventional linguistic resources.

LOOKING AHEAD: PROSAIC COMPLEXITIES AND EXPECTED CONSEQUENCES

The practicum course for new teaching assistants is moving beyond an "inoculation" model of translingual scholarship; a single engagement with a single essay, however well written or widely cited, can't do much to inculcate a translingual reorientation among new graduate teaching assistants far more strongly invested in SWE than their students (see Kehoe 2015). Like students in the translingual sections of ENG 101, new teaching assistants *also* need a substantial frame of reference for these new ways to rethink language. Practicum assignment sequences have been revised to ask graduate students to engage with the intersubjectivity of language (Giltrow 2003) and the historical origins of "academic English" (Connors 2000; T. Miller 1997) as well as work originating from language-acquisition traditions (Atkinson et al. 2015; Tardy 2015) before encountering emerging ideas in translingual scholarship.

New challenges come into view as old ones are met: UMaine has been cultivating relationships with international undergraduate headhunting companies who offer to deliver a certain number of international tuition-paying undergrads each year. As some of our fellow contributors have also noted, the comparatively wealthy clientele of such companies have thrown traditional BW/FYC/ESL operating assumptions of "working poor," or "urban poor" or "aspirational striver," into sharp relief. As this comparatively wealthy and coveted clientele moves through our curriculum, we are likely to encounter additional pressures to help ensure that these students "succeed" (a sensation that will be familiar to readers at institutions with powerful athletic programs).

Yet as experienced workers in—and now across—BW/FYC/ESL divides, we call these complexities *prosaic* because they have become part of the never-completed work of running progressive writing programs. We look to our field and to our fellow contributors for wisdom on how and when to best pick the next battles; meanwhile, at UMaine, the translingual dispositions fostered in these sections are slowly becoming more aligned with a local documentary society enabling progressive uptakes and enabling L1 and ML writers alike to carry these practices of considered negotiation into WID coursework and beyond. In the very longest term, these parts we all can do will aggregate. Provided we are also careful to revise more prosaic documents like paper prompts, course descriptions, rubrics, and rater comments that might otherwise send powerful countermessages (and some of which are sure to survive us), we steadily advance on all fronts, reducing the everyday insistent pressure of pedagogical contradictions, monitoring, and self-censorship (Jerskey 2013, 202; Young 2013, 140).

Notes

1. Even though the conventions of rubric writing seem to discourage such tinkering, consider, for example, the 2014 revisions to the 2001 Council of Writing Program Administrators Outcomes Statement for FYC. The previous iteration envisioned students and instructors working to "control surface features"; now they are imagined as working to "develop knowledge of linguistic structures . . . through practice in composing and revising."

2. Although, ironically, word-and-phrase-level eradication of language differences enjoys a near monopoly on popular perceptions of what FYC is and what it's for.

3. This picture is improving. Thanks to ongoing outreach, IEI now refers its students to our translingual section early in their careers and has developed a course to run parallel to and support it.

4. A largely oral variation of Quebecois French known as *Franco* is still common in the upper third of the state. Like other attempts to regulate "foreign" speech in the United States (e.g., Scandinavian languages in the upper Midwest and Spanish in the Southwest), Franco communities were targeted by state laws prohibiting the use of any "foreign" language in public schools. These laws remained in effect until 1976.

5.   We refer to "native" speakers as *L1* to emphasize both their belief that English is their "first" and "only" language, and we refer to their counterparts as *ML* for *multilingual.*
6.   Also adapted from Lalicker (2013).
7.   We find an analogue in the Citation Project, which has mapped a useful category of "patchwriting" between the former original/plagiarized binary (and in so doing, enabled instructors to better see patchwriting as part of a developmental continuum).

APPENDIX 9.A

Portfolio Assessment Rubric

> *English 101 Final Portfolio Assessment Rubric (version 4.0)* **Writer Name**
> *University of Maine, Department of English* **Section Number**

An ENG 101 Final Portfolio consists of one critical reflection and two substantially redeveloped and revised academic essays that exhibit the academic writing abilities the writer has developed during the term.

Writers satisfy the University of Maine's ENG 101 requirement by submitting a portfolio for assessment. During ENG 101 portfolio assessment, each portfolio is read by at least two ENG 101 instructors other than the writer's instructor; they must independently agree that it demonstrates the ability to meet course outcomes. These readers will comment on the portfolio's demonstration of each of the traits outlined below. *After* writing comments, using the back of this form if necessary, readers will make an overall judgment.

A critical reflection should demonstrate a reflective awareness of the writer's negotiations of academic discourse conventions. In order to engage reflectively with their own work, the writer should cite and analyze passages from the two accompanying essays to situate their work (create a critical context for it) in conversation with course texts (whether previously published or produced by colleagues), concepts, and/or outcomes. The writer can situate their work by analyzing the contexts, audiences, and/or purposes that occasioned the composition decisions evident in the portfolio.

How would you describe the critical reflection's demonstration of reflective awareness?

All portfolio essays should demonstrate conventions of academic discourse:

Are the writer's ideas adequately situated in relation to sources? Are important names and terms adequately defined? Are lines of inquiry adequately revealed and followed by such strategies as pursuing lines of reasoning, substantiating arguments, extending examples, providing quotations, paraphrasing, synthesizing, and summarizing?

Are documentable claims supporting these inquiries adequately and consistently cited in-text and accompanied by appropriate reference page(s)?

Are controlling purposes apparent?

Do portfolio texts holistically suggest the ability to sufficiently negotiate conventional mechanics and usage to avoid misleading or confusing readers and/or to further the writer's purposes?

How would you describe this portfolio's demonstration of academic discourse conventions?

Further, the portfolio should demonstrate the ability to critically interpret texts:

Does this interpretation extend and/or complicate the original uses of the texts in order to adequately establish and convey the writer's purposes?

Does the portfolio provide analysis of passages from works read within the contexts of the controlling purposes? Does the portfolio provide critical contexts through which at least a few passages are examined; is one text used to provide a context for understanding another?

How would you describe the portfolio's demonstration of the ability to critically interpret texts?

Does this portfolio demonstrate the ability to meet course outcomes and thus pass review? _____Yes _____No

Revisions adopted 11 August 2015
Reader Number_____

APPENDIX 9.B

ENG 101 "Translingual" Assignment Sequence, Spring 2016.

Assignment 1. We'll start by collaborating on a contract to help us agree on how you'd like me to respond to your writing. Please start by thinking about these questions: What is important to you in your writing? What are your writing strengths? What writing strategies, skills, and techniques do you hope to learn? What kinds of writing do you expect to do in your major/minor and future profession? What would you like me to focus on as I comment on your writing? Can you think of any additional question(s) that you would like me to ask you?

Assignment 2. William Lalicker, a colleague at West Chester University, has developed questions like these to help his students engage with readings like ours. We'll use these questions as a way into all our readings this semester. Please read through them and discuss what you find significant with a colleague. Today, we'll practice applying these questions to Hogarth's image *Gin Lane*.

1. What might be the author/designer's purposes or points in their composition?
2. What does the composer seem to bring to their composition, in terms of assumptions, details, supportive examples, arguments, anecdotes, autobiographic or biographic details, to support their purposes/points?
3. What are the cultural perspectives of the composer (from her, his, or zir national heritage, historical era, community experience, or individual experience)?
4. What are the cultural perspectives that I have, as a reader (from my national heritage, historical era, community experience, or individual experience)?
5. What knowledge or experience do I need in order to fully understand and respect this composer's points? Do I like them? Do I think they are valid?

Tonight, read the excerpt from Thomas Malthus's "An Essay on the Principle of Population." Apply the five questions from our discussion today.

Assignment 3. As we discuss the insights Lalicker's questions enabled you to discover in Malthus, we'll continue developing our writing contract. We'll decide what conventions your writing needs in order to qualify as satisfactory for peer review. We'll also decide **when** you should give me your writing to receive my comments.

Assignment 4. For your next assignment, annotate "Language and Rhetoric" (467–469) and the introductions to Aristotle's *Rhetoric* on page 489. After your reading make some notes on how Hogarth employs the rhetorical appeals Aristotle describes. Compose a few paragraphs that address these questions.

Assignment 5. To further what we've learned thus far about rhetorical situations, annotate Austin's guide for "Reading Visual Texts" on pages 558–561. How might you revise your reading of *Gin Lane*? After your reading, select an image of your choosing to bring to our next class. You may bring a painting, advertisement, or brochure. Compose a few paragraphs by using the Lalicker questions 1–3 to help you discuss the rhetoric of this image.

Assignment 6. For your next assignment, read John Locke's "Of Ideas in General, and their Original," on page 126, and its introduction on page 125. Please annotate key ideas and terms and write about why or how these ideas and terms seem important to you or to Locke's text. In a few paragraphs, describe your initial thoughts, responses, and ideas. Jot down some connections you might make among Locke, Hogarth, Malthus, and the five Lalicker questions. After class discussion today, you'll draft an essay that develops these ideas.

Assignment 7. After reviewing our *Writing Contract,* today we'll read an anonymous essay written by one of your colleagues. As a group we will work on developing potential kinds of evidence for the claims in this essay, and discuss potential additional connections it might make to our course readings. For next class, please expand your own essay by specifically focusing on one or two of the Lalicker questions. Use these questions to revisit your initial interpretation of Locke's text, and to more thoroughly incorporate your experience, or additional texts, into your current essay.

Assignment 8. For your next assignment, annotate the Beatus Map on page C–5, and its introduction on pages 381–383, and 387. Focus your annotations on identifying the rhetorical appeals this map suggests. The Lalicker questions 1–3 will help your analysis. For this assignment, we'll need to decide whether to use your insights generated from this reading to form a new essay, or if you'd like to rewrite your Assignment 7 in light of this reading.

Assignment 9. Today in class we'll continue our work on Assignment 8 by identifying rhetorical appeals and applying the Lalicker questions to the Beatus Map, to your responses to Assignment 4, to Ptolemy's chart of the universe and to Wright's painting, *An Experiment on a Bird in the Air Pump.* For our next class, please work to incorporate your original responses to Locke's text and expand them with the additional connections generated from these new documents.

Assignment 10. For your next assignment, read Benedict's "The Individual and the Pattern of Culture" (133–142) and its introduction on page 132. Please annotate key ideas and write about why or how they further John Locke's points and/or help you apply the Lalicker questions to your interpretation of the texts introduced in Assignment 8.

Assignment 11. Tonight, read Canagarajah's "The Place of World Englishes in Composition: Pluralization Continued." Think of experiences you've had that might shed light on the issues Canagarajah is engaging. Contextualize these experiences in a few draft paragraphs.

Assignment 12. Canagarajah describes how communication strategies we use outside of school can increase our skills both in and outside of school. To investigate this possibility, please list the kinds of communication you do (audio, visual, or written).

1. What types of communication are you most invested in? Why?
2. What types of communication are you least invested in? Why?
3. What do you consider to be your most successful piece of communication in school? Why? (Least successful? Why)
4. What do you consider to be your most successful piece of communication outside of school? Why? (Least successful? Why?)

Assignment 13. As we transition to investigating ideas we'll call "translingual," please revisit your Canagarajah annotations. Start by writing some further notes that explain why you annotated the quotes you did. Then please reread your annotations in our course description where we made claims like "regardless of monolingual or multilingual capabilities, we are all translingual thinkers and writers," and "college graduates who are able to work across linguistic borders are at an advantage intellectually, emotionally, and economically." Compose a few paragraphs that describe your current thinking about these claims, and reason through any connections you've made among Canagarajah and any authors we've read thus far, including anonymous samples read in class.

Assignment 14. For next class, please prepare two samples of your writing. Both samples should represent what you think is a "successful" piece of writing—for the context and purpose for which it was written. One should be in-school; the other from an outside-of-school context. Samples including (or entirely in) languages other than English are welcome. Our objective is to consider if any communication strategies from your outside-of-school sample could be incorporated into your academic work. Recalling our work earlier in the term on rhetorical theory and audience, assess each sample's "success" in terms of how strongly you think your target audience understood your main point(s).

Assignment 15. Please annotate the excerpt from Kenneth Bruffee's (2007) *A Short Course in Writing*. After reading, create a list of some discourse communities that you belong to, and some that you do not belong to. Please generate a list of specific language, such as word choice or idiom, that each discourse community you belong to uses, or chooses *not* to use.

Assignment 16. We'll continue reflecting on how each of us could be said to be communicating "translingually," or the strategies enacted by "people . . . at community boundaries" (Bruffee 2007, 190). Bruffee claims we "try to make what [we] have to say accessible to members of other . . . discourse communities, so that the members of those different communities can understand each other and get along. [We] do that by negotiating differences in language and by translating from one community language into another" (190).

To test Bruffee's and Canagarajah's claims, locate a *communication sample* from a familiar discourse. To select your sample, consider the writing you selected for assignment 13 and the lists you composed in response to assignment 14. Your communication sample could be a series of texts, facebook posts, music lyrics, a letter, a visual design, creative writing . . . it needs only to rhetorically engage with an audience that you are familiar with or belong to.

Assignment 17. For the first phase of class, share what you decided to bring and the reasoning behind your choice. In the space below, please list the various communication samples your colleagues collected, briefly describe the discourse communities they're associated with, and how your sample is appealing rhetorically to its target audience:

Communication Samples
Rhetorical Appeals
Discourse Communities

To prepare for your next writing assignment, please revisit Canagarajah and Bruffee, keeping our *Writing Contract* in mind. One of your purposes for this essay is to contextualize your communication sample for your colleagues. Another purpose is to contextualize Canagarajah and Bruffee's distinctions about Englishes, learning accomplished inside and outside of the English classroom, and discourse communities.

References

Atkinson, Dwight, Deborah Crusan, Paul K. Matsuda, Christina Ortmeier-Hooper, Todd Ruecker, Steve Simpson, and Christine Tardy. 2015. "Clarifying the Relationship between L2 Writing and Translingual Writing: An Open Letter to Writing Studies Editors and Organization Leaders." *College English* 77 (4): 283–86.

Aull, Laura. 2015. *First-Year University Writing: A Corpus-Based Study with Implications for Pedagogy.* New York: Palgrave Macmillan.

Austin, Michael, ed. 2010. *Reading the World, Ideas that Matter.* 2nd ed. New York: Norton.

Baldwin, James. 2008. "If Black English Isn't a Language, Then Tell Me, What Is?" In *Writing Conventions*, ed. Min-Zhan Lu and Bruce Horner. New York: Pearson Academic.

Bruffee, Kenneth. 2007. "Reaching Out to Members of Other Communities." In *A Short Course in Writing*, 189–97. New York: Brooklyn College City University of New York.

Canagarajah, A. Suresh. 2006. "The Place of World Englishes in Composition: Pluralization Continued." *College Composition and Communication* 57 (4): 586–619.

Cisneros, Sandra. 2008. "Little Miracles, Kept Promises." In *Writing Conventions*, edited by Min-Zhan Lu and Bruce Horner. New York: Pearson Academic.

Connors, Robert J. 2000. "The Erasure of the Sentence." *College Composition and Communication* 52 (1): 96–128.

Cumming, Alister. 1990. "Expertise in Evaluating Second Language Compositions." *Language Testing* 7 (1): 31–51.

Dryer, Dylan B. 2012. "At a Mirror, Darkly: The Imagined Undergraduate Writers of Ten Novice Composition Instructors." *College Composition and Communication* 63 (3): 420–52.

Eckes, Thomas. 2008. "Rater Types in Writing Performance Assessments: A Classification Approach to Rater Variability." *Language Testing* 25 (2): 155–85.

Faigley, Lester. 1989. "Judging Writing, Judging Selves." *College Composition and Communication* 40 (4): 395–413.

Giltrow, Janet. 2003. "Legends of the Centre: System, Self, and Linguistic Consciousness." In *Writing Selves/Writing Societies: Research from Activity Perspectives*, edited by Charles Bazerman and David R. Russell, 363–92. Fort Collins, CO: WAC Clearinghouse.

Hall, Carla, and Jaffer Sheyholislami. 2013. "Using Appraisal Theory to Understand Rater Values: An Examination of Rater Comments on ESL Test Essays." *JWA: Journal of Writing Assessment* 6 (1). http://www.journalofwritingassessment.org/article.php ?article=66.

Haswell, Richard H. 2010. "Hieroglyphic World: A Review of Five Background Readers for Novice Writing Teachers." *WPA: Journal of the Council of Writing Program Administrators* 33 (3): 104–15.

Horner, Bruce, Min-Zhan Lu, Jacqueline Jones Royster, and John Trimbur. 2011. "Language Difference in Writing: Toward a Translingual Approach." *College English* 72 (3): 299–317.

Horner, Bruce, Samantha NeCamp, and Christiane Donahue. 2011. "Toward a Multilingual Composition Scholarship: From English Only to a Translingual Norm." *College Composition and Communication* 63 (2): 269–300.

Huisman, Kimberly A. 2011. "Readers Theater as Public Pedagogy." In *Somalis in Maine: Crossing Cultural Currents*, edited by Mazie Hough, Kristin M. Langellier, and Carol Nordstrom Toner, 227–39. Berkeley, CA: North Atlantic Books.

Jerskey, Maria. 2013. "Literacy Brokers in the Contact Zone, Year 1: The Crowded Safe House." In *Literacy as Translingual Practice: Between Communities and Classrooms*, edited by A. Suresh Canagarajah, 197–206. New York: Routledge.

Kehoe, Eric. 2015. "Dispositions toward Written Language Difference: L1 and L2 Novice Composition Instructors." MA thesis, University of Maine, Orono.

Kim, Hyun Jung. 2015. "A Qualitative Analysis of Rater Behavior on an L2 Speaking Assessment." *Language Assessment Quarterly* 12 (3): 239–61.

Lalicker, William. 2013. *Written Rhetoric 210 Multicultural Writing Syllabus: English Dept., Guizhou University, Guiyang, Guizhou Province, China*. West Chester, PA: West Chester University.

Lu, Min-Zhan. 2009. "Metaphors Matter: Transcultural Literacy." *JAC* 29 (1/2): 285–93.

Lu, Min-Zhan, and Bruce Horner. 2008. *Writing Conventions*. New York: Pearson Academic.

Lu, Min-Zhan, and Bruce Horner. 2013. "Translingual Literacy, Language Difference, and Matters of Agency." *College English* 75 (6): 582–607.

Matsuda, Paul Kei. 2012. "Let's Face It: Language Issues and the Writing Program Administrator." *WPA: Journal of the Council of Writing Program Administrators* 36 (1): 141–63.

Matsuda, Paul Kei. 2014. "The Lure of Translingual Writing." *PMLA* 129 (3): 478–83.

Matsuda, Paul Kei, Tanita Saenkhum, and Steven Accardi. 2013. "Writing Teachers' Perceptions of the Presence and Needs of Second Language Writers: An Institutional Case Study." *Journal of Second Language Writing* 22 (1): 68–86.

Miller, Susan. 1991. *Textual Carnivals: The Politics of Composition.* Carbondale: Southern Illinois Press.

Miller, Thomas P. 1997. *The Formation of College English: Rhetoric and Belles Lettres in the British Cultural Provinces.* Pittsburgh, PA: University of Pittsburgh Press.

North, Stephen. 2011. "On the Place of Writing in Higher Education (and Why It Doesn't Include Composition)." In *The Changing of Knowledge in Composition: Contemporary Perspectives,* edited by Lance Massey and Richard C. Gephardt, 194–211. Logan: Utah State University Press.

Peters, Jason. 2013. "'Speak White': Language Policy, Immigration, Discourse, and Tactical Authenticity in a French Enclave in New England." *College English* 75 (6): 563–81.

Petraglia, Joseph, ed. 1995. *Reconceiving Writing, Rethinking Writing Instruction.* Mahwah, NJ: Lawrence Erlbaum.

Potholm, Christian, Yvon Labbe, Tony Brinkley, and Jacob Albert. 2013. "Contemporary Attitudes of Maine Franco-Americans." Franco American Centre Occasional Papers. 1.1. http://umaine.edu/francoamerican/occasional-papers.

Quintal, Claire. 1996. *Steeples and Smokestacks: A Collection of Essays on the Franco-American Experience in New England.* Worcester, MA: Institut francais, Assumption College.

Reiff, Mary Jo, and Anis Bawarshi. 2011. "Tracing Discursive Resources: How Students Use Prior Genre Knowledge to Negotiate New Writing Contexts in First-Year Composition." *Written Communication* 28 (3): 312–37.

Saenkhum, Tanita, and Paul Kei Matsuda. 2010. "Second Language Writing and Writing Program Administration." *WPA-CompPile Research Bibliographies* 4. http://comppile.org/wpa/bibliographies/Saenkhum_Matsuda.pdf.

Shuck, Gail. 2006. "Combating Monolingualism: A Novice Administrator's Challenge." *WPA. Journal of the Council of Writing Program Administrators* 30 (1/2): 59–82.

Tardy, Christine M. 2015. "Multilingual/ism." In *Keywords in Writing Studies,* edited by Paul Heilker and Peter Vandenberg, 114–19. Logan: Utah State University Press.

White, Edward M., Norbert Elliot, and Irvin Peckham. 2015. *Very Like a Whale: The Assessment of Writing Programs.* Logan: Utah State University Press.

Wiseman, Cynthia S. 2012. "Rater Effects: Ego Engagement in Rater Decision-Making." *Assessing Writing* 17 (3): 150–73.

Wolfe, Edward W., Chi-Wen Kao, and Michael Ranney. 1998. "Cognitive Differences in Proficient and Non-Proficient Essay Scorers." *Written Communication* 15 (4): 465–92.

Young, Vershawn Ashanti. 2013. "Keep Code Meshing." In *Literacy as Translingual Practice: Between Classrooms and Communities,* edited by A. Suresh Canagarajah, 139–46. New York: Routledge.

9

BECOMING GLOBAL
Learning to "Do" Translingualism

Chris Gallagher and Matt Noonan

Once a modest local school, Northeastern University has transformed itself into a highly selective university, shooting up the *US News & World Report* rankings to join the top fifty national universities. Over the past decade, Northeastern has added more than five hundred faculty members—going on a hiring spree while other universities have been retrenching to survive the economic recession—and it has more than doubled its external research funding (Northeastern University 2016).

Northeastern's meteoric rise can be attributed in large part to its leveraging of its long-standing cooperative education model, which has gained particular salience during these difficult economic times. The key to its success has been fusing this hundred-year-old tradition with *the global*.

> As a university where teaching and research are grounded in global engagement, Northeastern's impact is being felt in all corners of the world. Our students shape the world through experiential learning opportunities with nearly 3,000 partners on seven continents and through the common pursuit of knowledge on a dynamic campus that connects students from 134 countries. Our faculty members collaborate on research with colleagues on campus and on the other side of the world, with a focus on global challenges in health, security, and sustainability. Our alumni, prepared to be engaged citizens of the world before they graduate, are making a difference in 145 countries. In every point of global connection, we don't just show up, we transform. (Northeastern University 2014)

While Northeastern is not alone in claiming this mantle,[1] *global* is shot through the university's identity. In addition to the statistics quoted above, Northeastern reported a 407 percent increase in global co-ops and a 433 percent increase in international students (Northeastern

DOI: 10.7330/9781607326205.c009

University 2016) between 2006–07 and 2014–15. It also reported in 2014–15 that nearly 20 percent of its seventeen thousand undergraduates and over 30 percent of its eight thousand graduate students were international (Northeastern University Office of Global Services 2017).

This, then, is Northeastern University's *brand*.[2] As our colleague Neal Lerner (2007) suggests, an institutional brand is both a signature (an assertion of uniqueness, of distinction) and a promise (a statement of assurance). It says, *This is who we are; this is what we do*—a delineation and a declaration of institutional identity.

Institutional branding is hardly new. But it has taken on increased importance in this age of public disinvestment, leveling US student enrollments, public doubt about the value of higher education, emerging competitors around the world, "disruptive" technologies, and the federal government's advocacy for alternative credentialing approaches such as competency-based education. Higher education institutions are embracing the language and practices of marketing with remarkable fervor (Kirp 2003). Large marketing and communications units partner with armies of consultants and freelance graphic designers to forge and protect the identity of the institution through tightly controlled and patrolled logos, images, taglines, and mascots—right down to color, size, and typography. Schools pour enormous energy and resources into identifying institutional "differentiators" and collecting "proof points" to support their brand in the highly competitive, and largely reputational, higher education market.

This intense focus on institutional branding has important implications for writing programs. As Lerner points out, "Institutional identity—or brand—is represented at many levels and by many audiences. The identity of a writing program as part of this larger brand needs to be presented in rhetorically smart ways" (Lerner 2007, 31). Institutional brands both enable and constrain writing program identities—and these identities shape what can and cannot be done within these programs.

In this chapter, we chronicle, from two perspectives, the Northeastern University writing program's efforts to engage translingualism as our institution has been "globalizing." Chris writes from the perspective of writing program director, recounting larger programmatic shifts, while Matt writes from the perspective of an instructor and peer leader in the program. The story we tell from our two vantages is not one of "branding" the writing program, our classes, or ourselves *translingual*; rather, it's a story of learning to "do" translingualism in our particular institutional context and with (and from) our particular students.

It's a story, finally, of coming to understand translingualism not as an achievement or condition, and not as a topic or kind of writing, but rather as a dynamic set of practices emerging from the teaching, writing, and reading of teachers and students interrogating language difference together.

BEING OR BECOMING . . . GLOBAL (CHRIS)

The most important consequence of Northeastern's global brand for us in the writing program has been a shift in student identities. Our student body overall is increasingly better prepared according to traditional metrics. In 2006, the average SAT score for incoming first-year students was 1230, and 38 percent of those students ranked in the top 10 percent of their high school class; in 2015, incoming students averaged 1416 on the SAT, and 70 percent of them ranked in the top 10 percent of their class. At the same time, our student body is much more diverse in terms of nationality and ethnicity, owing mostly to the increase in international students. These students, too, have risen in academic preparation. While just a few years ago, students were admitted with overall TOEFL scores in the 70s, today students generally are not admitted with scores lower than 92 (and high bars are set for subscores as well).

Despite the shift in test scores, the reality on the ground is that Northeastern's international students continue to run a large gamut, from those who struggle to follow discussions in classes and show little facility with written English to those who are among the most adept English-language users and highly accomplished students at the university. Though we have seen an *overall* rise in academic preparation of our international students, the wide range persists—whether because the TOEFL and high-school GPAs are limited metrics or because, as some have charged, we are seeing many instances of academic fraud among our applicants (or both).

One result of this persisting range of ability is palpable ambivalence about international students on campus. On the one hand, administrators, faculty, and students laud cultural diversity, embracing the opportunity to teach and learn in a context in which a variety of global perspectives and experiences are brought to bear. On the other hand, we constantly hear worries and complaints about the language abilities of international students, who are often problematically conflated with "ESL students." As a 2012 Faculty Senate report on admissions and enrollment policies asserted, many faculty and administrators worry that students with limited English proficiency drag down the quality of the educational experience for all students, jeopardizing the "academic rigor" of the class because they "cannot participate" in the "expected activities" (Northeastern University Faculty Senate 2012).

The senate report caused quite a stir in the writing program. Though we all recognized that some of our students do struggle with English language proficiency, we chafed against the framing of L2 (or international) students as a problem—a nuisance for faculty and their classmates (read: white, American, native English speakers). From our perspective, statements like these suggest that while we are eager to tout ourselves as *being* global, not everyone has embraced the task of *becoming* global. We cannot behave as if "academic rigor" and "expected activities" are universal and unchanging if we want to respond to our shifting student demographics. We must not "lower standards," but we must *rethink* those standards in light of the fact that our classrooms and university are now polyglot sites of global contact.

With these ideas in mind, the writing program has sought not only to reconsider our own practices but also to attempt to shape conversations on campus. When I arrived at Northeastern in 2009, we began revising and publicizing changes to our curriculum. We deemphasized static conceptions of "academic discourse" in favor of a broader mission, captured in our philosophy and aims statement, published in 2011.

Effective writing takes many forms.

> Our overarching goal in our courses and in the Writing Center is to help students write effectively. We acknowledge that "effective writing" must be defined in the context of writers' goals, audiences' expectations, and situational factors such as available technologies. There is no all-purpose prose that serves writers equally well in all situations. Different academic, professional, and public discourse communities practice different conventions, and these—like the English language itself—evolve over time. In some contexts, in fact, writers are expected to move across dialects within English or even across languages. Thus, instead of teaching students a single "standard" dialect or set of conventions, we help them develop knowledge of and facility with the conventions that characterize (but never fully define or stabilize) the academic, professional, and public discourses and communities they wish to enter. (Northeastern University 2011)

Thanks to a modest gift from a former Northeastern faculty member, we were able to implement an annual symposium for teachers of international and second language writers beginning in 2010. The symposium has brought to campus L2 writing and translingualism luminaries, including Christina Ortmeier-Hooper, Paul Kei Matsuda, Bruce Horner and Min-Zhan Lu, Asao Inoue and Mya Poe, and Juan Guerra. Each year, the symposium facilitator (or facilitators) has met with key players on campus and has offered a public talk aimed at bringing the latest thinking about linguistic and cultural difference to our campus community.

Our diverse teaching staff has been particularly taken by the notion of translingualism. Our shifting student demographics have made it clear to us that "traditional ways of understanding and responding to language differences are inadequate to the facts on the ground" (Horner et al. 2011, 303). Perhaps because so many of our second-, third-, and fourth-language speakers are so capable, it has been hard for most of us *not* to see language differences as a "resource for producing meaning in writing, speaking, reading, and listening" (303). The notion of translingualism, specifically as an attitude of openness toward language difference, has helped us embrace and seek to make use of the varied linguistic and cultural assets we see in our students.

But ours is not a story of a heroic writing program battling a villainous institution. Translingualism, we have found, is easier to espouse than to practice; it is a not a state of being but rather a process we must learn and learn again. Deeply engrained attitudes toward language difference do not change overnight. Often, we are coming to understand, we do not even *know* we harbor assumptions and perceptions rooted in monolingual ideologies—until they rear their heads. Nowhere has this been clearer to us than in our guided self-placement (GSP) process.

We implemented GSP in fall 2010. This process is a variation of "directed self-placement" (Blakesley 2002; Royer and Gilles 1998, 2003). It begins with our students, who familiarize themselves with our course offerings, self-assess using guidelines we provide, share their concerns and questions with their advisors, register for their courses, write a short essay describing their prior experiences with writing and reading, and bring those essays to the first meeting of their writing class. At that first meeting, instructors explain course expectations and offer students an opportunity to ask questions or share concerns. After class, instructors read the essays and consult with writing program administrators about possible recommendations for changes in course selection. If the writing program administrators agree, a recommendation is sent to students, who are asked to discuss a possible course change with their instructor, advisor, or the program administrators. Ultimately, students decide whether to accept the recommendation.

The then-director of first-year writing and I (as writing program director) had in mind several goals when we designed this process in consultation with our Writing Program Committee:

- to help students learn about our courses before taking them;
- to use multiple data sources for placement (rather than only an in-class essay, as we had been doing);
- to empower students in the course-selection process by trusting them as informants about their own learning experiences and needs and as decision makers;
- to involve program administrators and instructors as consultants to students rather than as judges and juries; and
- to provide instructors a wealth of information about students' literacy experiences and self-perceptions at the beginning of the class.

The last two goals were critical in the context of our shifting student demographics: we envisioned GSP as a tool for learning about and from students how we could best teach them. And we have—though that process has been more difficult than we could have imagined.

The first two weeks of fall 2010 were chaotic. We writing program administrators seemingly could not hold enough office hours to accommodate the instructors who lined up outside our offices, nervously clutching stacks of student essays. When it was finally their turn, these instructors—seasoned as well as newer teachers—all said some version of the same thing: *I can't teach these students.*

The whole program, it seemed, was having what I term *a Shaughnessy moment.* I'm thinking here of Mina Shaughnessy's (1979) description, at the beginning of *Errors and Expectations,* of reading a stack of error-ridden student papers and despairing of ever being able to help the poor souls who penned them. Of course, Shaughnessy *did* go on to help her students, and in order to do so, she had to learn to confront the sheer unfamiliarity, the overwhelming *foreignness,* she felt as she read the papers. But in that initial moment of confrontation, there was for Shaughnessy, as there was for many instructors in our program, a kind of existential terror, a feeling of being utterly out of one's depth.

What gave rise to our program-wide Shaughnessy moment? A small number of essays were incomprehensible or much too short to develop an idea. But a much larger number of essays contained fairly minor but consistent patterns of error—missing articles, for instance. Many of these essays were fascinating: students recounted learning two, three, or four languages while living in many places around the world. And yet, some of the instructors who brought these essays were having just as powerful a Shaughnessy moment as those with the short, undeveloped essays.

I cannot say my own readings of these essays were always fair or generous, either. Like many of the instructors, I sometimes had a difficult time overcoming my initial response to error and imposing an "ideal text" on the essays I was reading. Perhaps because the stakes seemed so high—students' college-writing experiences hinged on our decisions!— I found myself fixating on "errors" and ignoring the meaning making in the texts I was reading. I had to remind myself repeatedly to read more carefully and to talk with the instructors about the other sources of information we had available to us—especially the students, with whom either I, or the instructor, could have a conversation to learn more. Often through this process, instructors and I were able to see that the textual issues were minor and that the student would bring valuable perspectives and experiences to the classroom. Other times, students' perspectives on where they were most likely to succeed swayed us one way or another.

One criticism of DSP is that multilingual students are not always in a strong position to make curricular choices, whether because they do not understand well the options available to them because they struggle to assess and evaluate their own literacy abilities against expectations of which they are only dimly aware, or because they identify strongly with native English speakers (Bedore and Rossen-Knill 2004; DasBender 2012; Lewiecki-Wilson, Sommers, and Tassoni 2000). Our experience with GSP suggests that many *instructors and administrators* may be unprepared to help students make sound decisions because they are ill equipped to confront language difference. Virtually *all* the essays instructors brought to me that first semester were from multilingual writers. Their (and sometimes my) difficulty in distinguishing fundamental language problems from surface errors suggests the level of disorientation we were feeling upon being confronted for the first time with this magnitude of language difference.

These consultations occurred directly on the heels of Christina Ortmeier-Hooper's symposium workshop, which emphasized that difference is not deficiency and that multilingual students bring rich cultural and linguistic resources. Of course we cannot expect a single workshop will somehow "inoculate" anyone against such responses. At the same time, it was striking that within days of Ortmeier-Hooper's workshop, we were at times giving voice to the very attitudes she warned us against.

In retrospect, given the lack of preparation, our collective Shaughnessy moment was not surprising. More surprising, to me, was what happened next—namely, a precipitous decline in the number of GSP consultations and recommendations over a few short semesters—from several dozen in fall 2010 to a small handful by fall 2014.

What happened over that time period? Again, students, including international students, were increasingly better prepared; our admissions requirements were raised each year. We also worked with advisors to improve initial placement, so more students began in our sections for multilingual writers. But I also believe that as a program, we confronted our Shaughnessy moment in a way Shaughnessy would approve—by learning about, with, and from our students how to teach them. We read and talked constantly about linguistic and cultural diversity and the need to learn from our students. As a program, we engaged the field's emerging translingual literature, beginning with Bruce Horner et al.'s (2011) "Language Difference in Writing." I taught a graduate course in which we took up L2, "cross-language relations" (see Horner, Lu, and Matsuda 2010), translingualism, and World Englishes literatures. As he describes below, Matt and colleagues piloted World Englishes versions of first-year writing. We revamped the first-year writing curriculum in light of the philosophy and aims statement quoted above, and we renamed our Speakers of Other Languages (SOL!) course First-year Writing for Multilingual Writers. We embarked on a multiyear, mixed-methods study devoted to answering the question, who are our multilingual students at Northeastern? "We are all teachers of multilingual writers" became a program mantra.

We still saw markers of language difference in students' GSP essays. As a program, however, we enacted a slow, collective shift in attitude toward language difference. Rather than treating it as an obstacle or a problem, we began to embrace it as a resource for meaning making. In our reading of the GSP essays, we became much better at distinguishing surface-level errors from deeper problems—and we learned to value language differences that were neither errors nor problems. Some of the instructors most freaked out in fall 2010 began saying that unless they came across a student who simply could not communicate in English, or who insisted on changing courses, they would not bring me any placement recommendations; they valued the cultural and linguistic diversity in their classes too much to let these students go, and they felt they had the capacity to teach a broad range and variety of English-language users.

While we have seen these salutary shifts in the program, my enthusiasm is tempered in a few ways. First, our decision to provide *all* instructors with opportunities to study, discuss, and practice multilingual and translingual writing pedagogies represents a tradeoff. Though we do our best to staff the sections for multilingual writers with instructors who have ESL experience, there is little difference in the staffing or the content between the standard and multilingual sections. (As we tell students, the courses have the same learning goals; the differences are that multilingual sections are capped at fifteen, while standard sections are capped at nineteen, and the multilingual sections devote more class time to explicit language instruction. That's it.) We do not have a formal ESL training program. Nor do we systematically introduce our instructors to L2 writing literature. So we are vulnerable to Dwight Atkinson et al.'s (2015) charge that writing programs and professionals often show insufficient regard for the field of L2 writing. But given our particular combination of student demographics, a diverse teaching staff (part- and full-time lecturers, graduate-student TAs, and tenure/tenure-track faculty), and available resources—shaped in no small measure by our institution's "brand" as a global university—we believe translingualism opens up conversations about language difference and diversity in useful and approachable ways. It has helped us engage more thoughtfully and responsibly in our GSP process as we learn how to "become global." It has challenged us to inspect our dispositions toward language difference and has promoted openness and generosity—preconditions of learning from, with, and about our students.

Second, I cannot say *every* instructor now eagerly embraces language difference and knows how to make it a resource in their teaching. The fact is, I have been generalizing for the sake of narrative coherence. A couple of mandatory workshops a year and an invitation to attend optional ongoing conversations has little effect on instructors (or administrators) not willing to think hard about language difference. This may be particularly true for our non-tenure-track and especially part-time instructors, some of whom find it difficult to find the time or the motivation to attend (to) our ongoing program conversations and activities given their high teaching loads and insufficient remuneration. In addition, some of our instructors teach at other institutions, which may hew closely to monolingual ideologies and practices. We work hard to involve all instructors in program activities and to value everyone's contributions, but labor conditions in our program, as in any writing program, surely condition responses to, and preparedness for, language difference, and not always for the better.

Third—and perhaps most important—changes at the institutional and programmatic levels may create the conditions for, but do not guarantee, changes at the classroom level. While we certainly see more openness to language difference in syllabi and assignments, as well as in our periodic class observations, we cannot always be sure translingualism is being enacted with students. And as Matt shows in the next section, translingualism is a work in progress even for those who embrace it.

MISREADING DIFFERENCE: A PRACTICE UNFOLDING (MATT)

There are realities, and there are responses to those realities. As Chris has outlined, the university has changed dramatically, and so too have the students. These realities required a change in attitude. World Englishes is a reality, a phenomenon—a fact made visible by those who study it. Translingualism is a response to language difference, an approach to the facts. And both are concepts that describe and shape practice. Both are theories that require testing, theories that align (and don't) with practice.

In the fall of 2012, three instructors in our program piloted a new course—College Writing: World Englishes. The course was an outgrowth of ongoing conversations within the program, conversations focused on the changing and growing demographic of multilingual writers. Translingualism as a concept was not part of these conversations early on, but translingualism became a focus of my version of the course.

This is a story of missed opportunities and misunderstanding. It is a story familiar to most who teach. A story of good intentions, a story of a teacher struggling to see clearly the bigger picture, a story of a teacher taking his eye off the ball, a teacher learning—slowly. It is a story of reading the latest literature, a story of desire— the desire to stay current and adopt the novel language of the field. It is a story about the messy work of merging theory and practice.

In the first iteration of the course, I fumbled around with the direction and larger goals of the course. I invited writers to explore the idea of World Englishes and the implications of this phenomenon for their work as writers and for their sense of linguistic identity. From the syllabus:

> What is the nominal subject of the course? As you can see from the title, this is a college writing course, one that has the descriptor "World Englishes" attached to it. But what does marking the course in this way mean? First, and perhaps most obviously, it announces a topic that will be a point of focus in the course. It marks, that is, a direction, a jumping off point for our reading and thinking and writing. Second, and perhaps more important, this naming is misleading. Let me explain. By my titling the course in this way, you may be led to think the course is *about* "World Englishes" (about code switching and code meshing, about the politics of language, about the broader questions of representation and identity and power), when in fact the course is about *your* writing (and reading and thinking). By focusing on "World Englishes" you may overlook the name "College Writing." And why wouldn't your attention be drawn to this? College writing seems so self-evident, while "World Englishes" is odd sounding, perhaps novel, certainly not self-evident. In this course, though,

we will be taking aim at both the self-evident and the not-so-self-evident. So, what is college writing? What does it mean to be a college writer? To answer these questions you may ask—what kind of writing will be valued in this context? These questions are at the heart of the course.

I had not yet worked out for myself, or for the course, the role translingualism would play. I knew I wanted to build on the work of Horner and Lu. Our second annual symposium for teachers of international and second language writers was held the first week of classes that year. Students in this class were encouraged (not required) to attend the public talk entitled "Resisting Monoligualism." Not all attended, but all had access to the PowerPoint slides of the talk and Horner et al.'s "Language Difference in Writing" (2011), published the prior year.

In talks with my colleagues about the course, questions about language, identity, and power held center stage. In addition, I wanted to introduce writers to conversations I was following, conversations that were starting to take shape within the program, conversations that had a longer history in the field of writing studies but that were now getting a new jolt of energy from a fresh term—*translingualism.*

But what definition of translingualism did I operate from? As Laura Gonzales (2015), Paul Matsuda (2014), and Atkinson et al. (2015) all suggest, the concept of translingualism is a many-headed beast. As Matsuda (2014) notes, "A relatively new term, *translingual writing* is still in search of its own meaning" (478). My sense of the concept was still being worked out when I invited the writers in this class to work on defining it with me. For me, the motivation was not, as Matsuda claims it often is for those drawn to the term, a "moral imperative"—an impulse to do "the right thing." Rather, it was curiosity: I wanted to see what it could offer the writers in my classes.

Gonzales offers the following working model:

> Translingualism . . . provides a lens by which to examine (and value) "how writers deploy [and combine] diction, syntax, and style, as well as form, register, and media" (Horner, Lu, Royster, and Trimbur, 'Language' 304). Translingualism, as I will be using the term, does not define or represent students' linguistic backgrounds. . . . Rather, translingualism gives us a framework for understanding the fluidity of modalities and languages, a framework that we can use . . . to further understand how our students draw on their linguistic experiences to make meaning through their composing practices. (Gonzales 2015)

My initial reading of translingualism did not focus so much on the practice (particular acts of writing) or the background of the students but rather on the attitude adopted by Horner, Lu, Royster, and Trimbur

(2011) that I summarized in my head as *student voices should be valued, pay attention to what students bring to the classroom, move away from the deficit model.* And this attitude was nothing new. In fact I am sure that one reason translingualism appealed to me, or that I heard it at all, was that it was familiar. It validated what I and others in the program were already thinking and talking about, what the field of writing studies has been thinking through since its inception.

That first year, Horner's and Lu's presence at our university was an opportunity I did not want to let pass. Looking back, I see now that I did miss an opportunity. And, in some important ways, I missed the point. At the time, I thought World Englishes (WE) could be a way into discussions of language difference, a way to unsettle the notion (held by many of my students) that there is a single correct way to write. And it was. For a short time at the start of the first semester, students paid lip service to the ideas presented by Horner and Lu. Dutifully, in class discussions and in discussion-board posts, they echoed the sentiments found in the talk—for example, drawing attention to the "absurdity" of monolingualist ideology by offering examples of language difference in their own lives. They built connections between the videos we watched about World Englishes and translingualism, between the description of the phenomenon and the approach. I struggled to help them see this difference between WE—the phenomenon we were looking into—and translingualism—an approach to language difference. Too caught up in the moment, I was not thinking about this difference or where it could/would lead. And where did it lead? How did the saying lead to doing? How did these conversations impact the writing they were doing? In what ways did engaging with these ideas help them see themselves as writers, as users of language?

Two facts stood in the way of a richer exploration of these ideas. The first was out of my control—only three of the fifteen writers in the class had the resource of a language other than English to work with. Like me, the majority had experience learning other languages in high school. This is the first example of me missing the point. At the time I saw the absence of multiple language resources within the class as a problem, an excuse, a reason the course didn't fully realize my initial aims—aims set by conversations with my peers, conversations about the changing population and preparation of our multilingual writers. We initially chose WE as a focus to acknowledge the complexity of the linguistic scene. I wanted to unsettle the notion held by many of my students that there is a single correct way to write. Had the course stayed WE focused, had I not muddied the water by introducing translingualism into the mix, perhaps my mind wouldn't have been fixated on different languages as the key difference. Or perhaps I could or should have acknowledged, as Horner et al. (2011) do, that language difference is a reality and a resource even among monolingual students.

The second fact, the design of the course, was in my control. In this first iteration there was, from the start, an irreconcilable tension in the way I built the course. On the one hand, I wanted us to look at common texts and explore common questions. On the other hand, in an effort to encourage greater student agency, I asked them to design projects they were interested in. The common texts and questions served as a launching pad and most (for better and worse) went far away from my initial ideas about the course.

What do you make of it (our common text) and what can you make from it? These two questions framed each project. Only one writer built his first project by reconnecting to conversations around language difference and identity and power. And, moving forward, no writer looked back to these ideas (save for the occasional mention in the reflections that accompanied each project). Because I had not yet thought through translingualism, I was not able to make it a resource for their writing. And the same can be said of WE. I couldn't or didn't direct them in ways that helped them carry our thinking about WE forward into their own writing.

During the following fall (2013), I had another opportunity to teach the course. World Englishes redux started in a different place. Without Horner and Lu to anchor that first week, I offered Suresh Canagarajah's (2006) "The Place of World Englishes in Composition: Pluralization Continued." Following Canagarajah's lead, I foregrounded code meshing as a *strategy*: this time around I wanted to work from examples, to look at texts that enact as well as describe. I also thought the students would be interested in the historical frame Canagarajah builds, the context he provides for his examples. His text was a resource set in the background of the course; we did not spend much time writing or talking in class about his article. In those brief moments we did discuss his work, I offered a quick overview of translingualism as another way of talking about changing attitudes toward language difference. But I did not have the class read or view the materials as I had the previous year. In the foreground of our class conversations was the kind of work I wanted them to do as readers and writers. From the syllabus:

> What does it mean to be a reader? This may seem a curious question to start an overview of a writing course. But in this writing course we will be

thinking about what it means to be a reader. We will be looking at the ways reading and writing entwine. This is a good point to pause and take a look at what our writing program has to say about this relationship: http://www.northeastern.edu/writing/philosophy-and-aims/.

In this second iteration of the course, thirteen of the nineteen students were second language writers. However, this linguistic diversity was no longer a requisite component of my idea of translingualism. The previous year, I had been focused on the language resources students brought to the course, and I understood (misunderstood) or took (mistook) the plurality of languages to be a key factor in the success of the course. I failed to think carefully about language difference. We read about and talked about these ideas and concepts, but I failed to create situations (opportunities/conditions) in which these writers could use all their linguistic resources.

In order to foreground this enactment, I had to limit the amount of freedom I gave the writers. I guided the direction of the projects with common prompts, surrendering a little student freedom in favor of coherence. This allowed me to extend the attention of the writers in the class, to extend the time and the ways they thought about language and identity. For example, for the second project, the jumping-off point was John Edgar Wideman's (2010) "Our Time." As a writer, Wideman is pre-occupied with the representation of people and places; the drama of a writer making consequential choices takes center stage. Students were invited to write about a place and its people. From the prompt: "I want you to experiment with the limits of language to bring this place to life for your reader. I want to you use language descriptively. Build from what you know. What are the stories and the places (and the people) that have shaped you?"

Many writers in the class built projects that moved between languages. I say *projects* because they did not produce papers; writers in this course constructed multimodal compositions using an ePortfolio tool. They were able to write about subjects that meant something to them, and I was able to keep the conversation on the "doing," on the ways they were writing and representing these subjects, on the choices they were making as writers.

In the first iteration of the course, the readings were the content, but they were not used to model writing strategies. We did not think about these texts as a series of choices, as composed by writers making choices. The most significant change in the second iteration of the course had to do with our approach to the course readings. I selected readings that enacted the ideas of the course—"how writers deploy [and combine] diction, syntax, and style, as well as form, register, and media" (Horner et al. 2011, 304). For example, the first project used Susan Griffin's (2011) "Our Secret" as a model. We looked at how she collages together multiple discourses and how she changes style and diction and voice over the course of her essay. And we talked about the consequences of these choices.

This change in reading practices aligned with a shift of emphasis in the way I think about translingualism. At first this approach signaled to me a more generous attitude toward difference. Translingualism provided me with a way to talk about and value what writers were doing. Like many of my peers, I searched for examples of "translingual writing." I wanted examples to share with students. Now I see translingualism as a *reading* practice. My initial attempt to encourage writers in my class to take up questions of language and identity failed to account for their identity as readers. In the first version of the course, I did not design a course that enabled them to think in this way. I missed an opportunity. To have productive conversations about language and identity, I needed to think about how the writers in the course were readers first and how the way they were reading impacted what and how they wrote. The broader changes to the program Chris has described echo here. My peers and I are changing as readers too; we confronted our Shaughnessy moment and are different readers.

I am still thinking through what translingualism means to me and what it might mean to writers in my classes. What I do know is that translingualism must be more than a course topic or a "kind" of writing; in order for it to be meaningful and productive for students, it must be integrated into, must emerge from, their reading and writing practices.

CONCLUSION

As we have drafted this chapter, we have been mindful of Paul Kei Matsuda's (2014) bracing critique of those who "uncritically" accept and celebrate translingualism "not for its intellectual value but for its valorized status" (479). Matsuda rightly warns of the dangers of "linguistic tourism" among those who are fascinated by "exotic" writing but unwilling or unable to do the hard work of understanding and engaging linguistic diversity.

Let us be clear: we have no interest in "branding" the Northeastern writing program or our classes as "translingual." Translingualism is not, for us, an accomplishment or a status. It is instead an orientation to language difference and the reading, writing, and teaching practices that emerge from that orientation. We cannot claim to *be* translingual; we can only learn to practice translingualism.

We do so, as we believe all writing program administrators and instructors must, where we are, within the constraints and affordances of our institution, including *its* brand. Northeastern's commitment to "the global" has brought us students from all over the world, and it has challenged our campus community. We are continually learning how and when to leverage and sometimes challenge the institution's claims about linguistic and cultural diversity in what we hope are "rhetorically smart ways" (Lerner 2007). Perhaps most important, we are learning with and from our students, who themselves are learning to "do" translingualism as readers and writers. Because their linguistic and literacy experiences, perspectives, and practices are constantly evolving, this learning process has no end. And that's a good thing.

Notes

1. A few examples: the University at Buffalo (SUNY) touts its *global reach* (University of Buffalo n.d.); the University of California Berkeley trumpets its *global engagement* (University of California Berkeley n.d.); and New York University—which is challenging the very notion that a university should be associated exclusively with a US-based campus—describes itself (as Northeastern has also begun to do) as a *global network* (New York University n.d.).

2. By all accounts, the brand is effective. Northeastern's rise in the rankings has been accompanied by an explosion in the number of applications, now topping fifty thousand for twenty-eight hundred spots in the entering class. For many students in the United States and abroad (especially China, India, Saudi Arabia, and Central and South America), Northeastern has moved from "safety school" to "reach school" status.

References

Atkinson, Dwight, Deborah Crusan, Paul Kei Matsuda, Christina Ortmeier-Hooper, Todd Ruecker, Steve Simpson, and Christine Tardy. 2015. "Clarifying the Relationship between L2 Writing and Translingual Writing: An Open Letter to Writing Studies Editors and Organization Leaders." *College English* 77 (4): 383–86.

Bedore, Pamela, and Deborah F. Rossen-Knill. 2004. "Informed Self-Placement: Is a Choice Offered a Choice Received?" *WPA: Journal of the Council of Writing Program Administrators* 28 (1–2): 55–78.

Blakesley, David. 2002. "Directed Self-Placement in the University." *WPA: Journal of the Council of Writing Program Administrators* 25 (3): 9–39.

Canagarajah, A. Suresh. 2006. "The Place of World Englishes in Composition: Pluralization Continued." *College Composition and Communication* 57 (4): 586–619.

DasBender, Gita. 2012. "Assessing Generation 1.5 Learners: The Revelations of Directed Self-Placement." In *Writing Assessment in the 21st Century*, edited by Norbert Elliott and Les Perelman, 371–84. New York: Hampton.

Gonzales, Laura. 2015. "Multimodality, Translingualism, and Rhetorical Genre Studies." *Composition Forum* 31.

Griffin, Susan. 2011. "Our Secret." In *Ways of Reading*. 9th ed. Edited by David Bartholomae and Anthony Petrosky, 335–382. Boston, MA: Bedford/St. Martin's.

Horner, Bruce, Min-Zhan Lu, and Paul Kei Matsuda, eds. 2010. *Cross-Language Relations in Composition*. Carbondale: Southern Illinois University Press.

Horner, Bruce, Min-Zhan Lu, Jacqueline Jones Royster, and John Trimbur. 2011. "Language Difference in Writing: Towards a Translingual Approach." *College English* 73 (3): 299–317.

Kirp, David L. 2003. *Shakespeare, Einstein, and the Bottom Line: Marketing of Higher Education*. Cambridge, MA: Harvard University Press.

Lerner, Neal. 2007. "Rejecting the Remedial Brand: The Rise and Fall of the Dartmouth Writing Clinic." *College Composition and Communication* 59 (1): 13–35.

Lewiecki-Wilson, Cynthia, Jeff Sommers, and John Paul Tassoni. 2000. "Rhetoric and the Writer's Profile: Problematizing Directed Self-placement." *Assessing Writing* 7 (2): 165–83. http://dx.doi.org/10.1016/S1075-2935(00)00020-9.

Matsuda, Paul Kei. 2014. "The Lure of Translingual Writing." *PMLA* 129 (3): 478–83. http://dx.doi.org/10.1632/pmla.2014.129.3.478.

New York University. n.d. "Global Network." https://www.nyu.edu/global.html.

Northeastern University. 2011. "Philosophy and Aims." Writing Program, Northeastern University. http://www.northeastern.edu/writing/philosophy-and-aims/.

Northeastern University. 2014. "Focused Messages." Marketing and Communications Guidelines, Editorial. https://www.northeastern.edu/guidelines/editorial/focused messages.html.

Northeastern University. 2016. "Institutional Accomplishments: A Decade of Expanding Global Impact." https://accomplishments.northeastern.edu/.

Northeastern University Faculty Senate. 2012. "Report of the 2011–2012 Enrollment and Admissions Policy Committee." Boston, MA: Northeastern University.

Northeastern University Office of Global Services. 2017. https://www.northeastern.edu /ogs/.

Royer, Daniel, and Roger Gilles. 1998. "Directed Self-Placement." *College Composition and Communication* 50 (1): 54–70. http://dx.doi.org/10.2307/358352.

Royer, Daniel, and Roger Gilles, eds. 2003. *Directed Self-Placement: Principles and Practices*. New York: Hampton .

Shaughnessy, Mina. 1979. *Errors and Expectations: A Guide for the Teacher of Basic Writing*. New York: Oxford University Press.

University of Buffalo. n.d. "Global Reach." http://www.buffalo.edu/global_reach.html.

University of California Berkeley. n.d. "Global Engagement." http://globalengagement .berkeley.edu.

Wideman, John Edgar. 2010. "Our Time." In *Ways of Reading*. 9th ed. Edited by David Bartholomae and Anthony Petrosky, 655–94. Boston, MA: Bedford/St. Martin's.

PART 4

Responses

10

CROSSING, OR CREATING, DIVIDES?
A Plea for Transdisciplinary Scholarship

Christine M. Tardy

The construct of translingualism is meant to highlight the fluidity across and between languages, taking a holistic perspective rather than compartmentalizing different codes. This notion in and of itself is valuable in that it seems to capture the lived experiences of people, most of whom use more than one language on a regular basis. Whether it is fundamentally distinct from multilingualism is perhaps worthy of debate, but the term intends to draw attention to language fluidity in a way some feel *multilingualism* does not (see Juan Guerra and Ann Shivers-McNair in this collection). Within this volume, translingualism is described primarily as an ideology about, approach to, or disposition toward language and language difference (Dryer and Mitchell; Guerra and Shivers-McNair; Horner) and as an attitude about the valuing of student voices (Gallagher and Noonan). Several contributors refer to Bruce Horner et al.'s description of a translingual approach as seeing "difference in language not as a barrier to overcome or as a problem to manage, but as a resource for producing meaning in writing, speaking, reading, and listening" (Horner et al. 2011, 303). This use of *translingualism* to refer to an ideology or paradigm has potential value, assigning a name to a phenomenon in order to make it more visible.

The pedagogical applications of the term, however, are where confusion often begins: in this collection, *translingual courses* are defined as those that purposefully blend populations of native English users with L2 writers (Dryer and Mitchell; Lalicker); *translingual strategies* or *practices* refer to code meshing (Gallagher and Noonan) or to courses that emphasize negotiation of meaning over decontextualized grammar (Malcolm); and *translingual documents* refer to the written texts of multilingual writers (Dryer and Mitchell). Because these kinds of courses,

DOI: 10.7330/9781607326205.c010

practices, and texts have long existed, it is not clear to many why new labels are needed. Indeed, the use of new terminology for established ideas can ultimately restrict our understanding of an issue by occluding relevant scholarship from view (MacDonald 2007; Matsuda 2013).

As this book is about crossing divides, I need to acknowledge up front the disciplinary perspective I bring to this conversation. With degrees in Russian, TESOL, and applied linguistics, I identify primarily as an applied linguist. Because of my interest in writing, I have overtly tried in my own scholarship and thinking to cross disciplinary divides—more aptly, perhaps, to ignore them, drawing on any work that can inform my understanding of the issues I am engaged in: second language writing, academic writing development, and the policies and politics of English. This has meant attending CCCC and other composition conferences when possible, keeping up with new composition scholarship, and taking several courses in composition studies as a graduate student.

Given my personal commitment to interdisciplinary writing scholarship, I was excited by the interest in multilingual writers in two special issues published in 2006: one in *College English* and another in *WPA*. I attended the 2010 Watson Conference, at which language was a prominent theme, and I was happy to endorse Horner et al.'s (2011) position piece that called for thinking about language difference and diversity as a resource rather than a deficit. From my perspective at the time, it seemed as though some synergy was beginning to form, some potential for conversations across distinct but related bodies of scholarship. Unfortunately, I have since become discouraged that the promise of crossing divides has not come to fruition. Somewhat surprisingly, the recent interest in translingualism among compositionists has not brought on serious engagement with related work in applied linguistics (including the fields of second language writing, World Englishes, and second language acquisition), but instead decades of relevant research, theory, and practice are routinely ignored or dismissed as traditional or monolingualist. And I now find myself concerned that, rather than crossing divides, current discussions of translingualism may be exacerbating the disciplinary division of labor that Paul Matsuda (1999) wrote about years ago. In the remainder of my response, then, I'd like to highlight three important themes from this collection and probe further how scholarly discussions in these areas could be strengthened through a more interdisciplinary (or transdisciplinary) approach. Particularly central to my discussion is the third theme of teacher education.

One point that emerges in several chapters is the value of understanding how translingualism—as a disposition or attitude—might influence or shift our practices at the programmatic and institutional levels. Asao Inoue, for example, offers the excellent example of how directed self-placement (DSP) can create conditions that allow such dispositions to take hold within a program—specifically, the conditions of respecting and listening to students and allowing students to play a role in how they are assessed. Inoue's arguments resonate with positions articulated by Tony Silva (1997) in a piece titled "On The Ethical Treatment of ESL Writers." Like Inoue, Silva emphasizes that his approach is "based on the notion of respect" (359) and that to treat ESL writers ethically requires, among other things, an informed and equitable approach to assessment. Deborah Crusan (2011) has also been a strong advocate for respectful approaches to assessment and, like Inoue, has called attention to DSP because of the agency and autonomy it grants to L2 writers. Though L2 writing scholars like Silva and Crusan are rarely referenced in discussions of translingualism, their dispositions and the institutional practices they call for align well with those in this volume and could enhance discussions. Similarly, existing research into cross-cultural composition could inform explorations of blended "translingual courses," which appear to be synonymous. Scholarship on these courses (Matsuda and Silva 1999; Miller-Cochran 2012; Ruecker 2011; Shuck 2006) has established some of the same challenges described in chapters in this collection by William Lalicker and Dylan Dryer and Paige Mitchell while offering additional perspectives too. When brought into conversation, such scholarship may provide a broader pool of theoretical and practical resources for program administrators and instructors.

A second prominent theme from this collection relates to the interrelations of language, identity, agency, genre, and discourse. This theme is brought out most visibly in chapters by Bruce Horner, Patricia Bizzell, and Sara P. Alvarez, Suresh Canagarajah, Eunjeong Lee, Jerry Lee, and Shakil Rabbi; these authors compel us to see language difference from a rhetorical perspective. As Horner argues, judgments of what is "different" or "conventional" are often variously assigned among readers. He notes the need to take into account writer positions, social identities, writing forms and modes, and time and space of text reception. Canagarajah (2013), too, has acknowledged that such elements play a role in how language difference is perceived, and chapters here by Dryer and Mitchell, Chris Gallagher and Matt Noonan, and Katie Malcolm all illustrate practitioners' sense that code meshing for code meshing's sake is insufficient—language difference and its reception must be considered as part of a larger, complex eco-social system (Tardy 2016).

Applied linguistics scholarship on identity, agency, genre, and discourse can be informative to this conversation. Work by Bonny Norton (2013), for example, illustrates not only the complexity and shifting nature of identities but also the role they play in language acquisition. Sue Starfield's (2002) critical ethnographic research in South Africa sheds light on the interrelations of racial identities, written language, and assessment of student writing. Ken Hyland's (2012) theoretical and methodological tools provide useful means for understanding identity in academic writing as constructed through linguistic and rhetorical choices writers make from socially available options. And Vijay Bhatia's (2006) exploration of relations between genre and World Englishes contributes additional frameworks for understanding the extent to which different genres (and contexts) may be more or less amenable to language difference. Though the questions, contexts, and disciplinary paradigms are not identical, these strands of research share similar concerns, and engagement with existing scholarship could go far in enhancing current understandings and conversing across so-called disciplinary divides. The relations among language, identity, genres, and discourses are obviously complex and are a perfect example of an area of scholarship that may be best approached through transdisciplinary efforts.

The third theme I will discuss is the one that, to me, seems most urgent, and that is the importance of teacher knowledge and support in successfully adopting a translingual disposition at the classroom and program levels. This concern underlies nearly every chapter in the collection but is most explicitly discussed by Dryer and Mitchell, who state that a social orientation to writing instruction "has almost completely displaced training in the study of English *as a language*." This argument has also been made by Susan Peck MacDonald (2007) and Matsuda (2014), among others, but it seems particularly imperative at a moment in which composition studies has taken greater interest in valuing students' linguistic resources. As Hyland has pointedly stated, "Teachers of *writing* clearly need to be teachers of *language*" (Hyland 2007, 151). A sophisticated knowledge of language (including grammar, lexical grammar, and discourse) is, to quote Hyland, "central to teacher education programs" (151).

Metaknowledge of language allows teachers (and students) to analyze and discuss writing in valuable ways, including how linguistic and discursive choices might shape meanings for different readers. In MA-TESOL programs, pedagogical or descriptive grammar is a common course requirement because it equips teachers with knowledge of how language works at a structural (but not prescriptive) level; also often required, courses in sociolinguistics or discourse analysis raise teachers' awareness of language variation and difference, and they provide tools for analyzing patterns of use within social spaces. Courses in second language acquisition build teachers' understandings of how language proficiency might be defined and supported, along with exploration of the many social and cognitive factors that influence it. Language proficiency is mentioned in several chapters of this collection, and Canagarajah (2013) has also acknowledged that translingual practice "demands proficiency in established varieties" (125), so it seems a strong understanding of language and development is essential for teachers interested in supporting and valuing their students' linguistic resources. Yet such courses are rarely obligatory or even optional for composition teachers. Carrie Byars Kilfoil (2014) has shown that the percentage of rhetoric and composition programs that include core or elective courses in linguistics, TESOL, and basic writing has dropped from 92 percent in 1987 to a mere 6 percent in 2007. The content of such coursework, instead, is relegated to single class sessions of other courses or orientation programs for new teachers, often represented only through a reading or two and possibly a guest visit from an expert—far too little time or attention for teachers to develop the complex knowledge of language that should be considered essential for writing instructors, particularly those working with linguistically diverse students.

As a result, many writing teachers feel ill equipped to support students with language-related questions or language development or even to implement pedagogies that draw on students' multiple linguistic resources (Matsuda, Saenkhum, and Accardi 2013; Tardy 2011). Without the metalanguage and the content knowledge of language and language learning, avoidance of such concerns becomes a common strategy. In my graduate course Second Language Writing, we always spend some time on topics such as language feedback and second language and academic literacy development. Many of the students/teachers in the class struggle with practices such as prioritizing language-related feedback areas or developing activities to help students explore lexicogrammatical conventions in genres. Inevitably, some express concern that these kinds of issues have not been addressed in their preparation for teaching first-year writing or in their graduate programs in rhetoric and composition. "Why," they ask, "is this not part of the orientation or practicum course for *all* writing instructors?" Given the relatively small proportion of writing instructors who have the opportunity to take courses that address language—let alone writing pedagogy—it is clear we have some considerable challenges to overcome in writing-teacher preparation. But, as MacDonald (2007) states, without knowledge about language, the field will "lack the resources to respond to students who are now coming to us from all corners of the world" (619).

In graduate education, the devaluing of language-related knowledge is at times reinforced through the elimination of a foreign-language proficiency requirement in many rhetoric and composition graduate programs, so teachers often miss out on the first-hand experience of advanced language learning and use. Even programs that retain this requirement tend to give minimal attention to it (Horner et al. 2011), so, in Christiane Donahue's (2009) words, "Our classrooms may well be multilingual, but our writing faculty and scholars are quite often not" (227). Certainly, there are many reasons behind the diminished attention to language in rhetoric and composition graduate education, at least some of which relates to the field's disciplinary origins and relations that link it more strongly to the humanities and areas like cultural studies than to social sciences and fields like applied linguistics (see Aull 2015; Matsuda 1999; and Silva and Leki 2004 for extended discussions of these issues). Nevertheless, it should be a significant concern to faculty and students in these programs that serious attention to language study has virtually disappeared just as our campuses have become more and more linguistically diverse.

There is, however, a growing body of research relevant for teachers wishing to acknowledge and value the linguistic resources of writers who are still developing English-language proficiency. The following list touches, too briefly, on some of what this scholarship has demonstrated:

- Second language development is nonlinear, gradual, and dependent on factors such as "readiness," what is measured, and in what tasks (including considerations of genre, topic, and task complexity) (Ortega 2012).
- The learning opportunities and affordances of different linguistic environments play an important role in L2 development and are highly individualized in relation to learners' circumstances and choices (Ortega 2014).
- Multilinguals' composing processes may differ qualitatively when writing in different languages, as they draw on their L1 and additional languages for different functions and resources (Kobayashi and Rinnert 2013).
- Bilingual writers may draw variously on their stronger languages for procedural or conceptual tasks to facilitate processing. They may also exploit genre knowledge across languages, but doing so likely requires a certain threshold of language proficiency and some degree of similarity in the genre's realization across the two languages (Gentil 2011).
- Use of one's L1 during L2 writing appears to be common across writers but may be less prominent for those with stronger general writing

proficiency, regardless of L2 proficiency (van Weijen et al. 2009), and
may vary in relation to genre (Wang and Wen 2002).

Such scholarship is not simply applicable to discussions of translingualism—it is central to it. With such knowledge, teachers will be far better
equipped to understand, support, and facilitate the multi(or trans)lin-
gual development of their students, to make pedagogical choices that are
broadly informed and context sensitive, and, ultimately, to adopt dispositions that value and build upon the linguistic resources of their students.

I understand the challenges teachers face in accessing and familiar-
izing themselves with such scholarship, but if we are to take issues of
language seriously, these challenges must be addressed. Facilitating
interaction among graduate programs in rhetoric and composition
and applied linguistics would be ideal, where institutionally possible, as
would encouraging graduate students to take relevant coursework across
programs. Where such interactions are not possible locally, rhetoric and
composition faculty might consider regularly inviting speakers with language and writing expertise or assigning language-related readings in
graduate courses, followed by online/video discussions with the authors.
Ideally, rhetoric and composition programs will begin to hire "hybrid"
scholars as faculty who can also play roles in writing program administration, where they can support writing teachers most directly. Of course,
graduate students cannot be expected to learn entire additional fields
of scholarship in the four or five years it takes to earn a PhD, but they
can become more comfortable with some of the terminology, journals,
scholars, and methods of inquiry in language studies so they can continue to engage with such scholarship as faculty and administrators.

The title of my response states my position fairly plainly. I hope I have
illustrated here, at least in part, the untapped potential of a truly transdisciplinary approach to language and language difference in writing
studies. We have the resources and the scholarship at our disposal, but
we need an open mind, a willingness to do the work, and a commitment
to moving beyond the borders we profess to disavow.

References

Aull, Laura. 2015. *First-Year University Writing: A Corpus-Based Study with Implications for Pedagogy*. London: Palgrave Macmillan.

Bhatia, Vijay K. 2006. "Genres and Styles in World Englishes." In *The Handbook of World Englishes*, edited by Braj B. Kachru, Yamuna Kachru, and Charles Nelson, 386–401. Malden, MA: Wiley-Blackwell.

Canagarajah, Suresh. 2013. *Translingual Practice: Global Englishes and Cosmopolitan Relations*. New York: Routledge.

Crusan, Deborah. 2011. "The Promise of Directed Self-Placement for Second Language Writers." *TESOL Quarterly* 45 (4): 774–80.

Donahue, Christiane. 2009. "'Internationalization' and Composition Studies: Reorienting the Discourse." *College Composition and Communication* 61 (2): 212–43.

Gentil, Guillaume. 2011. "A Biliteracy Agenda for Genre Research." *Journal of Second Language Writing* 20 (1): 6–23.

Horner, Bruce, Min-Zhan Lu, Jacqueline Jones Royster, and John Trimbur. 2011. "Language Difference in Writing: Toward a Translingual Approach." *College English* 73 (3): 303–21.

Hyland, Ken. 2007. "Genre Pedagogy: Language, Literacy, and L2 Writing Instruction." *Journal of Second Language Writing* 16 (3): 148–64.

Hyland, Ken. 2012. *Disciplinary Identities: Individuality and Community in Academic Discourse.* Cambridge: Cambridge University Press.

Kilfoil, Carrie Byars. 2014. "The Language Politics of Doctoral Studies in Rhetoric and Composition: Toward a Translingual Revision of Graduate Education in the Field." PhD diss., University of Louisville.

Kobayashi, Hiroe, and Carol Rinnert. 2013. "L1/L2/L3 Writing Development: Longitudinal Case Study of a Japanese Multicompetent Writer." *Journal of Second Language Writing* 22 (1): 4–33.

MacDonald, Susan Peck. 2007. "The Erasure of Language." *College Composition and Communication* 58 (4): 585–625.

Matsuda, Paul Kei. 1999. "Composition Studies and ESL Writing: A Disciplinary Division of Labor." *College Composition and Communication* 50 (4): 699–721.

Matsuda, Paul Kei. 2013. "It's the Wild West Out There: A New Linguistic Frontier in U.S. College Composition." In *Literacy as Translingual Practice: Between Communities and Classrooms*, edited by A. Suresh Canagarajah, 128–38. New York: Routledge.

Matsuda, Paul Kei. 2014. "The Lure of Translingual Writing." *PMLA* 129 (3): 478–83.

Matsuda, Paul Kei, Tanita Saenkhum, and Steven Accardi. 2013. "Writing Teachers' Perceptions of the Presence and Needs of Second Language Writers: An Institutional Case Study." *Journal of Second Language Writing* 22 (1): 68–86.

Matsuda, Paul Kei, and Tony Silva. 1999. "Cross-Cultural Composition: Mediated Integration of U.S. and International Students." *Composition Studies* 27 (1): 15–30.

Miller-Cochran, Susan. 2012. "Beyond 'ESL Writing': Teaching Cross-Cultural Composition at a Community College." *Teaching English in the Two-Year College* 40 (1): 20–30.

Norton, Bonny. 2013. *Identity and Language Learning: Extending the Conversation.* 2nd ed. Bristol, UK: Multilingual Matters.

Ortega, Lourdes. 2012. "Epilogue: Exploring L2 Writing-SLA Interfaces." *Journal of Second Language Writing* 21 (4): 404–15.

Ortega, Lourdes. 2014. "Ways Forward for a Bi/Multilingual Turn in SLA." In *The Multilingual Turn: Implications for SLA, TESOL and Bilingual Education*, edited by Stephen May, 32–53. New York: Routledge.

Ruecker, Todd. 2011. "Improving the Placement of L2 Writers: The Students' Perspective." *WPA: Journal of the Council of Writing Program Administrators* 35 (1): 91–117.

Shuck, Gail. 2006. "Combating Monolingualism: A Novice Administrator's Challenge." *WPA: Journal of the Council of Writing Program Administrators* 30 (1–2): 59–82.

Silva, Tony. 1997. "On the Ethical Treatment of ESL Writers." *TESOL Quarterly* 31 (2): 359–63.

Silva, Tony, and Ilona Leki. 2004. "Family Matters: The Influence of Applied Linguistics and Composition Studies on Second Language Writing Studies—Past, Present, and Future." *Modern Language Journal* 88 (1): 1–13.

Starfield, Sue. 2002. "'I'm a Second-Language English Speaker': Negotiating Writer Identity and Authority in Sociology One." *Journal of Language, Identity, and Education* 1 (2): 121–40.

Tardy, Christine M. 2011. "Enacting and Transforming Local Language Policies." *College Composition and Communication* 62 (4): 634–61.

Tardy, Christine M. 2016. *Beyond Convention: Genre Innovation in Academic Writing.* Ann Arbor: University of Michigan Press.

Van Weijen, Daphne, Huub van den Bergh, Gert Rijlaarsdam, and Ted Sanders. 2009. "L1 Use During L2 Writing: An Empirical Study of a Complex Phenomenon." *Journal of Second Language Writing* 18 (4): 235–50.

Wang, Wenyu, and Quifang Wen. 2002. "L1 Use in the L2 Composing Process: An Exploratory Study of 16 Chinese EFL Writers." *Journal of Second Language Writing* 11 (3): 225–46.

11
THE INS AND OUTS OF TRANSLINGUAL WORK

Thomas Lavelle

The chapters in this book demonstrate both the importance and the difficulty of doing translingual work while dominant classroom and assessment practices, academic policies, language theories, and linguistic ideologies all insist implicitly upon a conception of English (and other languages) that is reified, stable, standardized, and replicable. Given the exigencies of better learning environments (Lavelle and Shima 2014; Sohan 2014), fairness (Horner et al. 2011), sustainable theories of language (Cooper 2014; Lu and Horner 2013), and progressive ideologies of literacy (Horner 2013), I will take for granted here the importance of doing translingual work and make a case that analyzes aspects of the difficulty and suggests one way through it. After clarifying briefly what I see as translingual work, I will model a dynamic I see as critical to its success. The model loosely resembles a Lakatosian model of inquiry, and I suggest it can clarify and help rectify some of the challenging circumstances facing translingual efforts, as exemplified in some of the other chapters here.

As I understand the issue, the exigency for translingual work lies in unfair and ineffective teaching and policies, that is, student writers are poorly taught and treated unfairly because of perceived or purported differences between their Anglophone writing practices and some imagined ideal usage. That unfair treatment rests upon and seeks legitimacy through a language ideology—monolingualism—that relies in turn upon a deeply flawed theory of language. That theory, however tacit and incoherent, portrays languages as largely autonomous, largely stable systems.

In responding to this theory and this ideology, translingual efforts distinguish themselves from other research and teaching traditions working for academic fairness. Bruce Horner (this volume) correctly characterizes many strands of those traditions as accommodationist

DOI: 10.7330/9781607326205.c011

in their stance vis-à-vis language difference and therefore unlikely to succeed. Moreover, within those traditions, pathways to fairness generally rest upon appeals for tolerance, assertions of rights, and demands for equal treatment. In sharp contrast, translingual work goes beyond those legitimate appeals, assertions, and demands and marshals a body of scholarship to discredit claims of autonomy and stability and thereby show languages are not the Saussurean systems proffered by grammar handbooks and formalist linguistics. One objective, therefore, of translingual work is to demonstrate that unfair treatment of linguistic difference is indefensible not solely on ethical grounds but also indefensible intellectually.

On these theoretical and ideological bases, translingual research evokes and explains a deessentialized notion of English (and other languages) compatible with writer agency. This compatibility does not enable agency, which, as Lu and Horner (2013) make clear, is always both available and inevitable. What it does, however, is make agency explicit and thereby change the discourse around language conventions.

Driven, then, by exigent fairness and always informed by an anti-Saussurean understanding of language, translingual workers (i.e., teacherscholars) examine the agentive production of student writers and its interaction with academic institutions and habitus in order first to identify and eradicate obstacles to fairness and then to facilitate—through research and teaching—informed choices by student writers about visible linguistic difference. Implicit in this work of examination and facilitation is an active interplay between theory and practice, an interplay that can productively be modeled as what I call here *centripetal* and *centrifugal dynamics.*

That model, or metaphor, resembles very generally a Lakatosian structure of inquiry (Lakatos 1970), in which certain theoretical commitments are central and further work extends outward from them to account for diverse phenomena, conditions, and environments. In Imre Lakatos's work, those central commitments constitute an unquestionable set of core beliefs, and while Lakatos himself, a staunch rationalist, would have rejected a characterization of his "hard core" (Lakatos 1970, 133) as beliefs and commitments, he stipulates that any successful research program incorporates a set of tenets methodologically immune to either theoretical or observational refutation, that is, immune to modus tollens arguments (Lakatos 1970, 133). His bestknown illustration is the early research program around Newtonian gravitation, in which the hard core of commitment was to action at a distance and Newton's three laws of dynamics. In that program, this network of beliefs was protected, a priori, from the large body of observational challenges and counterexamples that existed at that time, all of which rested upon pre-Newtonian theoretical assumptions (133). With that core in place, the work of Newtonians, then, consisted of explaining, reinterpreting, or accounting for this body of "facts" in terms consistent with action at a distance, and Lakatos locates this type of work in a "protective belt" (134) existing outside the core position it serves.

This spatial framing of methodological (or ideological) priorities can also frame the dynamics I suggest here for successful translingual work in composition. Centripetal, inward-looking work attends to core commitments. Centrifugal, outward-looking work attends to innovations and interventions that improve local conditions, resist entrenched practices, and challenge resistant habitas, all of which rest in various ways on monolingualist assumptions about the nature of language, just as "evidence" against Newtonian gravitation rested upon classical assumptions about motion, mass, and inertia. This analogy, however, is an admittedly imperfect one. First, the supposition of a complete and wholly coherent "core," as in Lakatos's example, is probably too strong a stance for an emergent field like translingual writing studies. Nevertheless, if *translingual* is to have any semantic import, some core commitments must coalesce around a performative, agentive understanding of linguistic resources and how they function within social contexts. Second, the ends of an applied research program like translingualism differ from those of a basic research program like Newtonian physics, and, accordingly, the work that extends from core translingualist commitments is best construed not as a protective belt but rather as a proactive one.

Given this imperfect fit, I have recast Lakatos's static spatial distinction between hard core and protective belt into directional dynamics within the metaphorical space of an applied research program. In that space, centripetal work refers to work that turns inward and either specifies, articulates, or refines translingual beliefs about the nature of languages or explicitly evokes those beliefs in contested arenas. In this volume, Juan Guerra and Ann Shivers-McNair do this by clarifying and modifying the metalanguage and conceptual underpinnings available for doing translingual work. Likewise, centrifugal work turns outward to challenge manifestations of monolingualism in classrooms, in curricula, or among colleagues. Examples in this collection include the course designed and implemented by Dylan Dryer and Paige Mitchell, the efforts with directed self-placement described by Chris Gallagher and Matt Noonan, and by Asao Inoue, the classroom engagement with mixed-language texts tried and evaluated by Bruce Horner, and the accelerated learning program developed by Katie Malcolm.

Each of those chapters chronicles mixed results, and local conditions—material and ideological—unquestionably influence the outcomes, but those conditions are the starting point for translingual efforts, the dominant givens against which translingual work works. The proportion then of more or less successful outcomes depends largely on the interplay, or its absence, between centripetal and centrifugal work, that is, between the articulation or evocation of translingual commitments and the reform of unfair and misleading monolingualist practices. Horner's chapter, for instance, does and reports on substantially successful work because the chapter balances these two dynamics. Some of its work engaging translingualism's core concerns is straightforwardly evident. It clarifies the ideological distinctions among three approaches to language difference and reiterates the strong theoretical claim made for translingualism as "an inevitable feature of all writing" (88). Later, it clarifies the implications of translingualism's status as an ideology in opposition to other language ideologies, specifically monolingualism. The chapter's centrifugal work addresses the local classroom practices through which Horner attempts to "break with dominant frameworks" (89), specifically reading mixed-language writing and assigning an essay that requires fairly extensive engagement with both translation and notions of translation.

One could at this point say, "well and good," Horner combines theory and practice, looks to and looks after the tenets of translingualism, and teaches accordingly, all of which is in fact well and good. More relevant, however, is that this chapter attends to Horner's basic commitments *even while* enacting them pedagogically. His discussion of reading mixed-language texts acknowledges "the potential value of introducing students to such writing" (89) and offers nuanced characterizations of the texts and students' responses to them, but that centrifugal effort relies upon regular reference to the tenets Horner hopes to enact: that "dominant definitions of what counts as difference in language" should be resisted (89) and that "difference in language [is] always emergent and contingent" (91). There is a similar interplay of centrifugal and centripetal concerns in his depiction of the translation assignment. Horner operationalizes his assignment in a way that actively rejects assumptions of "the discrete character of languages and the internal uniformity of each" (93) and thus resists monolingualist notions of languages and their relationships. Simply put, every outward move is made with an inward reference to the core commitments of translingual work as he understands and articulates them.

Combining centrifugal and centripetal steps is demanding work, but necessary. Many chapters here show that the representations of language, the textual behaviors, or the assessment and placement practices that follow from and reinforce essentialist language ideologies seep into any conceptual or institutional space not actively occupied by an alternative representation, behavior, or practices. It is that seepage that limits the efficacy of some translingual work described in this volume, and I argue that active evocation of core beliefs about language is what could sustain the alternative representations, behaviors, and practices that can prevent such seepage.

Understandably, in a volume largely devoted to translingual practices, outward, local engagement dominates, and there is an underattention to inward-directed work, to core translingual commitments, however authors might specify them. In some cases that imbalance is so striking that an author's or authors' tenets remain unclear, but in what follows I consider four strongly centrifugal chapters in some detail not simply to substantiate my centripetal/centrifugal analysis but to suggest how more symmetry within that dynamic can help translingual workers better meet the challenges posed by intransigent ideology and institutions.

Each in its own way, the chapters by Malcolm, Dryer and Mitchell, Gallagher and Noonan, and Inoue all tell success stories. Malcolm's account does and describes work that accelerates writing instruction, introduces translingual practices at multiple institutional levels, and intentionally disrupts monolingual ideologies—clearly many wins emerging from a mix of centripetal and centrifugal work. Dryer and Mitchell also recount a curricular innovation, designated sections of 101 that foster translingual dispositions in order to meet the needs of writers traditionally seen as multilingual and those traditionally seen as English only, and this innovation too is a qualified success. The work reported on by Gallagher and Noonan is both more wide ranging and more exploratory, but the success stories seem to center on placement reforms and staff-training initiatives reflecting what I characterize as a cultural shift, a shift embodied perhaps in the frank, retrospective account of pedagogical development in the World Englishes writing section. Finally, Inoue's chapter attempts to leverage local institutional successes with self-placement and contract grading into an argument that makes these specific institutional structures prerequisites, or enabling conditions, for successful translingual work, an argument that fails even while his local reforms seem to be successful.

Malcolm's chapter both reports success and demonstrates a high degree of inward/outward balance, but the persistent challenges she identifies are signs of ideological seepage. The challenges, which she always addresses and sometimes overcomes, include students' concessions to monolingual reading and writing practices, practices that require recursive attention throughout a quarter. Malcolm also refers to prevalent monolingual ideologies among instructors and warns with prescience that structural or curricular changes, like the acceleration work she does and describes, will likely reinforce monolingualist responses to language difference in the absence of ongoing translingual work with pedagogy. So while the chapter blends centrifugal and centripetal efforts, with regular references to monolingual ideology contra translingualism, those references usually invoke a fairly general notion of translingualism (rather than, say, an explicit set of tenets). This leaves Malcolm with a strategy of disruption aiming to derail, deter, detour an entrenched ideology when what might be required is a replacement, such as a strong and explicit commitment that language is only ever located in practice. While derailing, deterring, and detouring are necessary elements of translingual work, those actions are not sufficient to fill intellectual and institutional spaces and block the essentializing linguistic ideologies that will otherwise seep in. That oppositional work requires a more elaborate and more explicit set of core commitments.

Dryer and Mitchell portray their successes as more qualified and annotate that portrayal with cautionary observations and lessons learned, often observations and lessons incorporated into ongoing adjustments to their curricular innovation. Nevertheless, I suggest that the factors they identify as obstacles to their implementation of translingual dispositions are traceable to a shortfall in work with core translingual theory in relation to their ambitious pedagogical project. That shortfall is somewhat surprising because the authors declare their ambition to do both kinds of work: contribute to our understanding of what translingual writing is and isn't (1), certainly a core concern; provide an account of their own engagement with that writing and the local structures and documents constraining it (1), which clearly represents work within a proactive belt; and then return to the conceptual center with an attempt to theorize the unexpected consequences of these efforts. However, their core conceptual efforts are relatively modest in comparison to their extensive work with local structures and documents, and that work most often refers to a general version of translingualism, defining it solely as dispositions of openness to language difference. While certainly among any imaginable set of translingual commitments, this definition says too little about what translingual writing is.

Again, not saying—avoiding the work of articulating beliefs about language and ideology—allows for ideological seepage and for dominant practices and policies to continue more or less unaltered. For example, Dryer and Mitchell identify difficulties around portfolio assessment: after years of work to create more open dispositions, the authors report on and richly illustrate unfair portfolio assessment, unfair inasmuch as assessors grant themselves license to ignore rubrics and comment idiosyncratically in response to *some* kinds of language difference. I suggest that in their detailed account there are theoretical gestures that could certainly explain and perhaps reform this monolingualist practice if the authors had drawn those gestures into a coherent translingual stance of their own. For instance, they refer to Susan Miller's insightful characterization of prevailing language ideology—the attraction and retreat of promise unfulfilled, a figuration of some good English as available and desirable, yet elusive, receding and ultimately unattainable, and to her characterization of composition programs and practitioners—both heavily invested economically and symbolically in that promise unfulfilled—as complicit in sustaining and reproducing that ideology. Similarly, they are well aware of the institutional structures that proscribe training instructors to think about language or language difference. These insights, worked centripetally, could create an explicit explanatory arc linking language ideology > individual and institutional complicity > insufficient training in thinking about language > unfair portfolio assessments. Such explanations, I submit, provide a more effective tool for working against the monolingual practices that seem in some measure to be subverting Dryer and Mitchell's local translingual work.

Questions of ideological seepage do not actually apply to the chapter by Gallagher and Noonan because the chapter takes no explicit ideological stance even as it sets about its pragmatic work. The chapter records a writing program's successful introduction of more progressive placement policies and broader understandings of language difference. The centrifugal work of that record is an elaborate chronicle of cultural and even personal evolution within a complex architecture of local particulars. It is a detailed and reflective account of visiting speakers, placement practices, and two iterations of a writing course all aimed at more generous readings of apparent differences in language and all playing out within the institutional and ideological framework carefully and affirmatively described in the chapter's opening (1–2). The centripetal work is nearly as extensive, but without the depth of detail.

The most specific account of core commitments comes in a citation of Laura Gonzales's definition of translingualism (Gallagher and Noonan, 171), which can be effectively summarized as, translingualism is a lens and a framework. Beyond that there are primarily tropes of emergence: "still being worked out" (171), "fresh term" (171), "nothing new" and "familiar" (171–72), "not yet thought through" (173), "a shift . . . in the way I think" (175), "now I see . . ." (175), "we can only learn to practice" (175); these tropes are helpful exactly to the extent that they indicate emergence from something to something else, but no clear end or starting points are identified. This attention to core commitments, elaborate but vague, falls far short of what Guerra and Shivers-McNair ask for in their chapter in terms of clarifying our conceptual apparatus (19–20) and seems to ignore their own reference to Paul Matsuda's admonition "to use translingual writing for its *intellectual value*" (Matsuda 2014, 479; emphasis added). Nevertheless, Gallagher and Noonan's chapter closes with apparent confidence in the success of the work it has done, work which on my reading is to add a patina of accommodationist tolerance for some language difference within an organization that eradicates other kinds of language difference through its use of TOEFL scores and other recruitment/admission strategies.

Inoue's chapter begins with substantial attention to translingual tenets, which he harnesses to the work done in establishing directed self-placement and contract grading in his local setting, so on the basis of this account there is little space for ideological seepage. He carefully identifies a cluster of assumptions derived from translingual literature and aligns them with the aims and outcomes of his institutional innovations. Those innovations do not, however, necessarily create conditions supportive of translingual work. In fact, contract grading and self-placement have no necessary connection to translingualism; it is wholly possible, perhaps likely, that they would be employed in courses or programs fully committed to essentialist theories of language and monolingualist ideologies, this even in light of Inoue's accurate analysis of fairness and power.

Nevertheless, the chapter does identify affinities between translingual work and Inoue's efforts with placement and assessment, and it also helps identify some limitations of my centripetal-centrifugal metaphor as a tool for understanding and guiding translingual work. Even with a strong, inward-looking account of translingual assumptions, as Inoue selects them, and meticulous work on the rationale for local innovation, this chapter, whatever its other merits, does not appear to document or do any actual translingual work. A further limitation to my metaphor, one not explored here, is an asymmetry that shows inward-looking, more purely theoretical work on translingual thinking unfolding successfully without explicit regard for its outward-looking instantiation. The chapter by Guerra and Shivers-McNair is an example of such unidirectional success. That imbalance, however, remains a question for another setting, one safely deferred because, as I have suggested here, translingual labor is not hampered by too much attention to its core tenets. It will, rather, become increasingly successful in its local enactments as it attends to that core more rigorously.

References

Cooper, Marilyn. 2014. "The Being of Language." In *Reworking English in Rhetoric and Composition: Global Interrogations, Local Interventions*, edited by Bruce Horner and Karen Kopelson, 13–30. Carbondale: Southern Illinois University Press.

Horner, Bruce. 2013. "Ideologies of Literacy, 'Academic Literacies,' and Composition Studies." *Literacy in Composition Studies* 1 (1): 1–9.

Horner, Bruce, Min-Zhan Lu, Jacqueline Jones Royster, and John Trimbur. 2011. "Language Difference in Writing: Toward a Translingual Approach." *College English* 73 (3): 303–21.

Lakatos, Imre. 1970. "Falsification and the Methodology of Scientific Research Programmes." In *Criticism and the Growth of Knowledge*, edited by Imre Lakatos and Alan Musgrave, 91–196. Cambridge: Cambridge University Press.

Lavelle, Thomas, and Alan Shima. 2014. "Writing Histories: Lingua Franca English in a Swedish Graduate Program." In *WAC and Second Language Writers: Research towards Linguistically and Culturally Inclusive Programs and Practices*, edited by Terry Myers Zawacki and Michelle Cox, 439–63. Anderson, SC: Parlor.

Lu, Min-Zhan, and Bruce Horner. 2013. "Translingual Literacy, Language Difference, and Matters of Agency." *College English* 75 (6): 582–607.

Matsuda, Paul Kei. 2014. "The Lure of Translingual Writing." *PMLA* 129 (3): 478–83.

Sohan, Vanessa Kraemer. 2014. "Relocalized Listening: Responding to All Student Texts from a Translingual Starting Point." In *Reworking English in Rhetoric and Composition: Global Interrogations, Local Interventions*, edited by Bruce Horner and Karen Kopelson, 191–206. Carbondale: Southern Illinois University Press.

12

LANGUAGE DIFFERENCE AND TRANSLINGUAL ENACTMENTS

Kate Mangelsdorf

In reading over the chapters in this collection, I was struck by the diversity of programmatic and pedagogical initiatives that can fall under the umbrella of *translingual*. This diversity is not surprising, given both the highly contextualized nature of writing programs, as well as the complexity related to the term *translingualism*. Paul Matsuda has noted that "a relatively new term, *translingual writing* is still in search of its own meaning" (Matsuda 2014, 478), and I would modify that statement in regard to these chapters as "*translingual programs and pedagogies* are still in search of their own practices." Just as the notion of translingual writing has been adopted, resisted, complicated, and deepened, translingual enactments are experiencing a similar process. I am not implying, however, that these practices are in any way imperfect; quite the contrary, they are significant improvements over what they are replacing. My point is simply that translingual enactments are developmental; due to the entrenched nature of institutional structures, they take a long time to implement, involve a great deal of compromise, and can initially lead to resistance and confusion.

Different perspectives toward translingualism are given in these chapters. In their 2011 *College English* article, "Language Difference in Writing: Toward a Translingual Approach," Bruce Horner, Min-Zhan Lu, Jacqueline Jones Royster, and John Trimbur note that a translingual orientation includes honoring the ability of language users to employ language for their own purposes, recognizing the variety of languages throughout the world, and working against English monolingualist ideology through teaching and research (Horner et al. 2011, 305). Throughout this piece, they emphasize engagements with language differences: a translingual approach "sees difference in language not as a barrier to overcome or as a problem to manage, but as a resource for producing meaning in writing, speaking, reading, and listening" (303).

DOI: 10.7330/9781607326205.c012

"Difference as resource" gives writers the agency to negotiate language strategies and repertoires when communicating meaning and identity. It is similar in some ways to the notion of plurilingualism, which Ofelia García explains as "the understanding that language use in the twenty-first century requires differentiated abilities and uses of multiple languages as citizens cross borders either physically or virtually" (García 2009, 54). But a key feature of translingualism is that *all* language users are translingual, not just those who know more than one language, because all utterances are fluid, relational, and contingent.

Reductive notions of language difference can easily lead to misinterpretations of translingualism. Horner et al. (2011) emphasize that translingualism is an orientation toward language rather than a particular type of writing or writers. However, language difference has often come to mean *visible* language differences, with the result that translingualism is often associated only with multilingual writers and the marked language "differences" typical of second language or English-dialect writers. As a result, translingualism has sometimes been conflated with second language writing studies, to the detriment of both.[1] And this focus on only *visible* language differences reinforces the idea that discourse lacking visible differences (as seen through a monolingual[2] lens) is somehow *not* different, that instead it consists of an unchanging display of conventional structures aimed at particular audiences.

Two chapters in this volume do much to rectify this reductive notion of translingualism, in particular with their assertions concerning language difference. In his chapter, Bruce Horner writes that translingualism is an "inevitable feature of all writing, whatever forms that writing might take. . . . . Hence even those utterances that appear merely to reiterate conventional linguistic forms are renewing those forms and thus producing difference by their iteration of these forms in a different spatial and temporal location" (88). A key facet of language as always emergent, always transforming is the coconstitutive nature of rhetorical acts. Juan Guerra and Ann Shivers-McNair note that "difference" is "a contingent iterative performativity" resulting from the "*intra-action*" of identities (Barad cited in Guerra and Shivers-McNair). Both Horner and Guerra and Shivers-McNair acknowledge some overlap between translingualism and an accommodationist view of language in that both paradigms desire to honor so-called unconventional language uses. However, translingual ideology sees difference as an inherent characteristic of all language practices, even that which appears unmarked by difference. Horner's "double translation" work with his students helps them see how languages are "complex, indeterminate assemblages of possibilities" (94) and that communicative acts are both iterative and contingent. In this view, "standard" English practices are intrinsically translingual, and multilingual students (such as those at my university on the US-Mexican border) might prefer to produce "standard" English in conventional formats, despite their bilingual fluencies. Since no language is isolated from its context and no language iteration is truly the same, the standard English language forms they create are as translingual as any overtly code-meshed language.

Since translingualism is about *all* language practices, not just those that appear different, administrators and teachers attempting to enact translingualism must work against common writing program structures in which students are separated into different classes according to language background and measured proficiencies and in which student writing that exhibits marked differences might be valorized but will still be constrained to drafts or minor assignments. In reading the chapters in parts 2 and part 3 of this volume, I was interested in the successful programmatic and curricular engagements described and even more interested in the struggles and tensions encountered. These struggles speak to challenges of changing ingrained monolingual ideologies seldom questioned in the day-to-day activities of program directors and writing instructors.

Two successful attempts to implement translingual writing orientations are described in chapters by Katie Malcolm and Asao Inoue. Both these chapters describe significant changes in writing programs. In Malcolm's community college, basic writers had been placed in a linear course sequence, a step-by-step approach that assumes rhetorical development is a smooth progression toward "good" writing. Malcolm and her colleagues developed an accelerated program in which students are placed immediately in college-level courses with a studio course as a corequisite. While accelerated learning programs have become fairly common, the focus in these programs has been on increasing the pace at which students are allowed entry into college-credit classes. In contrast, in her chapter Malcolm concentrates on students' language dispositions. Malcolm gives examples of students' negotiating conventional essay formats and language structures through online and class discussions, writing that "the institutional thirdspace of English 100 allowed us to critically examine"—for college credits—"the various ways UCC defined 'writing' [and] how the students could turn to one another and themselves as writing resources" (115). Conversations in class and online showed that students became more self-reflective readers and writers, more prone to questioning conventional academic discourse, and more confident about their language use.

Like Malcolm, Inoue in his chapter demonstrates how programmatic changes can create conditions for translingual practices. In his view, "Translingualism itself is a call for new and better ways to conceive of and practice the assessment of student writing in college and secondary classrooms" (121). Inoue argues that directed self placement (DSP) and labor-based contract assessment help create practices that are translingual in nature. Rather than course placement being determined according to linguistic "adequacy," DSP allows students to select their own placement level. Grading contracts in which students negotiate how much work they will accomplish in a course replaces evaluations driven by predetermined standards. Since grades are not based on a preconceived notion of writing quality, students' histories and backgrounds can be valued, not judged, and teachers and students can work together as the writing evolves. According to Inoue, both DSP and labor-based grading contracts promote a more critical stance toward language: "Fairness comes from not ranking but considering language performances on more critical terms that embrace failure as places of negotiation, discussion, and potential" (133). I imagine a key feature of the success of contract grading in particular is the preparation of teachers, for teachers (and their students) are likely to insert their ingrained ideas about language standards even in an assessment system grounded in more critical perspectives on language.

Inoue focuses on a writing-assessment ecology that encompasses classrooms and programs—and, I would add, larger administrative structures in which programs operate. The different components of a writing program (individual students and teachers, labor contracts, textbook decisions, pedagogy courses, curriculum committees, budgetary practices, and so on) are also located within the ecology of the larger field of rhetoric and composition. In their chapter, Dylan Dryer and Paige Mitchell situate the challenges they faced enacting a translingual pedagogy not only within their largely white, rural, New England campus but also within the discipline of rhetoric and composition, which turned away from issues of language several decades ago in what is commonly described as the *social turn*. They acknowledge that their initial foray into translingualism, in which they combined domestic and international students in the same classroom, resulted in misunderstandings. However, they persevered, and change started to slowly happen: they introduced translingualism to teaching assistants; experimented with course readings and sequencing; intervened in peer-review interactions to encourage risk taking and openness; and worked to interrupt instructors' habituated reading practices that tended to implicitly or explicitly penalize visible language differences. Their attention to the practices of raters evaluating student portfolios is especially illustrative of the challenge of dislodging a view of language as static, contained, and nonrelational. As they emphasize, "Translingual pedagogies like the one we've described here ask us to attend to the word-and-phrase levels of meaning as students work across language relations" (137). This was work their portfolio raters initially were unprepared to do.

In their chapter, Chris Gallagher and Matt Noonan highlight what they call a "Shaughnessy moment" that seems similar to the experiences of Dryer and Mitchell when working with portfolio raters. Referring to Mina Shaughnessy's sense of desperation when she read her CUNY student essays, Gallagher and Noonan recall their instructors' "feeling of being utterly out of [their] depth"(166) when reading essays from students who were able to self-select their writing courses, students who otherwise would have been isolated from "regular" composition. At this point in Gallagher and Noonan's discussion, practicing translingualism seems to mean attending to visible language differences in multilingual students' writing, a topic the field of second language writing has examined in depth. However, the authors note that theirs is a "a story of learning to 'do' translingualism in our particular institutional context and with (and from) our particular students" (162). As their program continued to change, the notion of translingualism became more complex as the authors come to perceive translingualism as pertaining to all students; significantly, they began to think of it as a *reading* practice that involves attending to the linguistic and modal movements within texts. Their story, they write, is still evolving: "This learning process has no end. And that's a good thing" (176).

Gallagher and Noonan introduce their translingual work as a reaction to their institution's efforts to brand itself as *global*, something many schools are doing in order to attract more international students and maintain their competitive status. While the adoption of *the global* within the higher education industry in the United States might make the field of rhetoric and composition more open to attending to language, the novelty of the global move can obscure important ethical considerations. Some institutions, for instance, are accepting large numbers of international students without providing resources for helping those students achieve basic English-language proficiency. The tendency is to celebrate obvious differences in language, appearance, and customs without critically studying the power dynamics in which languages are enmeshed. Patricia Bizzell's chapter on English in Korea is a good example of how English, a language traditionally associated with the global powers of

First Circle countries, is not owned by any particular country or group of people but rather is being managed and altered in localized settings. Furthermore, while languages are a social construct, they are also what Alastair Pennycook has called "sedimented products of repeated acts of identity" (Pennycook 2007, 13). The chapter in this volume by Sara P. Alvarez, Suresh Canagarajah, Eunjeon Lee, Jerry Won Lee, and Shakil Rabbi gives examples of the interplay between identity and language as the authors describe how they have experienced, resisted, transformed, and conceded to traditional categories of ethnic identity as related to their language practices. Most striking to me is the authors' descriptions of uptake, of how their translanguaging practices were perceived by others. Often, translanguaging is a powerful way to perform a desired identity, but it also can lead to being ascribed an undesired identity, as it does for Jerry Won Lee, who is frequently perceived as being ABC (American-born Chinese). As noted in the conclusion, "Jerry's narrative therefore shows identity is not constructed through language resources alone. . . . Sometimes we become ethnicized by others in ways we may not always expect or even comprehend" (44). Translingual practices cannot be isolated from the cultural, racial, and material contexts in which they exist.

These chapters on translingualism in writing programs and pedagogies demonstrate the imperfections and even hazards of these enactments in a field that for so long has neglected *language* as a part of rhetoric. Perhaps the most effective way to enact change is to improve the graduate programs in rhetoric and composition that prepare future writing and rhetoric professionals. While graduate students read an article or two about translingualism in their coursework, the programs in which they are enrolled still remain stubbornly monolingual English and US-centric in their orientations. To challenge monolingual ideologies in graduate programs, critical language theory, drawn from scholarship in applied linguistics and education, can be integrated into core classes. Students can learn about critical discourse analysis, ethnography, and other research methodologies appropriate for research into language practices in educational and community contexts. Students can be given the opportunity to write theses and dissertations that are multilingual and multivocal.

However, contesting monolingual language ideologies in graduate programs will not be easy, particularly in those plagued by tensions over specializations and turf. A zero-sum attitude toward curricular change can make faculty worry that if language is foregrounded, another topic will be eclipsed. Because translingualism tends to be connected to only language-minority or ESL students, faculty wishing to do translingualism might be kept apart from the "real" work of teaching rhetorical theory and history into which language issues seldom intrude. Finally, questions might arise about how well a translingual approach can prepare students for the job market: will students be hired if they espouse "radical" changes in writing programs? No doubt there will be resistance to changing graduate programs, just as there is resistance to changing writing programs.

Other areas related to translingualism must be explored. For instance, more attention must be devoted to developing a critical awareness of "conventional" language and how communicators negotiate language norms. And as Cindy Selfe (2014) has said, there are clear connections between translingualism and multimodal communicative practices that must be studied. Scholarship from the field of second language writing can help administrators and writing instructors work more effectively with second language writing students. Translingualism as a practice is just beginning to take shape, and as the chapters in this volume demonstrate, good work is starting to be done.

Notes

1. For an explanation of the problems that this conflation has caused, see Dwight Atkinson et al. (2015).
2. Throughout this response I am using *monolingual* only as a convenience. No language practice is truly monolingual.

References

Atkinson, Dwight, Deborah Crusan, Paul Kei Matsuda, Christina Ortmeier-Hooper, Todd Ruecker, Steve Simpson, and Christine Tardy. 2015. "Clarifying the Relationship between L2 Writing and Translingual Writing: An Open Letter to Writing Studies Editors and Organization Leaders." *College English* 77 (4): 383–86.

García, Ofelia. 2009. *Bilingual Education in the 21st Century: A Global Perspective.* Malden, MA: Wiley-Blackwell.

Horner, Bruce, Min-Zhan Lu, Jacqueline Jones Royster, and John Trimbur. 2011. "Language Difference in Writing: Toward a Translingual Approach." *College English* 73 (3): 40–67.

Matsuda, Paul Kei. 2014. "The Lure of Translingual Writing." *PMLA* 129 (3): 478–83.

Pennycook, Alastair. 2007. *Global Englishes and Transcultural Flows.* New York: Routledge.

Selfe, Cynthia L. 2014. "The Disciplining Disposition of Print." Presentation at the Annual Convention of the Conference on College Composition and Communication, Indianapolis, IN.

ABOUT THE AUTHORS

Sara P. Alvarez is a PhD candidate in rhetoric and composition at the University of Louisville and multilingual writing fellow at Queens College, CUNY. Sara's research interests intersect the fields of critical applied linguistics, bilingualism, and education. Sara is the winner of the 2015 National Council of Teachers of English (NCTE) Early Career Educator of Color Leadership Award and the co-recipient of the 2015 Conference on College Composition and Communication (CCCC) Research Initiative Award.

Patricia Bizzell is distinguished professor of English at Holy Cross, where she teaches introductory academic writing courses every year. Other interests include literature by cultural and linguistic border crossers. Among her honors are NCTE's Outstanding Book Award for *The Rhetorical Tradition*, the Exemplar Award from CCCC, and the 2016–17 Cardin Chair in Humanities at Loyola University–Maryland. She is a past president of the Rhetoric Society of America and a two-term member of MLA's Publication Committee, along with other professional responsibilities.

Suresh Canagarajah is Edwin Erle Sparks Professor of Applied Linguistics and English at Penn State University. He teaches language socialization, composition research, and World Englishes.

Dylan B. Dryer is associate professor of composition studies at the University of Maine. His qualitative research findings have won the Braddock (2013) and Bruffee (2014) awards (the latter with Irvin Peckham). Current corpus-informed projects on the disciplinary identity of writing studies and composition teachers' construct validity aim to responsibly integrate qualitative and quantitative methods. Graduate training in research methodology remains a particular teaching interest.

Chris Gallagher is associate dean of teaching, learning, and experiential education and professor of English at Northeastern University. His books include *Radical Departures: Composition and Progressive Pedagogy* (NCTE), *Reclaiming Assessment: A Better Alternative to the Accountability Agenda* (Heinemann), *Teaching Writing that Matters* (with Amy Lee, Scholastic), and *Our Better Judgment: Teacher Leadership for Writing Assessment* (with Eric Turley, NCTE). His articles have appeared in a variety of journals in writing studies and education.

Juan C. Guerra, current director of NCTE's Cultivating New Voices among Scholars of Color, is professor of English and chair of the Department of American Ethnic Studies at the University of Washington at Seattle. His scholarship is highlighted in two earlier books: *Writing in Multicultural Settings* (1997) and *Close to Home: Oral and Literate Practices in a Transnational Mexicano Community* (1998). His most recent book is titled *Language, Culture, Identity, and Citizenship in College Classrooms and Communities* (2016).

Bruce Horner is Endowed Chair in Rhetoric and Composition at the University of Louisville, where he teaches courses in composition, composition theory and pedagogy, and literacy studies. His recent books include *Rewriting Composition: Terms of Exchange* and the coedited collections *Economies of Writing: Revaluations in Rhetoric and Composition* and *Reworking English in Composition: Global Interrogations, Local Interventions*.

Asao B. Inoue is professor of interdisciplinary arts and sciences, director of University Writing and the Writing Center, a member of the Executive Board of CWPA, and the program chair of the 2018 CCCC convention. He has written many articles and chapters on writing assessment and race and racism studies, as well as two books. He has won the 2014 CWPA Outstanding Scholarship Award and the NCTE/CCCC Outstanding Book Award in 2014 and 2017.

WILLIAM B. LALICKER (PhD, University of Washington, Seattle) is professor of English at West Chester University, where he teaches written rhetoric at every level. He has taught, presented, or researched in England, Poland, Costa Rica, the Netherlands, Hungary, France, and China. His publications and presentations focus on composition and basic writing pedagogies, writing program administration, rhetorical theory, and intercultural rhetoric. He is chair of the Pennsylvania State System of Higher Education's International Education Council.

THOMAS LAVELLE directs the Center for Modern Languages at the Stockholm School of Economics (SSE), where he teaches a range of courses in areas as diverse as professional rhetoric and communication, multilingual pedagogy, and creative writing. In addition to this work at SSE, he has taught at other universities in Sweden as well as in the United States, the United Kingdom, and China. The theme that unifies his teaching is the relationship among language, culture, and learning.

EUNJEONG LEE recently earned her doctoral degree in applied linguistics at Pennsylvania State University. Her dissertation explores the relationship between a writing instructor's disposition and multilingual writers' textual negotiation and rhetorical attunement. Her research interests include translingual practice, second language writing, Global English, and composition pedagogy and teacher education for multilingual writers.

JERRY WON LEE is assistant professor of English at the University of California, Irvine. His publications appear in journals such as *College Composition and Communication, College English, Critical Inquiry in Language Studies,* and the *International Journal of Applied Linguistics.* His monograph, *The Politics of Translingualism,* is forthcoming with Routledge.

KATIE MALCOLM is an instructional consultant at the University of Washington's Center for Teaching and Learning, where she consults with faculty and TAs across campus on their teaching, particularly designing and assessing writing assignments for multilingual students. Previously she taught basic writing and composition courses in the Seattle community colleges. She received her PhD in rhetoric and composition from the University of Wisconsin–Milwaukee and currently researches translingual writing pedagogies across the curriculum.

KATE MANGELSDORF is professor of rhetoric and writing studies at the University of Texas at El Paso, where she has served as the director of University Writing Programs. She has published on cross-border literacies, second language writing, and writing program administration and is currently coauthoring a book on graduate students' experiences becoming ethnographers and academic writers. She is the coauthor of the sixth edition of *Choices: A Writing Guide with Readings* (Bedford/St. Martin's).

PAIGE MITCHELL directs the University of Maine's Writing Center and is a PhD candidate concentrating in writing center administration, literacy, and writing studies. She obtained her MA in English, concentrating in gender and critical analysis, and her BA, with a double concentration in creative writing and professional and technical writing, and was an Honors College graduate. Her research interests include writing center collaborative practice, multimodal design, assessment, and translingual pedagogy.

MATT NOONAN is an associate professor of teaching in the Writing Program at Northeastern University. His research interests include teacher inquiry, multilingual writers, and assessment.

Sʜᴀᴋɪʟ Rᴀʙʙɪ is a PhD candidate in the Department of English at the Pennsylvania State University. His research on academic literacies looks at graduate students and their disciplinary writing practices, with a focus on internationals being socialized in US higher education institutions. He has previously worked as a lecturer in English literature and composition in Bangladesh and as a primary school teacher in Thailand.

Aɴɴ Sʜɪᴠᴇʀs-McNᴀɪʀ is an assistant professor and director of professional and technical writing at the University of Arizona. Her work has appeared or is forthcoming in *Technical Communication, Kairos, Across the Disciplines, Basic Writing e-Journal, College Composition and Communication,* and *FORUM: Issues about Part-Time and Contingent Labor,* as well as edited collections and conference proceedings. Previously, she was a predoctoral instructor and assistant director of the expository writing program at the University of Washington.

Cʜʀɪsᴛɪɴᴇ M. Tᴀʀᴅʏ is professor in the English Applied Linguistics and interdisciplinary Second Language Acquisition and Teaching (SLAT) programs at the University of Arizona; she also serves as the Writing Program's associate director for second language writing. She has published widely in areas such as genre and discourse studies, second language writing, and the policies and politics of English. Her most recent book is *Beyond Convention: Genre Innovation in Academic Writing* (University of Michigan Press)

Eʟʟɪᴏᴛ Tᴇᴛʀᴇᴀᴜʟᴛ is assistant professor in the English department and affiliate faculty in Women's, Gender, and Sexuality Studies at University at Albany, SUNY. He also served as assistant director of the University Writing Center at the University of Louisville, is the recipient of the Mina Shaughnessy Prize and the Gloria Anzaldúa Rhetorician Award, and has published in Enculturation, QED, Journal of GLBTQ Worldmaking, Computers & Composition Online, and Peitho.

INDEX

AAVE. *See* African American Vernacular English
ABC. *See* adult basic education track
academic discourse, 37
accelerated learning program (ALP), 101–2
acceleration programs, 10, 101–2; adoption of, 106–7; English 101+100, 104, 105, 107–16; impacts of, 116–17
accommodationist approach, 87–88
Adams, Peter, 101
administration, writing program, 11, 202–3
adult basic education (ABC) track, 105
African American Vernacular English (AAVE), 3
after-school programs (*hakwans*), in South Korea, 71–75
agency, 28, 183, 184
agentive states, South Korea as, 70–71
ALP. *See* accelerated learning program
applied linguistics, 182, 184
argumentation, styles of, 90–91
Aristotle, *Rhetoric*, 155
assessment, 197–98; mesopolitics of, 123–24; practices and processes, 122–23, 202–3; student-driven, 129, 183; translingual pedagogies and, 120–21, 131–33; writing, 10–11; writing portfolio, 148–50

Baldwin, James, "If Black English Isn't a Language, Then Tell Me, What Is?," 140
Bangladesh, 44, 46(n13, n14); literacy and identity, 38–39, 40
Barad, Karen, 29; on language performativity, 27–28; *Meeting the Universe Halfway*, 26
Bazerman, Charles, 81
Benedict, Ruth, "The Individual and the Pattern of Culture," 142, 156
Bhabha, Homi, 107
bicultural context, 38
bilingualism, 36, 38, 186
blending, 25
borrowing, 25
Bourdieu, Pierre, 7, 95

Bruffee, Kenneth, *A Short Course in Writing*, 157–58
Business & Organizational Writing class (West Chester University), 62, 63, 67; structure of, 57–61
Butler, Johnnella E.: on performativity, 27–28; *Writing in Multicultural Settings*, 22

California Acceleration Project (CAP), 101–2
Calvet, Louis-Jean, 124
Canagarajah, Suresh, "The Place of World Englishes in Composition," 144, 156–57, 173
CAP. *See* California Acceleration Project
CCBC. *See* Community College of Baltimore County
Center for Franco-American Studies (UMaine), 139
centripetal and centrifugal dynamics, 191, 192–94
children, Korean, 76–77
Chinese, 9; identity, 41
choice, 126
Cisneros, Sandra, "Little Miracles, Kept Promises," 140
classrooms: evaluation of, 120; translingual FYC, 135–36
code meshing, 32, 45(n1), 183
code switching, 21, 25, 32, 103–4
College Writing: language difference and, 172–73; syllabus, 173–74; World Englishes, 170–71, 175
Colombian New Yorker, identity as, 36
coming to develop, 125–26
commodity, English proficiency as, 76
communication strategies, negotiative, 142–43
communicative practices, 145
Community College of Baltimore County (CCBC), 101
community colleges, 10
COMPASS, as evaluation tool, 105, 106, 116, 117
compassion, 130
competence, translingual, 145–46

CompPile.org research bibliography, 138
composition, 12, 143, 186
composition classes, 4, 6; curriculum, 139–42; internationalization, 53–54, 65–66; peer review, 143–44; Sogang University, 77–82; translingual, 8–9, 51–53, 64–65. *See also* English 101 (University of Maine); English 101/English 100, Critical Literacy for College,
conceptual frameworks, developing, 114–15
Conference on College Composition and Communication, Students' Right to Their Own Language, 3
contracts, 75. *See also* grading contracts
conversation practice, in South Korean schools, 75
cooperative education model, global, 161–62
Council of Europe, on plurilingualism, 83
critical discourse analysis, 62
cross-language experimentation, 146–47
cross-language work, 13
culture, 143; and equitable-exchange courses, 56; and translingual writing, 141–42
curriculum, 194; in composition courses, 139–42

developmental courses, 102
Dhaka, 46(n12); literacy education in, 38–39
difference. *See* language differences
diffraction, 8, 26
directed self-placement (DSP), 119, 183, 197–98, 202; fairness in, 124–27; grading contracts in, 131–33
directional dynamics, 191, 192
discourse, in trilingual composition classes, 52–53
discourse practices, as negotiations, 104
documentary orientation, 136
double translation exercise, 92–94
DSP. *See* directed self-placement

ecologies, writing assessment, 121–22, 124, 130, 202
Edited American English, 53
editing practices, processes and labors of, 125–26
elites, 62
employers, South Korean, 73–75
English, 9, 37, 102, 136; at Holy Cross college, 83–84; in South Korea, 71–82; trilingual composition classes, 51–52

English as a second language (ESL), 105, 183; international students and, 39–40; at Northeastern University, 168–69
Englishes, global, 141, 144. *See also* World Englishes
English 101 (University of Maine), 136, 138; assignment sequencing, 142–43, 154–58; course description, 139–40; peer review, 143–44; Portfolio Assessment Rubric, 153–54; portfolio assessments, 148–51; readings for, 140–42; translingual practices in, 144–47
English 101/English 100, Critical Literacy for College, 104, 105, 111–15; evaluation of, 116–17; small-group discussions in, 109–10; thirdspace in, 107–9
English proficiency, and educational experience, 163–64
entanglement, 8, 28, 29; language differences as, 26–27
equitable-exchange classes, 54; Guizhou University, 55–57
eradicationist approach, 87
Errors and Expectations (Shaughnessy), 166
ESL. *See* English as a second language
essays: assessment of, 148–51; genre, 113
ethnic identity, ethnicity, 8, 33–34, 45; fluidity of, 31–32; hybridity of, 43–44; internationalism as, 38–40; and language, 35–36; role of, 41–42
Europe, plurilingualism, 83
evaluation, classroom, 120
exchange classes, 54–55; enacting, 64–65
expats, in South Korea, 73–77, 84–85

fairness: in directed self-placement, 124–27, 132; in grading contracts, 127–28, 202; in teaching and research traditions, 190–91
feedback: in grading contracts, 128, 129, 130; student exchanges, 108–9, 111–13, 123; translingual approaches to, 110–11
first-year composition (FYC), 137; translingual, 135–36
First-year Writing for Multilingual Writers (Northeastern), 168
French, as first language, 139, 152(n4)
Fresno State, DSP process, 124–27
"From a Native Daughter" (Trask), 89, 90–91, 92
funding, for study abroad courses, 65
FYC. *See* first-year composition

gender, in South Korea, 74–75, 80
genres, and language differences, 183, 184
global, the, 5, 71, 203–4; of cooperative education model, 161–62; in higher education, 62, 64–65; Northeastern's writing program, 163–69
global branding, 162–63, 176(n1, n2)
globally networked learning environments (GNLEs), 54, 55, 67; enacting, 64–65
grading, 122
grading contracts, 202; in directed self-placement, 126–27, 131–33; labor-based, 124, 127–30, 132
graduate students, translingual training, 151
Grego, Rhonda, 107
Griffin, Susan, "Our Secret," 175
GSP. *See* guided self-placement
Guerra, Juan C., *Writing in Multicultural Settings*, 22
guided self-placement (GSP), Northeastern University program, 165–69
Guide for the Development of Language Education Policies in Europe (Council of Europe), 83
Guizhou University (GZU), 67; equitable-exchange class, 54–55; Multicultural Writing course, 55–57, 61–62, 63

hakwans, 71–72; teaching English at, 75–77
Harvard University, English monolingualism, 20
heritage, performance of, 43
heritage languages, 8, 32, 33
Hern, Katie, 101
higher education, 135, 162; globalization and, 62–63, 64–65
"Historical Structure of Scientific Discovery, The" (Kuhn), 92
Holy Cross college, English-only attitude, 83–84
humor, in Korean language use, 73

"Ideas in General, and their Original, Of" (Locke), 156
identification-in-difference, 44
identity, identities, 32, 162, 183; ethno-linguistic, 8, 41–42; hybrid, 43–44; language and, 4–5, 24, 31, 204; and language difference, 91, 184; literacy education and, 38–39; multilingualism and, 22, 34–35; translingualism and, 35–36
ideology, 7, 197; language, 195–96
IEI. *See* Intensive English Institute

IEP. *See* international English Program
"If Black English Isn't a Language, Then Tell Me, What Is?" (Baldwin), 140
"Individual and the Pattern of Culture, The" (Benedict), 142, 156
institutional branding, 162, 176(n1, n2)
Intensive English Institute (IEI), 138, 152(n3)
international English program (IEP), 105
internationalization, 62; education, 63, 65–66; as ethnicity, 38–40
interviews: of expat teachers, 84–85; student, 143

Japan, and Korea, 72
Japanese, 9
job interviews, South Korea, 72
Journal of Second Language Writing, 3
judgment, 123, 132

knowledge, 53, 113, 126, 136, 184; language-related, 92, 186
Konglish, 9, 73
Korean, 9; identity as, 34–36; use of, 72–73, 83
Kuhn, Thomas, "The Historical Structure of Scientific Discovery," 92

labor, 123; in grading contracts, 119, 127–30, 132–33
Lakatosian structure of inquiry, 190, 191–92
Lalicker, William, 141, 154–55
language(s), 9, 32, 125, 132, 140, 142; fluidity of, 24–25, 200; and identity, 4–5, 31, 36; knowledge of, 185–86; metaknowledge, 184–85
language choices, 132
language differences/variation, 6, 7, 10, 52, 87, 95, 128, 137, 181, 191, 193, 199–201; approaches to, 21–23, 103–4; as entanglement, 26–27; knowledge of, 184–85; as resource, 119–20, 182; rhetoric of, 24, 183; translingualism and, 175–76, 195–97; World Englishes, 172–73; in writing, 88, 90, 150–51, 152(n1, n2); writing assessments, 120–21
language discourse, socially reinforced, 32
language ideology, 7, 33
language norms, plurality of, 44
language policies, 95–96
language practices, 92, 95, 181, 201; expanding range of, 89–90; legitimate, 3–4
language proficiency, 185, 186
languages-in-use, 26
language study, 12

language users, 26
learning, 186; in self-placement, 125
learning management system (LMS), 116
learning processes, 11–12, 203
Lee, Yo-An, 81
Lewiston-Auburn, Somalis in, 139
linguistics, 3, 113, 122; applied, 182, 184–
    87; decisions, 94
literacies, 39, 118(n2)
literacy education, and identity, 38–39
"Little Miracles, Kept Promises" (Cisne-
    ros), 140
living-English work, 60
LMS. See learning management system
Locke, John, "Of Ideas in General, and
    their Original," 156
"Loss of the Creature, The" (Percy), 90, 91
Lu, Min-Zhan, 60, 70, 103, 132, 164, 199
Lyons, Scott, code meshing, 32

Maher, John, 31
Maine, 135, 137, 152(n4); Somalis in,
    138–39
marketing, higher education, 162
MA-TESOL programs, 184
Matsuda, Paul, 138
Meeting the Universe Halfway: Quantum Phys-
    ics and the Entanglement of Matter and
    Meaning (Barad), 26
memory, 27
mesopolitics, 123–24
metaknowledge, 184–85
metalanguage, 192
metroethnicity, 31–32
metrolingualism, 32
Miller, Carolyn R., 81
Miller, Susan, 136
mimicry, and literacy education, 38–39
mixed-language writing, 89
monolingualism, 4, 6, 9, 19, 29, 36, 38,
    195; challenging, 7, 21–22, 204–5;
    history of, 20–21; and language differ-
    ence, 10, 22–23, 88, 103–4
multiculturalism, and writing, 54–55,
    141–42
Multicultural Writing course, Guizhou
    University, 55–57, 61–63
multilingualism, 19, 20, 29, 36, 39, 40, 92,
    186; approaches to, 21–22; and identi-
    ties, 34–35; in South Korea, 70–71,
    82–83

national sovereignty, 71
negotiation, 27, 39, 104, 130; in directed
    self-placement, 126–27

"New Literacy Studies and Time: An
    Exploration" (Tusting), 27
New Yorkers, identity as, 36
non-native English speakers, 105
nonproficiency, and identity, 41, 42
North Americans, as expat English teach-
    ers, 74–75
Northeastern University, 176(n2); Col-
    lege Writing: World Englishes, 170–75;
    global cooperative education model,
    161–62; guided self-placement at, 165–
    69; international students at, 163–64;
    writing program at, 11, 162–63; writing
    symposium at, 164–65

Ojibwe, code meshing in, 32
online learning, 116
Ortmeier-Hooper, Christina, 167
Otsuji, Emi, on metrolingualism, 31–32
"Our Secret" (Griffin), 175
Oxford English Dictionary, in double transla-
    tion, 93

parents, and English proficiency, 76–77
PARs. See Portfolio Assessment Rubrics
passing, 41–42
peer review, in composition classes, 143–44
Pennycook, Alastair, 27, 204; on metrolin-
    gualism, 31–32; on passing, 41–42
Percy, Walker, "The Loss of the Creature,"
    90, 91
performance, of ethnicity, 43
performativity, 27–28; of translanguaging,
    42–43
placement, 120, 196–97
"Place of World Englishes in Composition:
    Pluralization Continued, The" (Canag-
    arajah), 144, 156–57, 173
plurilingualism, Council of Europe, 83
Portfolio Assessment Rubrics (PARs), 148,
    153–54
portfolios, 140, 174; assessment of, 148–50,
    202–3
postsecondary writing, 10
physical characteristics, racialized, 41

Queens, translingualism of, 36
quotations, and conceptual frameworks,
    114–15

racism, 3, 74
ranking, student, 122
reading(s), 201; academic, 102–3; in
    UMaine English 101, 140–42, 144,
    154–58

reading practices, 142, 150, 195; processes and labors of, 125–26
Reading the World: Ideas that Matter, 141
recruitment: of English teachers, 74; of international students, 137–38
repetition, sedimenting, 27
representations, 124
research practices, fairness in, 191–92
resistance, ethnic identity as, 32
Rhetoric (Aristotle), 155
rhetoric: intercultural, 51; language and, 204–5; readings in, 155
rhetorical styles, 142, 201

Saenkhum, Tanita, 138
Samsung, English use at, 72
SAT scores, and Northeastern admittance, 163
second language acquisition/development, 3, 12, 184–85, 186
sedimenting, 27
Serbian language, 146–47
Severino, Carol, *Writing in Multicultural Settings*, 22
Shaughnessy, Mina, 168, 203; *Errors and Expectations*, 166
Short Course in Writing, A (Bruffee), 157–58
Singapore, English in, 72
Slovaks, and English-language learning, 73
small-group discussions, structure of, 109–10
Sogang University: linguistic environment of, 82–83; teaching English at, 77–82
Somalis, in Maine, 138–39
South Asia, multilingualism of, 40
South Korea: English in, 9, 72, 203–4; English proficiency in, 77–78; expat English teachers in, 73–77, 85–86; language use in, 70–71; linguistic environment in, 82–83; teaching English in, 78–82
sovereignty, Korean, 72–73
space, 27
Speakers of Other Languages (SOL), 168
speech communities, 145
SRTOL. *See* Students' Right to Their Own Language
Standard English, 53, 102
Standard Written English (SWE), 144, 151; and translingual composition, 145–46
Student Assessment Services, 105
students, 5, 7, 129, 136, 140, 183, 203; accelerated learning program, 101–2; in acceleration programs, 108–17; and alternative Englishes, 144–46; classroom interactions among, 142–43; and

developing conceptual frameworks, 114–15; and directed self-placement process, 124–27; double translation exercise for, 92–94; in equitable-exchange classes, 61–62, 64–65; evaluating, 10–11; international, 39–40, 135, 137–38, 151–52, 161–62, 163–69; and labor-based contracts, 132–33; peer review by, 43–44; at Sogang University, 77–82; in studies abroad, 63–64, 65–68; writing assessment ecologies for, 120–22, 202
Students' Right to Their Own Language (SRTOL), 3
student-teacher relationships, 128, 130
studio approach, 107, 125
study-abroad programs, 63; enacting, 64–65; students and, 65–68
Symposium on Second Language Writing, 3

teachers, teaching, 130, 133(n4, n5), 151; fairness in, 190–91; linguistic knowledge of, 184–87; in South Korea, 9, 73–77, 84–85
teaching staff, Northeastern University, 164–65
TESOL, 3
texts, 136, 193
thirdspace theory, 104; application of, 107–9, 113, 117
Thompson, Nancy, 107
Thoreau, Henry David, *Walden*, 92
time, 27
Title III grant, 107
TOEFL exam, 40, 163
transdisciplinary studies, vocabularies of motive, 23–24
translanguaging, 45(n5), 204
translation, 89; double, 92–94
translingual approach/pedagogies, 88–89, 94–95, 126; assessment within, 120–21, 131–33, 202–3
translingualism, 4, 7, 12–13, 19, 28, 29, 44, 66, 104, 181–82; in composition classes, 8–9, 51–53, 145–46; cultural perspectives, 141–42; feedback, 110–13; and identity, 35–36; language fluidity and, 24–25; and language difference, 22–23, 91, 195–96, 199–200; language practice, 95, 201; literacy education and, 38–39; as orientation, 175–76; performativity and, 42–43; practicing, 165, 171–72; as threat to ethnicity, 32, 33; in UMaine English 101, 140–41

Trask, Haunani-Kay, "From a Native Daughter," 89, 90–91, 92
Tusting, Karin, "New Literacy Studies and Time: An Exploration," 27
tutoring, directive, 39, 40

UCC: acceleration program at, 106–17; English proficiency, 105–6
University of Maine, 11; English 101, 136, 139–51; Portfolio Assessment Rubric, 153–54; student recruitment at, 137–38, 151–52; translingual assignment sequence at, 154–58
University of Washington Tacoma, DSP process, 124–27
urban contexts, metrolingualism in, 32

vocabularies of motive, in transdisciplinary studies, 23–25

Walden (Thoreau), 92
Watson Conference, 182
West Chester University (WCU): Business & Organizational Writing class, 57–61, 62, 63, 67; equitable-exchange class, 54–55
white men theory, and expat English teachers, 74
word choice, and translingualism, 146–47
World Englishes, 12, 144, 168, 172, 184, 194; courses for, 170–75; readings in, 174–75
writer's block, 37

writing, 12, 37, 89, 94, 136, 147, 152(n1), 164, 201; academic, 102–3, 112–13; alternative Englishes and, 144–46; assessment of, 120, 131–33; bilingualism and, 186–87; conformity vs. difference, 90, 91–92; corporate, 58; language differences and, 87–88; meso-politics of, 123–24; translingual, 51–52
writing-abroad programs, 64–65
writing-across-the-curriculum programs, Sogang University, 81, 82
writing centers, Sogang University, 81
writing classes, accelerated, 104, 105–17
Writing Conventions, 140
Writing in Multicultural Settings (Severino, Guerra, and Butler), 22
writing practices, 195; bilingual and multilingual, 186–87; processes and labors of, 125–26
Writing Program Committee, Northeastern University, 165–66
writing programs, 152; administration of, 202–3; in globally networked learning environments, 53–54; guided self-placement and, 165–69; internationalization of, 65–66; international students in, 39–40; learning processes in, 11–12; at Northeastern University, 162–63, 164
writing scholarship, interdisciplinary, 182
writing studios, 125
Written Rhetoric 210: Multicultural Writing, 141

Zhaozhe, 142